The End of
Silen...

KAREN ARMSTRONG was a Roman Catholic nun for seven years. After leaving the religious life, she wrote a thesis on Tennyson, taught modern literature at London University and English at a girls' school in Dulwich. Since 1982 she has been a freelance writer and broadcaster. Her television work includes, *The First Christian* (a six-part documentary series on St Paul), *Tongues of Fire* and *Varieties of Religious Experience*. Her books include *The Gospel According to Woman*, *Holy War*, *The English Mystics of the Fourteenth Century*, *Muhammad* and, most recently, the acclaimed *A History of God*.

The End of Silence

Women and the Priesthood

Karen Armstrong

FOURTH ESTATE · *London*

First published in Great Britain in 1993 by
Fourth Estate Limited
289 Westbourne Grove
London W11 2QA

A catalogue record for this book is available from the British Library.

ISBN 1–85702–145–2

Typeset by York House Typographic Ltd, London
Printed in Great Britain by Biddles Ltd, Guildford

Contents

'Women are to remain silent in the assembly.'

1 Corinthians 14:35

Acknowledgements

My thanks to Joyce Bennett, Janet Grierson, Christian Howard, Diana McClatchey and Christina Rees for their kind encouragement and generous help.

Introduction

O N 15 NOVEMBER 1992, a priest climbed into the pulpit to deliver his Sunday sermon but, to the consternation and distress of the congregation, he told them that he was tendering his resignation. The Church of England, he said, had made an irrevocable error which, at a stroke, negated some four hundred years of noble Christian endeavour. It was no longer the institution that he had loved all his life and served so gladly.

What was the crime of the Anglican Church? Had it denied a fundamental Christian doctrine, such as the existence of God or the divinity of Christ? Had it decided to throw in its lot with the neo-fascists of Europe? What had it done that was worse than any of the Christian atrocities of the past? Like most other religions, Christianity has not always lived up to its high ideals. The crusades, inquisitions and persecutions of Western Christendom had been a flagrant denial of the compassionate ethos of the Gospels. Even the tolerant Church of England had oppressed Roman Catholics in the past, had connived at an iniquitous social system and had allied itself rather too closely with the aggressive colonialism of the British Empire. But the Anglican priest who could no longer serve his beloved Church had come to terms with these unhappy episodes. What had finally driven him out was the historic decision of the Synod a

few days earlier, on 11 November 1992, to admit women to the
priesthood.

The debate about the ordination of women had attracted a
good deal of media interest and was thus carried out in an
unusual glare of publicity. Even non-believers were fascinated
by the issue and were eager to know what the Church was
going to do. It was difficult for many outsiders to understand
what all the fuss was about. Women had been invading
traditionally male preserves for so long that the idea of women
priests seemed a natural development. But many Christians –
women as well as men – were passionately opposed to a female
priesthood and it was not always easy to follow their theological arguments. As I write this, at the end of March 1993, it seems
that the Church of England will be irrevocably split by the
decision to ordain women. Some of the opponents of women
priests are considering joining forces with the Roman Catholic
Church, while others are in the process of forming a separate
province of the Church of England which has been described as
a 'Church within a Church'. The Anglican communion has
been known for its liberal attitudes and its ability to embrace a
wide range of religious opinion, but the issue of women priests
has apparently been too much for it. The November decision in
Synod has also gravely damaged ecumenical relations between
the Anglican Church and the Roman Catholics and Greek
Orthodox: the patriarch of the Russian Orthodox Church has
refused to receive Dr George Carey, Archbishop of Canterbury,
during his forthcoming trip to the former Soviet Union. What is
it about a female priesthood that stirs up such desperate and
intransigent emotion?

Both sides of the dispute have been able to produce an
impressive armoury of texts to back up their position. Opponents of the ordination of women argue that Jesus chose only
men as Apostles and that a woman cannot represent a deity
who is conceived of in predominantly masculine imagery.
Supporters of women priests point to the egalitarian spirit of
the New Testament, which states that in Christ there is neither
male nor female. Both sides claim St Paul as their authority. It is
also argued that the Anglican Church has no right to take this
major step alone and that the Synod's decision means that

Anglicans can no longer regard themselves as members of the Universal, Catholic Church. Others lament the damage to Church unity and claim that by pandering to the women's movement and to the fashions of the day, the Church of England has lost its integrity. They protest that in the Gospels women are regarded as equal to men but different: their Christian calling is not identical with that of a man. It is, they believe, as ludicrous for a woman to seek ordination as it would be for a man to hope to bear a child. On the other side, the supporters of women priests have insisted that on the contrary the Church will lose its integrity and credibility if it does not ordain women.

Both sides have constantly looked back to the past in the course of this long debate which has raged in the Anglican communion and in other Churches for over twenty years. Both believe that history and tradition are on their side. This is inevitable, since Judaism, Christianity and Islam – the three religions of Abraham – take history very seriously indeed. Where Hindus believe that history is an illusion and where the Greek rationalists of antiquity claimed that history was less serious and philosophical than poetry, Jews, Christians and Muslims have discovered their God in the mundane events of this world. Christians have gone so far as to claim that God actually entered human history by being born into a particular culture and a particular time. God revealed himself definitively in the man Jesus, who was the last divine Word to humanity. Historical events have continued to be crucial and formative in the Christian faith. Roman Catholics, Greek Orthodox and Anglicans, unlike Protestants, all claim that tradition is an authoritative guide in the current search for truth. Not all the facts are to be found in scripture but Christians must take notice of Christian practice and teaching over the centuries. Yet history can be as ambiguous as scripture, as the present debate about the ordination of women makes clear. Since both sides claim that their position can be supported by Christian history and tradition, many people are understandably confused. Did Jesus want women – or, indeed, anybody at all – to be priests? Will admitting women to the priesthood constitute a major break with tradition, or is this innovation a logical Christian development, on a par with the abolition of slavery in the nineteenth century?

This brief book will examine some of these questions. Since history is so important in the conflict about women priests, it will trace the development of priesthood in the Christian tradition, alongside the Christian attitudes to women, sexuality and gender. Since the question is of particular urgency in Britain at the time of writing, the later chapters will focus on the debate in the Church of England, though the position of other Churches will not be neglected.

This will be a history of the ideas and theology regarding women and the priesthood. It will not deal with the more political aspects of the conflict within the Churches, detailing the factions, personalities, pressure groups and committees that have contributed to the debate. The ideas themselves are not difficult to grasp. The issues are fairly clear-cut. In 1978 the Synod of the Church of England decided that there were no fundamental theological objections to admitting women to the priesthood, but this has not prevented further disputes and divisions. Questions of gender and sexuality are notoriously sensitive and the prospect of women priests seems to touch upon anxieties that exist far below the rational level. What has happened in Christian history to make it possible for some people to accept women doctors but not women priests? Why is it acceptable for a woman to be Prime Minister but not a bishop? Is this simply a matter of cultural conditioning, as some claim, or is there something about women that makes them incompatible with priesthood and the sacred?

Although I was a Roman Catholic nun for seven years, I never had any desire to be a priest. My calling was, I thought, to the monastic life which is a different vocation: the fact that many Christian monks are also priests should not blur this distinction. Like the shaman in traditional societies, monks and nuns are seeking a personal religious experience. So are priests, of course, but they are also officials of a cult and institution. A society will worship its gods in a particular way and for nearly six thousand years priests – and priestesses – have been ordained to carry out this ritual. In the Christian world, priests have also acquired other jobs: they have become ethical guides and guardians of doctrinal orthodoxy. I never felt attracted to the cultic, ethical or doctrinal functions of a Christian priest, so I have no personal axe to grind. But in recent years, many women of obvious integrity have felt deprived by their exclusion from Holy Orders and I have been dismayed by the hostility that this has inspired, from women as well as from men.

None of the major world religions has been particularly good to women. They have usually become male affairs and women have been relegated to a marginal position. Centuries of Christian conditioning have made the very idea of a woman presiding at the altar emotionally impossible for many people. We should try to understand why this has happened and whether this revulsion is justified. The kind of ungovernable fear that the spectre of women priests inspires is partly the result of a long tradition of Christian misogyny which has constituted one of the major failings of the Churches over the centuries. A faith which finds it so difficult to accommodate half the human race and which has long found it almost impossible to take a balanced view of human sexuality has serious problems. When did women become relegated to the sidelines of holiness and why did Christians find it inconceivable that a woman should represent them in the Sanctuary? To answer these questions we must return to the institution of priesthood in the ancient world, when women priests were accepted as a perfectly normal phenomenon. We should also look back to the Jewish priesthood, which was the priestly institution with which Jesus and the first Christians were familiar. We shall then begin to see how surprising it was that Christians should have decided to have priests at all.

— 1 —

Priest and Priestess in the Ancient World

A s soon as men and women became recognizably human, they felt the need to live a spiritual life. This has not always involved subscribing to a creed or an institutional Church but was primarily an attempt to articulate and develop a sense of mystery and wonder in life and a conviction that, despite much distressing evidence to the contrary, life has ultimate meaning and value. Thus human beings created their religions in much the same way as they created works of art. Like their paintings and music, their religious systems were not concerned with objective fact or with verifiable scientific and historical truth but were inspired by a more elusive, imaginative experience. When they wanted advice about the best way to live a spiritual life, they consulted experts – as in other matters. They sought help from shamans, prophets, sages and seers. One religious institution developed by nearly all the cultures of antiquity was the priesthood, which, as a matter of course, included both men and women.

Indeed, at a very early date, women were considered central to the spiritual quest. The origins of religion are obscure and there is much that we shall never know, but it is generally agreed that one of the earliest symbols of the ultimate was the Great Mother Goddess. In Europe, the Middle East and Asia, archaeologists have unearthed hundreds of little figurines

dating from the early Neolithic period which probably represent her, but have found scarcely any male effigies. Artists
depicted the Creator of Heaven and Earth as a naked, pregnant
woman. Yet in the recent discussions about the ordination of
women to the Christian priesthood, many of the opponents of
women priests have seemed disturbed by female sexuality. This
is partly because, as we shall see, Christians in the West have
found it particularly difficult to integrate women and sexuality
into their sense of the sacred. But at the dawn of human history,
women's sexuality was seen as a holy force. At a time when
agriculture was being developed, the fertility that was trans-
forming human life was revered as a sacred mystery. The Earth
produced plants and nourished them in rather the same way as
a woman gave birth to a child and fed it from her own body. The
magical power of the Earth seemed vitally interconnected with
the mysterious creativity of the female sex. The image of the
Great Mother Goddess was a personification of that energy
which gives life to forms and nurtures them; it encouraged men
and women to view themselves, the divine and the natural
world as bound up with one another, sharing the same predica-
ment and the same substance and force. Before the connection
between the sexual act and procreation was properly understood, it may well have seemed that women alone possessed
this fecund power, that the mystery of life was somehow
female, and men may have felt somewhat marginal and
redundant.

The cult of the Mother Goddess may also have been linked
with vague memories and impressions left over from infancy,
when, psychologists tell us, the body of the mother constitutes
the whole of reality. In a similar way, the Goddess was all that
there was; she was identical with the universe which had
emerged from her belly. Everything that people could experience or imagine, as well as all things that had concrete existence, were within her and had been produced by her alone. In
more traditional societies, men and women still revere the Earth
as sacred in a way that is no longer possible in our technolo-
gized society which has tethered the natural world and made it
serve our own needs. The cult of the Goddess had emerged at a
stage of human development when women played a leading

role in planting and harvesting, when people were beginning to settle in one place and become domestic. Later, when they had invented the plough which cut into the earth in a more efficient way, and later still, when they had started to build cities, more masculine qualities were revered and personified in male gods. But people did not forget the Mother Goddess. She was absorbed into the pantheons of deities and remained a powerful figure. She was called Inanna in Sumer, in ancient Mesopotamia, Ishtar in Babylon, Anat or Asherah in Canaan, Isis in Egypt and Aphrodite in Greece. In all these cultures, people told remarkably similar stories about her to express her role in their spiritual lives. She was still revered as the source of fertility and, since there is no life without death (a fact mirrored in the cycle of the seasons), she was also venerated as Lady of the Underworld. When rituals were devised to enact the sense of these spiritual truths, the role of the Great Mother was naturally represented by women who functioned as priestesses alongside the male priests.

In our own day, many of the discussions about the nature of the priesthood have focused on the notion of representation. We shall see that many Christians, including women as well as men, believe that female priests cannot properly re-present the divine. Because the Judaeo-Christian God has usually been conceived as male and became incarnate in a man, it has been argued that a woman cannot stand in for Christ at the altar. Others claim that since male and female were both created in God's image, we need both men and women as priests to present a fuller and more rounded icon of the divine. Both sides are correct in seeing re-presentation as central to the whole notion and institution of priesthood. It is the reason why some monotheists have decided to jettison the priesthood altogether: we shall see that Jews were beginning to move away from the institution of priesthood even before their Temple was destroyed by the Romans in 70 CE, that Muslims have never had priests and that some Christian sects decided that priesthood was no longer appropriate. Since God was beyond all human expression, it could be blasphemous – or, at the very least, misleading – to have a man or woman represent 'him'. Since all three of the monotheistic religions that subscribe to the worship of the One God have developed a strongly egalitarian ethos, the idea of having a priest to mediate between this God and the faithful has also been unacceptable to Jews, Muslims and some Protestant Christians: all have come to the conviction that each individual has free access to the divine and does not need to rely on a privileged élite. Roman Catholics, Greek and Russian Orthodox and Anglicans, however, have all retained a representative priesthood, although they do not see the office of re-presentation in quite the same way as the pagans and the Israelites of antiquity.

In the ancient world, it was widely believed that everything on earth was simply the replica of a heavenly reality. Mundane life was clearly frail and overshadowed by mortality but if men and women participated in the life of the gods, they would discover their true potential. Indeed, it was only by sharing this divine life that you could become fully human. Thus it was said, in myth and fable, that the gods had shown men how to build their cities and temples, which were copies of the gods' homes in the celestial realm. The sacred world of the gods was seen as the archetype or the original pattern on which our world had been modelled, a perception underlying the mythology, ritual and social organization of most cultures in antiquity as well as some traditional societies today. Plato's theory of the Eternal Forms or archetypal Ideas as the substantial reality of which our earthly life is a mere shadow can be seen as a philosophical attempt to articulate this perennial, imaginative conception. Religious rituals were devised to help men and women participate in the divine life by imitating the actions of their gods and goddesses. The *imitatio dei* has also been a factor in monotheism: people still rest on the Sabbath and eat bread and wine – actions which are insignificant in themselves – because they believe that in some sense God once did the same.

The *imitatio dei* of pagan antiquity depended upon mythology. In our more secular and rational society, we often use the words 'myth' or 'mythical' to refer to an event that did not actually happen or to a fraudulent account of history. This is rather reductive, however. The mythology of the ancient world was always seen as primarily symbolic. When people evolved myths about the Creation of the world, for example, they did not consider these to be accurate or scientific accounts of the origins of life. Nobody had been present at Creation, so this unimaginable event could only properly be recounted in a symbolic mode. Similarly, when people told the story of the descent of the Great Mother Goddess to the Underworld, they were not giving an account of an historical event. This expressed a spiritual truth: that an enhanced life must sometimes be wrested from the jaws of death or that it might be necessary to journey to the darkest depths of sorrow or the self to achieve salvation. In our own century, Freud and Jung turned instinctively to ancient mythology to chart their own interior quests.

The mythical stories of the gods and goddesses were not describing an impossibly distant reality, of course, since the divine and human were so closely interconnected. When they tried to imitate their various deities in stylized ritual, people of antiquity were not struggling to cross a gulf that yawned ontologically between humanity and the gods. The pagan vision was essentially holistic: there was no gulf between human beings and the divine world such as has been experienced since. The gods, plants, animals, rocks, rivers, men and women were all believed to share the same nature. All participated in the same divine life, had been derived from the same primordial divine substance. The gods had the same problems and the same needs as human beings. The only difference was that these deities were more powerful and would never die. In the sixth century BCE, Pindar expressed this holistic vision in his ode on the Olympic Games:

> Single is the race, single
> of men and gods;
> From a single mother we both draw breath.
> But a difference of power in everything
> keeps us apart;
> For one is as nothing, but the brazen sky
> stays a fixed habitation for ever.
> Yet we can in greatness of mind
> or of body be like the Immortals.[1]

Pindar's athletes are seeking to imitate the superhuman feats of the gods during the Games because they were the pattern of all human achievement. It was by seeking to 'be like the Immortals' in mind and body that men and women could live up to the potential of their own essentially divine nature. The *imitatio dei* of the pagan world did not mean a painful struggle for an alien or impossible perfection.

The same was true of the temple rituals as for athletics, but this time the feats of the gods and goddesses were imitated by their priests and priestesses. By taking part in one of these ritual dramas, either as an actor or a spectator, people felt that they were actually experiencing a mythological life and learning how to live in a spiritual manner. The rite was thought to activate the mysterious divine forces symbolized by the myths. People lived in a city built around a temple, because the gods lived there and they wanted to get as close as possible to this divine power and effectiveness. The *Enuma Elish*, the Babylonian Creation epic, shows the gods building the city of Babylon as their home on earth; it tells us how the great god Marduk erected the ancient ziggurat. The Babylonians who chanted this poem during the New Year Festival knew perfectly well that the ziggurat of Marduk had been physically built by their own ancestors, but the story expressed their sense of its true meaning. Civilization was modelled on the archetypal divine world and would only endure if it participated in the powerful life of the gods. Babylon was actually called 'the gate of the gods' (*bab-ili*); it was their home, and people became conscious of this during the New Year rites which symbolized participation in the divine and made it a reality in the consciousness in an imaginative way that reached far deeper than cerebral, rational understanding. The various dramas of the Festival re-enacted the symbolic events of the Creation, projected the worshippers outside profane time and into the sacred time of the gods, activated the divine energies and made them a potent reality in the mundane city. This ensured that chaos and disintegration would be held at bay for another year. The priests and priestesses were not just actors. When they represented the gods and goddesses, they became identical with them and were the outward sign of this real divine presence.

Because the female had long been a powerful image of the divine, a female priesthood was considered entirely appropriate. The first women priests on record served in the Temple of Eanna in about 4000 BCE in Uruk in what is now Iraq. The temple was said to have been given by Anu, the Sumerian Sky God, to his consort Inanna, the Queen of Heaven. It continued to function for about four millennia: archaeologists of the site have found eighteen different layers. Some early seals, dating from about 3100 BCE, show the goddess Inanna sitting on a throne worshipped by a procession of devotees bearing gifts of produce. The famous Uruk vase, of about the same date or slightly later, shows Inanna standing at the gate of her temple to receive the first fruits of the harvest from another procession of worshippers. Scholars believe that these scenes of temple life in fact depict a priestess who is dressed up as Inanna and standing in for her. This is a distinction that would probably have seemed artificial and unnecessary to the Sumerians. During these sacred rites, the priestess *was* Inanna. Just as everything here below had its fuller, divine replica in the celestial world, the deities also had their human representatives who helped to re-produce this archetypal reality. Later cult statues have been found in Sumeria which may have dispensed with the need for a priestess to sit in Inanna's place and take the offerings on her behalf. But this did not render the priestly office unnecessary: there was still a great deal to do. The job of the male and female priests of Uruk and the other great cities of Sumer was to maintain the connection with the divine world. In this earliest urban society, civilization was felt to be a fragile achievement. It depended economically upon an agricultural surplus produced by the peasantry in the countryside and would fail if it outran its resources. Since women were such a potent emblem of fertility, it was natural to equate this necessary agricultural abundance with Inanna and her priestess. The Sumerians expressed their gratitude for this divine gift by symbolically returning the produce to its source. The temples of both male and female priests were also centres of administration. Priestesses engaged in business, trade and the purchase and maintenance of real estate. A number of seals and plaques show rows of women engaged in various crafts, such as pottery and weaving. Crafts and other skills of civilization were also divine activities; they had been transmitted to human beings by the gods themselves. Early texts describe Inanna as a carpenter, a weaver and a potter. The earliest examples of human writing were discovered in the Temple of Inanna in Erech.

Other temples to male and female deities, served by the appropriate priesthood, were built by the Sumerians in their cities of Ur, Eridu, Erech, Nippur and Kish. Later the region was conquered by Semitic peoples from the north, who adopted the Sumerian religion, culture and language. The Akkadians ruled in Mesopotamia from about 2340 BCE, and the Amorites, who made Babylon their capital and became known as 'Babylonians', from about 1800. The Mesopotamian tradition affected the mythology and religion of Canaan, which would become the Promised Land of the ancient Israelites. Thus, distant as it may seem, this pagan vision would influence the spirituality of our own Judaeo-Christian tradition.

Both the Akkadians and the Amorites held the male and female priesthood in high esteem. It was a complex institution with varying ranks and offices. We know most about the *naditu* priestesses, who were often dedicated to their goddesses as young girls. Drawn from the aristocracy, the *naditu* were privileged women who lived together in community. Relics of their 'convents' (*gigparu*) have been found in Kish, Nippur, Larsa and Sippar, where, at the beginning of the second millennium, about 140 *naditu* lived under the guardianship of a High Priest. But it was no prison: the women had their own private quarters and were allowed to do business in town and buy and sell property. The *naditu* were powerful because they derived a divine authority from their goddess. Thus when King Sargon of Akkad conquered Ur in about 2340 BCE, he appointed his daughter as the High Priestess of the Moon God Nanna, patron of the city, to ease the transition and to give divine legitimacy to his rule. As the daughter of Nanna, the Princess Enheduanna became the sister of his daughter Inanna and acquired a quasi-divinity by this association. Enheduanna did not have an easy life: she was suspended from office when her father suffered a political and military setback. Archaeologists believe that the plaques erected in her honour were deliberately smashed, and hymns have been preserved which commemorate her desolation and sense of having been deserted by her divine patrons. Finally, however, Sargon triumphed and her cultus was restored in Ur. The songs which celebrate this blur the distinction between Enheduanna and Inanna. As far as she and her worshippers were concerned, as the re-presentative of the Goddess, she incarnated her divine presence on earth:

> The First Lady, the Reliance of the throne room has
>   accepted her offerings.
> Inanna's heart has been restored.
> The day was favourable to her, she was clothed
>   sumptuously, she was garbed in womanly beauty
> Like the light of the rising moon, how was she
>   sumptuously attired!
> When Nanna appeared in proper view they all blessed
>   [Inanna's] mother Ningal.
> The heavenly threshold cried 'Hail!'[2]

After her death, Enheduanna was held in such esteem that she was succeeded by two other High Priestesses who took her name. For over five hundred years, the Akkadian and Amorite rulers of Mesopotamia filled the post with their daughters to give their rule divine authority.

The female priesthood could thus be a channel for divine power on earth and necessary to the political stability of a dynasty. One of the chief ways in which this was expressed was in the ceremony of the Sacred Marriage. This has been much misunderstood, in large part because of the bad press it has got in the Bible which refers to it as temple prostitution. Because of the sexual taboos of our own religious tradition, we often imagine these fertility cults as shameless orgies. The very mention of the word 'priestess' tends to conjure up lurid images of erotic depravity, which has done the cause of the ordination of women to the Christian priesthood no good at all. Yet in ancient Mesopotamia as in India, the sexual act was regarded as sacred and as a powerful symbol of the mystery of life. In Neolithic times, the image of the Mother Goddess had personified the creative energy of the earth. Now the sexual union of the God and Goddess had become a symbol of the generation of the whole of being. During the New Year Festival in Sumeria and Babylonia, the divine marriages of the various gods and their consorts were celebrated in an elaborate ritual of great dignity. At Ur, the marriage of Nanna and his consort Ningal was commemorated; at Nippur it was the union of Enlil, god of the atmosphere, and his wife Ninlil, and at Uruk that of Inanna with the shepherd fertility figure Tammuz whom she had rescued from the Underworld. Not only were effigies of the deities brought together for this purpose but in the inner sanctum of the main temple the King celebrated the holy nuptials with the High Priestess. Together they incarnated the divine maleness and femaleness, joined in an apotheosis of wholeness and harmony. By this act of *imitatio dei*, all the participants – actors and congregation alike – were able to ally themselves symbolically with the rhythms of nature.

The gods, it will be recalled, were not distant beings to the people of Mesopotamia. Not only were they immanent and near but they shared the same life as human beings and the natural world: everything had been created from the body of the Goddess, as it were. The gods were all in all; there was nothing that they were not. Like humanity, they were in and of nature. Human passion, therefore, participated in the divine *eros*, and the ritual drama of the Sacred Marriage only made this perception explicit in the consciousness of the worshipper. By means of this sacramental act, men and women entered into the heart of the cycle of life and helped to regenerate it, activating the fertility of the whole land, together with its flocks, herds and peoples. Like human beings, the gods and goddesses needed to have their powers renewed; there was only so much energy available for deities, humans and the natural world. To ensure circulation of all the available divine energy, it was necessary for human beings to contribute annually to this constant battle against sterility and destruction which they were waging with their gods.

The 'fertility rite' was not a frenzied, chorybantic orgy but a disciplined, ordered drama. It was a privilege to be the *naditu* princess who was chosen to re-present the divine bride: she was called *nin-dinghir*, the Lady of the God, and trained very carefully. Before the ceremony she would bathe in the river, have her skin massaged with oil, dress elaborately in a costume decked with jewels, branches, flowers and ears of corn like the Mother Goddess herself. Meanwhile the King made a symbolic journey to his sacred bride in a boat decked with branches or a rich cart decorated with gold and lapis lazuli. He would bring a rich gift with him, such as a jewelled girdle. When he arrived, there would be a lavish banquet to represent the meeting of all the gods and their communion with men, and after the feast the couple would be led in procession to the inner shrine: this might be situated at the summit of the ziggurat, midway between Heaven and Earth, or at its base, in which case the royal pair would enter it as into the Underworld. Either way, their entrance symbolized a meeting and marriage between the celestial and the human, and the penetration of the divine into the mundane. Afterwards, the priest who had supervised the rites would emerge to announce that they had been fulfilled satisfactorily, the King's reign had been re-energized and ratified for another year, and the feasting was renewed. Necklaces have been found inscribed with a dedication to the *naditu* princess of the King of Ur, which may have been given to the *nin-dinghir* as a gift. Hymns have been put into the mouth of kings, dating from the third millennium, which show a humble and tender gratitude to the priestess, the sister of Inanna, for the gift of kingship and deification bestowed on him in the arms of the Goddess.

This type of communion service would not be possible for us today. We no longer share the holistic pagan vision and find the idea of such an *imitatio dei* alien and potentially blasphemous. Our God is above gender and sexuality. In our culture, sexuality in general and women in particular have been so divorced from the religious experience that to link them in this way seems profane. Yet these ancient myths, which were so vitriolically denounced by the prophets of Israel, would find their way back into the monotheistic vision. They would re-emerge in the myths of the Jewish Cabbalists, who speak reverently of the sex life of God and of the female aspect of the divine. Muslim Sufi mystics would speak of the knowledge of God in erotic terms and even hint that al-Lah had been incarnate in a woman. These

pronouncements were not intended to be taken literally, of
course. They were symbolic expressions of a spirituality which
is natural to humanity and attempts to feminize a religion that
had become too harshly masculine. Women and sexuality have
both been so gravely exploited in our own society that it would
be difficult to imagine the Sacred Marriage being performed in a
way that would not be degrading to a priestess. But in ancient
Mesopotamia, Canaan and Anatolia, the priestess who imper-
sonated the goddess in this ceremony was held in high honour:
it was she who conferred the kingship on the male ruler, she
was the channel of the divine power. This reflected the primitive veneration of the Great Goddess. Later myths speak of
gods such as Tammuz, Baal, Osiris and Adonis dying and
entering the Underworld. It is thought that this may originally
have been a punishment for an offence against the Goddess,
though this has been ironed out in the later developments of
the story. Certainly in some of these legends, it is Anat or Isis
who leaves the divine realm and goes in search of her consort
and brother, the other half of her soul, and she who brings life
to him and to the world. When Baal-Habad, the Canaanite god
who is mentioned in such unflattering terms in the Bible, dies
and descends to the world of Mot (god of death and sterility),
his sister and lover Anat goes to look for him, 'desiring him as a
cow her calf or a ewe her lamb'.[3] When she finds his body, she
makes a funeral feast in his honour, seizes Mot, cleaves him
with her sword, winnows, burns and grinds him like corn
before sowing him into the ground. Later, by some means that
are not clear to us, since our sources are incomplete, Baal is
brought back to life and restored to Anat. But this victory had to
be perpetuated on earth each year in Canaan by means of the
Sacred Marriage. By imitating the gods in this way, men and
women shared their struggle against sterility and ensured the
fertility of the earth for another year. Imitating Inanna or Anat
was not an ignoble role for a temple priestess but partook of the
Goddess's strength and effectiveness. Anat was no passive
recipient of male desire but the chief agent in the drama of
salvation and creativity.

   In a different way, the priestess was equally powerful in
ancient Egypt. There the deities were regarded as princes who

actually lived in their temples and who could command a major share of their revenue. The priests and priestesses were members of their household and attended to their needs, as royal servants attended the Pharaoh. From a very early date, the goddesses had been particularly important. In prehistoric times, they had been venerated as creator deities and as the protectors of the King. Later they were represented in this guise in animal form, as well as in a human female aspect. This in itself was an eloquent image of the holistic pagan vision, stressing as it did the inseparability of divine, human and natural worlds. By the beginning of the third millennium in Egypt, each city had its own pantheon of deities, usually consisting of a trinity with a male god, his consort and their child, such as Osiris, Isis and their son Horus. But the goddess was not a weakly, dependent figure. A consort like Sekhmet of Memphis was depicted as leading a wholly separate life from her divine spouse and had her own temples and households of priests and priestesses. Some goddesses were never paired with a male deity. Thus Neith, the patron of Lower Egypt, creator deity and huntress, was always completely independent and had never had a husband. Hathor ('The Golden One') was the Sky Goddess who was depicted as a cow – her rectangular body perhaps reflecting the long shape of Egypt itself. Hathor was a fertility goddess but also Mistress of the Underworld, Lady of Life and Death. Later her cult was merged with that of Isis, who herself enjoyed a huge cult in her own right. Depicted as a Madonna with her baby Horus (and perhaps contributing to the cult of the Virgin Mary in Christianity), Isis was venerated as the mother of the King who was the embodiment in human form of Horus for his generation. Her cult spread from Egypt to Europe during the Roman period; she even had a temple near London Bridge. These powerful goddesses reflected a need for positive images of the female. Even though there could be no goddesses in Judaism, Christianity and Islam, these images and cults would surface from time to time – sometimes as a psychic rebellion against an unbalanced spirituality which was dominated by a too male ethos.

In theory, at least, Egyptian women were positively affected by the veneration of these important goddesses and, indeed,

women enjoyed considerable status in Egypt until the fourth
century when the country was conquered by Alexander the
Great. The Greeks, as we shall see, had a far more negative
image of womankind and this would have an adverse affect on
Christianity. In ancient Egypt, property was inherited through
the female line; as in Mesopotamia, the Pharaoh's power came
to him through his consort. Royal women played an important
role as priestesses in the cult of the Pharaoh. In early days, the
Queen was closely identified with Hathor and as such represented the female aspect of kingship. Through ritual and stylized
dramatic evocations of such divine events as the death of Osiris,
she was also the means of its renewal. As in Mesopotamia, the
priestess would become the goddess she was impersonating
during the rite. Other lower-grade priestesses lived in the
temples as members of the divine household and were often
known as 'Concubines of the Gods'. This did not denote a
sexual function, however. In Egypt this 'concubinage' was
conceived and expressed in entirely cultic, symbolic form. The
concubines were often musicians and dancers of great skill who
had been trained carefully from infancy. They were not mere
entertainers but artists engaged in rites that were believed to be
essential to the preservation of the natural order. Even in our
own secular society, it is admitted that painting, music and
drama can yield an experience of transcendence, which touches
something deeply buried within us and seems to lift us beyond
ourselves so that we sense something greater. When dogma
and institutional religion have been devalued for many people,
art may be our only source of spirituality, and artists can
therefore be regarded as priests and priestesses, who lead us
skilfully into the experience.

In Egypt during the so-called New Kingdom (c. 1567–1068
BCE) we see the apogee of priestess power. It was at this time
that the Queen became known as the God's Wife, though again
this office had no explicitly sexual function. The first to assume
this position was Queen Ahmose Nofretani, who achieved
great distinction in the role. Her image was depicted on the
same scale as that of the King. Her chief priestly function was to
impersonate the consort of Amun, the Sky God, in rite and in
musical evocations of great erotic power. Thus she would

inspire and arouse the god, causing him to regenerate himself. This theological conception of women as the source of divine and kingly power actually made it possible for one woman – Hatsheput, the widow of Akheperenre Tuthmosis II – to become the sole ruler of Egypt through her regents from about 1456 to 1436 BCE. In theory, Hatsheput was the High Priest of every god in Egypt and contemporary monuments depict her in full sacerdotal regalia making the official offerings to the chief deities. Hatsheput was an exception, however. In general the men made it impossible for women to enjoy such power and they seem to have resented her: her monuments appear to have been smashed with great ferocity at a later date. But the great Queens of the Eighteenth Dynasty, such as Nefertiti, wife of Akhnaton (1367–50), had a unique status. Nefertiti played a central role in the worship of Aten, the Sun God; one of the temples at Karnak was built for her and its blocks depict her making priestly offerings to Aten, a job hitherto reserved exclusively for the King.

The position of the female was already in decline, however. In Mesopotamia, Egypt and India, Semitic and Aryan invaders from the north brought with them a male-oriented mythology which replaced the Goddess with more powerful masculine deities. These invasions had begun as early as the fourth millennium but became more and more devastating. We can sense the intensity of the conflict and the passions aroused during this period of transition in the Amorite myth of the goddess Tiamat's defeat as recounted in the *Enuma Elish*, composed in about 1750 BCE. Here Tiamat, the primal sea, has her supporters, but her originally creative role as the source of being is usurped by the younger male god Marduk, the patron deity of Babylon. In a fierce battle for supremacy, Marduk sends a whirlwind into Tiamat's belly which blows her up. Then he dismembers her corpse to create the Heavens and the Earth. In this myth, the goddess has been violently reduced to inert matter in the male god's hands. The story clearly represents on one level the political victory of the Amorites over the older Sumerian–Akkadian civilization, but it also marks the beginning of the end of the reign of the goddess. Henceforth masculine gods like Marduk, Zeus and the Hebrew Yahweh would become the supreme figures in the pantheon or cult of their worshippers and would introduce a more martial and aggressive spirituality. Priestesses would continue to take their parts in the ancient rites but they would be gradually pushed into a marginal position.

For our purposes, this process was particularly important in ancient Israel, where Yahweh eventually triumphed over the gods and goddesses of the area. It was a slow and painful business, however, achieved gradually and with many setbacks. Abraham had left the city of Ur in about 1850 BCE. After a sojourn in Harran in what is now eastern Turkey, he journeyed westward to the land of Canaan, the modern Israel. His God, often called Yahweh in the book of Genesis, promised Abraham that he would become the father of a mighty nation and that his descendants would one day own Canaan. This promise was not fulfilled until centuries later. Genesis tells us that the twelve sons of Jacob, Abraham's grandson who was renamed Israel ('May God show his strength!'), had settled in Egypt during a famine. After an initial period of prosperity there, the children of Israel became mere slaves. Later they claimed that their God Yahweh had seen their distress and led them out of Egypt under the leadership of his prophet Moses. The story is well known. Pharaoh was reluctant to let the Israelites go but Yahweh forced his hand by unleashing twelve terrible plagues upon Egypt. After their miraculous exodus in about 1250 BCE, the Twelve Tribes of Israel wandered for forty years in the Sinai peninsula. On Mount Sinai itself, Moses received the Law or the Torah and Yahweh entered into a special covenant agreement with the Israelites. Finally, after Moses's death, his successor Joshua led them into Canaan and eventually they conquered their Promised Land, each of the Twelve Tribes being allotted an area in which to settle, except the tribe of Levi, who were appointed the priests of Yahweh.

The religion of Abraham is usually known as monotheism, the worship of only one God. The God of Israel would later become the God of the Christians and the Muslims, who all regard themselves as the spiritual offspring of Abraham, the father of all believers. Yet it seems clear that neither Abraham nor Moses was monotheist as we usually understand the term.

The early Israelites were bound by the terms of their covenant to worship Yahweh alone but they believed that other gods existed. It is difficult to find a single monotheistic statement in the whole of the Pentateuch, the first five books of the Bible. Even the Ten Commandments given by God to Moses on Mount Sinai take the existence of other gods for granted: 'Thou shalt not have strange gods before me.' Consequently it was a great temptation to neglect the covenant and worship Yahweh's rivals, whose cults were attractive and who offered help which it seemed foolhardy to refuse. The Bible shows that time and again the Israelites turned to other deities, like Baal, Anat and Asherah. Indeed, while Moses had been with Yahweh on Mount Sinai, his brother Aaron had conceded to the pleas of the people and made them a Golden Calf, the effigy of El, High God of Canaan. As a punishment, the tribe of Levi had rallied to Yahweh and slain three thousand of the idolaters. When the editors of the Pentateuch put the story of this apostasy in stark juxtaposition with the awesome revelation on Mount Sinai, they were perhaps indicating the severity and bitterness of the division in Israel.

But the Israelites continued to worship other gods long after they had settled in the land of Canaan, in spite of the prophets who reminded them of the terms of the covenant. In the book of Judges, we are repeatedly told that in times of war the Israelites were faithful to Yahweh, who had proved his expertise in battle. But when things were easier they turned to the old pagan rites of their neighbours. To worship only one god would have been regarded as extremely eccentric in the ancient world: why turn down a source of power and influence? Why imperil the fertility of the Promised Land by neglecting the cult of Baal and Anat, who had kept Canaan fruitful for time immemorial? Prophets like Elijah tried to stamp out this pagan cult and show that Yahweh would supply rain for the crops, but they achieved no lasting success. Even important kings like Solomon worshipped the deities of his pagan wives and built shrines for them in the 'high places' round about Jerusalem. The great Temple built by Solomon in Yahweh's honour had pagan imagery: there was a huge bronze urn representing Yam, the sea god who had fought with Baal; there were also four pillars, similar to the fertility poles which marked the cult of Asherah, El's wife. Some Israelites appear to have thought that Yahweh himself had a consort: inscriptions have recently been unearthed dedicated 'To Yahweh and his Asherah'. There were other cultic centres besides Jerusalem, served by the Levites, at Hebron, Bethel and Shiloh where pagan rites were also celebrated alongside the traditional cults of Yahweh. Priests and kings connived at this and even encouraged it. In the tenth century, King Jeroboam set up cultic bulls in honour of El in the northern shrines of Dan and Bethel, which were still there two centuries later. Pillars of Asherah continued to adorn the Jerusalem Temple, and ninth-century kings set up official fertility cults in her honour, complete with the sacred priestesses.[4] In the eighth century, the wife of the prophet Hosea had become a priestess of Baal in Bethel and seems to have participated in ritualized sex. This painful experience gave Hosea an insight into the anguish Yahweh must have felt when Israel was unfaithful to him and went whoring after the pagan deities.

Numerous figurines of the naked Goddess figure dating from this period have been found in Israel. In comparison with the pagan rituals, Yahweh's own cult seems somewhat undeveloped. In the early days, the Levite priests had a number of functions, but none that demanded great skill or artistry. Levites looked after the various sanctuaries, consulted the oracle, carried the Ark of the Covenant (Yahweh's portable shrine) into battle, officiated at the sacrifices instituted by the kings and were the official judges of disputes. The only one of their jobs that demanded special training was consulting the oracle by casting the lots known as Urim and Thurrim, a skill that was probably passed down from father to son. It may have been thus that the idea of an hereditary priesthood developed in Israel. The only one of these Levitical functions that was liturgical was the sacrifice, but this does not seem to have become a specifically priestly duty until quite a late date. The Bible shows many people who were not priests offering an animal sacrifice to Yahweh: Gideon, David and Solomon were all able to perform this cultic function. In the early Israelite religion, offering the burned carcass of an animal to Yahweh or presenting him with the first fruits of the harvest was a sign of the Israelites' gratitude and obedience. Finally, by the seventh century the Levites had also become the authoritative interpreters of the Law. In the book of Deuteronomy, which was supposedly discovered in the Temple in 622 BCE, Moses is made to pay this tribute to the priestly tribe of Levi:

> Yes, they have kept your word,
> they hold firmly to your covenant.
> They teach your customs to Jacob,
> your law to Israel.
> They send incense rising to your nostrils,
> place the holocaust on your altars.[5]

The discovery of Deuteronomy inspired Josiah, King of Judah from 640 to 609 BCE, to reform the religion of Israel by wiping out the pagan opposition. As the second book of Kings tells us, he removed all the cult images of Baal, Asherah 'and the whole array of heaven' from the Temple and had them publicly burned. He 'pulled down the house of the sacred male prostitutes which was in the Temple of Yahweh and where the women wove garments for Asherah'.[6] He also 'smashed the sacred pillars, cut down the sacred poles and covered the places where they had stood with human bones'.[7] He desecrated the shrines which Solomon had built for deities such as Astarte, the fertility goddess of Sidon, and the male gods Chemesh and Milcom who were native to what is now Jordan. Finally he called in all the Levites from the shrines of Yahweh dotted round the country, which were tainted by pagan practice. Henceforth there would be only one official cultic centre in Israel: the Temple of Jerusalem. In theory, all the Levites were to be permitted to serve in the Temple now that they had lost their own shrines. Thus in Deuteronomy, Moses was made to say:

If the Levite living in one of your towns anywhere in Israel decides to come to the place Yahweh chooses, he shall minister there in the name of Yahweh his God like all his fellow Levites who stand ministering there in the presence of Yahweh, and shall eat equal shares with them.[8]

In practice, however, the Levites of Jerusalem made sure that their brethren from the provinces were reduced in status and performed only menial tasks in the Temple cult. An inner circle of senior priests was beginning to emerge.

Even Josiah's ruthless reforms did not make Israelites impervious to the lure of paganism, however. In the seventh and sixth centuries, the prophets Jeremiah and Ezekiel speak of Canaanite fertility cults flourishing in the 'high places' of Israel and in the Temple itself. Jeremiah mentions a special cult of Ishtar, Queen of Heaven, which was particularly popular among women, rituals performed in honour of the sun, and Ezekiel speaks of celebrations of the Mesopotamian deity Tammuz.[9] He also tells us that the pagan icons had crept back into the Temple and that the Levites themselves supported these abominable cults.[10] But political catastrophe put an end to all this. In 587 BCE Nebuchadnezzar, King of Babylon, conquered Jerusalem, destroyed the Temple and began to deport the Israelites to Mesopotamia. There they were settled in two colonies, one in Babylon itself and the other on the banks of a canal leading from the Euphrates called the Chebar, not far from Ur, in an area they named Tel Aviv (The Hill of Spring).

It was during their exile to Babylon that the Israelites lost all interest in paganism and the religion of Judaism was born. The catastrophe which might have caused them to lose faith in Yahweh in fact made them examine their conduct and embrace the serene monotheism preached by the anonymous prophet, known as Second Isaiah, who was active during the exile. Among the first batch of deportees to arrive in Tel Aviv was the prophet Ezekiel, who was also a priest. On the banks of the Chebar he had a terrifying vision of Yahweh seated on a throne pulled by four strange beasts. It proved that unlike most pagan gods, Yahweh was not confined to one locality but could visit and succour his people in exile. In Babylon, the prophets were beginning to see Yahweh as the Lord of history, who held all the nations in the palm of his hand and would one day lead his people home. In a vision, Ezekiel saw the glory of Yahweh entering the Temple again and looked forward to a reformed cult. But Yahweh warned him that the Israelites would have to abandon their filthy pagan practices once and for all. There must be no more foreigners in the new Temple, since they would import their alien rites into the reformed religion of Yahweh. They must also purge the priesthood. Most of the Levites had proved to be utterly unworthy. They had frequently served in the pagan shrines and condoned the foreign cults. Consequently, Yahweh said, they must be punished when the new Temple was built:

> They are to be servants in my sanctuary, responsible for guarding the Temple gates and serving the Temple. . . . Since they used to be at their service in front of their idols and were an occasion of sin in the House of Israel . . . they are never to approach me again to perform the priestly office in my presence, or to touch my holy things and to touch my most holy things; they must bear the disgrace of their filthy practices.[11]

When the exiles returned to Jerusalem, the Levites were to be mere servants in the Temple. They must never enter the Holy of Holies, the inmost sanctuary. Instead they were to act as doorkeepers, Temple servants, and take care of such chores as the killing of the sacrificial animals. The only Levites who were worthy to enter the inmost shrine and stand in God's presence were those who belonged to the clan of Zadok (a priest who had served Yahweh loyally under King Solomon).[12] Yahweh gave the Zadokite priests clear instructions for the reformed cultus. When they came to enter the Holy of Holies, they were to put on special clothes which, after performing the rites there, they were to take off when they returned to the people. They were not to marry widows or divorced women and were to take care not to be contaminated by touching a corpse.

There was a new emphasis on ritual purity. To purge themselves of the old pagan 'filth', the priests of Israel had a new task. As God said to Ezekiel, 'They are to teach my people the difference between what is sacred and what is profane and make them understand the difference between what is clean and what is unclean.'[13] This concern for purity reflected the Israelites' anxiety about their own racial integrity and social cohesion. In exile, they had become acutely conscious of the precariousness of their position. They were only a tiny minority: how could they hold on to their ethnic identity and avoid assimilation? In 722 BCE the Assyrians had conquered the northern territories of Palestine, the home of ten of the tribes of Israel who had also been deported. These tribes had disappeared from history. How were the exiles in Babylon to escape this fate? As a defence, the Israelites began to develop the laws of *kashrut*, the purity laws, to distinguish Jews sharply from their pagan neighbours and to prevent assimilation. As the anthropologist Mary Douglas has observed in her classic book *Purity and Danger*, the image of society is powerful and clear: 'it has external boundaries, margins, structures'.[14] Therefore rules that divide, demarcate and clarify the sense of identity of an endangered minority group bring a sense of order and safety:

> Ideas about separating, purifying, demarcating and punishing transgressions have as their main function to impose system on an inherently untidy experience. It is only by exaggerating the difference between within and without, above and below, male and female, with and against that a semblance of order is created.[15]

An obvious example were the *kashrut* laws about diet. Certain foods were declared to be 'unclean', depending upon their place in the order of creation to which they had been assigned. In each of the three elements – the heavens, the waters and the dry land – there were normative habits of locomotion, and only creatures which conformed to these norms were 'clean'. It was not allowed, for example, to eat sea creatures who crawled instead of swimming, the proper way to move in water. Predatory animals were also declared unclean, as was all blood since it was 'too closely associated with *nepes* (that is, breath and life) to be permitted'.[16] The dietary laws would not only define the Jewish identity by distinguishing the exiles from their pagan neighbours who did not observe these dietary laws, but would also help cultivate a respect for life.

The new priestly ethos was inspired by the ideal of holiness. The prophets had also emphasized the holiness of God. Holiness (*kaddosh*) did not mean moral excellence, though it came to signify this too, by extension. When Isaiah had had his vision Yahweh in the Temple in about 742 BCE, the seraphim around God's throne had cried: 'Holy! Holy! Holy!' What they meant was 'Yahweh is Other! Other! Other!' Instead of experiencing the immanence and kinship of the divine in the old pagan way, the prophets of Israel had stressed God's absolute separation from mankind. An encounter with God was a profound shock, a collision with a towering transcendence. Isaiah had felt that the divine impact had been fatal and was instantly conscious of his impurity. He had cried aloud in dismay:'What a wretched state I am in! I am lost, for I am a man of unclean lips and I live among a people of unclean lips, and my eyes have looked at the King, Yahweh Sabaoth.'[17]

In his important book *The Idea of the Holy*, the German scholar Rudolf Otto has described the experience of holiness as *mysterium terribile et fascinans*. It is profoundly shocking and 'terrible', since it takes the seer far from the consolations of normality, but also exerts a fascination and an irresistible attraction. It is beyond the concepts of rational thought in the same way as music and the erotic, appealing to a deeper, perhaps more primitive level of the mind.

In exile Ezekiel had also stressed the absolute 'holiness' of Yahweh in his frightening vision beside the Chebar, which left him, he says, like a man stunned for about a week afterwards. His own behaviour in Tel Aviv showed the dislocation that the experience of Yahweh brought with it. The prophet of Israel was to become as separate and strange as his God. When his wife died, Ezekiel was forbidden to mourn; he was commanded to lie on one side for 390 days and on the other for forty; once he was told to pack his possessions and walk around Tel Aviv like a displaced person. Holiness demanded that the people of Israel themselves became 'other', alien and abnormal in Middle Eastern terms. They must separate themselves radically from their neighbours. But this absolute 'holiness' would bring them close to their transcendent God.

Monotheistic spirituality enabled the Jews to survive the sorrow and pain of exile and to preserve a distinct identity. But they also experienced a loss. The old holistic vision which had celebrated the unity of the divine, the human and the natural had been replaced by a yawning gulf between God and man. When Moses had gone up Mount Sinai to meet his God, he had told the Israelites to keep their distance: 'Take care not to go up the mountain or to touch the foot of it. Whoever touches the mountain will be put to death. No one must lay a hand on him: he must be stoned or shot down by arrow.'[18] Only Moses could face the dangers of the divine impact on behalf of his people. In the old paganism, priests and priestesses had re-presented their deities because the divine was close and kin to them. This new type of God was so frightening in his holiness that only specially appointed people who observed complicated rules to protect themselves could enter his presence. It was a sad but necessary development. As men and women become more sophisticated, they begin to see themselves as separate from their environment in rather the same way, perhaps, as a child has to separate himself from the mother and become an independent person. In a sense, the achievements of civilization depend upon the ability to act upon the environment and make it do what we want. But like the dawning of individual maturity, this can be a painful experience, as the experience of a Moses, an Isaiah or an Ezekiel suggests. In the very early days, Yahweh had sat down and eaten a meal with Abraham as a friend. That kind of intimacy was no longer possible. It was becoming unbearable to contemplate an unmediated contact with the divine.

It was as a response to this experience that the new priestly tradition developed in Judaism during the exile. It continued after the Jews had been permitted by Cyrus, King of Persia (who had conquered Babylon) to return to the land of Israel and rebuild the Temple in 538 BCE. When they arrived home, the former exiles had to face not only a devastated and impoverished land but their own compatriots who had not been deported, had not shared the experience of exile and who consequently had very different notions of religion. Who was the true Israelite? Again, questions of identity were crucial and the new priestly spirituality emphasized the laws of *kashrut*. Priestly editors revised the earlier scriptures and produced the final version of the Pentateuch: they introduced new passages of their own, such as the first chapter of Genesis, to give their interpretation of the meaning of Jewish history, and added two whole new books – Leviticus and Numbers – to express the new priestly ideal.

Holiness and separation were crucial to the new priesthood. When the priestly author (usually known as 'P') described the Creation of the world in the first chapter of Genesis, separation was the key: Yahweh had made the cosmos an orderly place by separating night from day, water from dry land and light from darkness. At each stage, at the end of each symbolic 'day', God had blessed and sanctified what he had made, pronouncing it 'good'. At the end of the period of orderly creativity, God had rested on the seventh day, separating it from the rest of the week. When the Israelites observed the Sabbath rest henceforth they would imitate God, observing a ritual that Yahweh had originally observed alone. In the same way, the detailed dietary laws would become a ritual attempt to share the holy separateness of God, healing the painful severance between humanity and the divine. The Israelites would imitate God's creative acts on the day of Creation by separating milk from meat, clean from unclean. In this way they would bless and sanctify Creation, making it newly holy as Yahweh had done in the beginning.

Christians tend to have a rather misleading impression of this type of spirituality, which is described in a hostile way in the New Testament thanks to the first-century Christian polemic against Judaism. But the laws of *kashrut* are neither the crushing burden nor the pointless rules that Christians sometimes imagine. They are another form of ritual which have for centuries taught Jews how to live in a spiritual manner. The purity laws were another symbolic act of *imitatio dei* which every single Israelite could perform, whether he was a priest or not. P's watchword was the oft-repeated 'You must make yourselves holy, for I am Yahweh your God.'[19] By separating themselves from pagan practices and the lifestyle of their neighbours, the Israelites were going into a new type of exile which would bring them closer to God. They would themselves become a 'holy' nation, consecrated or 'set apart' for Yahweh: 'Be consecrated to me, because I, Yahweh, am holy, and I will set you apart from all these peoples so that you may be mine.'[20]

True, this idea of 'holiness' could lead to a sense of superiority or exclusiveness – a fault to which all religions are prone. But priestly laws of holiness also inculcated moral attitudes. Thus we have seen that they helped Jews to cultivate an appreciation of the principle of non-violence and respect for life. Because the Law forbade Israelites to use Creation as they wished – by eating exactly what they chose, for example – it reminded them that the world was not theirs to exploit and manipulate for their own uses, an attitude that is sorely needed today, as the planet becomes increasingly endangered. The so-called 'Holiness Code' of the nineteenth chapter of Leviticus does not simply concentrate on ritual purity but reminds Israelites that other people are sacred and have inalienable rights:

> You must not exploit or wrong your neighbour. . . . You must not curse the dumb, nor put an obstacle in the blind man's way, but you must fear your God: I am Yahweh. . . . You must not bear hatred for your brother in your heart. . . . You must love your neighbour as yourself: I am Yahweh. If a stranger lives with you in your land, do not molest him. You must count him as one of your own countrymen and love him as yourself – for you were once strangers yourselves in Egypt. I am Yahweh, your God.[21]

Long before the exile, prophets like Hosea and Isaiah had preached the necessity for the interior dimension of religion and the overriding duty of compassion. Isaiah had inveighed against a purely external observance of liturgy and Hosea had insisted that Yahweh wanted mercy rather than sacrifice. In its revised conception of the laws of holiness, the priestly tradition did not forget this insight.

But the Israelites had returned home to rebuild their Temple and create a new cult. This was crucial to P's spirituality. In his view, priesthood was about rebuilding the world. He included a long section in the book of Exodus about the Tent of Meeting where God had met with Moses in the desert. On Mount Sinai, Moses was said to have been given minute directions about the building of this Sanctuary, which was clearly not meant to be realistic. Nobody seriously imagined that the Israelites had built this elaborate shrine of gold, silver, bronze, silk, linen and acacia wood in the wilderness. Temple building was an act of *imitatio dei*, a symbolic act of re-creation. P's account is deliberately constructed to remind the reader of his Creation account at the very start of the Pentateuch. At each stage of the construction of the Sanctuary, Moses 'saw all the work' and 'blessed' the people like Yahweh. The Sanctuary is built on the first day of the first month of the year; Bezalel, its architect, is inspired by the Spirit of God that also brooded over the Creation, and both accounts emphasize the importance of the Sabbath. At the very end of the long list of instructions and requirements for the Sanctuary, Yahweh commands the Israelites to observe the Sabbath as a sanctuary in time, as 'a sign between myself and you from generation to generation to show that it is I, Yahweh, who sanctify you'.[22]

In rather the same way, the book of Leviticus gives equally detailed directions concerning the ordination and investiture of Aaron and his sons as priests of the new cult. Like Ezekiel, P does not believe that all Levites should serve as priests in the new dispensation. Ezekiel had assigned the priesthood to the clan of Zadok, able to do so because of his authority as a prophet. P does not have this right, so he ascribes the decision to limit the priesthood to Moses. Priesthood is now seen as far too difficult and dangerous for ordinary mortals, so, P says, God had decreed that it was Aaron and his descendants who were the true priests of Israel and the Levites were to serve only in subordinate roles. Moses constantly emphasizes the perils of approaching the holy God when he gives his instructions to Aaron. The requirements are intricate and must be followed to the letter: 'Do this and you will not die,' Moses explains.[23] Aaron obeys perfectly. He offers the sacrifices in the prescribed manner as an act of purification and God responds favourably. Because he has performed 'the sacrifice for sin, the holocaust and the communion sacrifice', Aaron is allowed to enter the Tent of Meeting with Moses and emerge unscathed: 'A flame leapt forth before Yahweh and consumed the holocaust and the fat that was on the altar. At this the people shouted for joy and fell on their faces.'[24] But then comes a tragedy. Nadab and Abihu, Aaron's eldest sons, break away from the ritual order

and act on their own initiative, offering something that God had
not asked for. What P calls 'strange fire' (*esh zarah*, which could
also be translated 'foreign fire', that is, coming from an alien
people) is not acceptable and Yahweh acts with hideous swift-
ness, sending another fire to consume Nadab and Abihu like
the holocaust that Aaron has just offered. The holiness of God is
a fearful, destructive force if not approached in the right way or
in foreign cults. Later P merely says that Nadab and Abihu
'drew near to Yahweh and perished'.[25] Proximity to God can no
longer be attempted spontaneously or with impunity: contact
with the divine must be made by the duly ordained personnel
who will approach God on behalf of their people, as their
representatives.

Not unnaturally, Aaron is distressed but, interestingly, he
appears surprised that he himself has not met the same fate,
and Moses approves of his penitence and caution. The names of
the two errant sons are very similar to Nadab and Abiju, the two
sons of King Jeroboam who had erected a Golden Bull in
honour of a Canaanite God in Dan and Bethel. Immediately, we
recall the story of the Golden Calf which Aaron had set up for
the people of Israel while Moses was on Mount Sinai. When
Nebuchadnezzar conquered Jerusalem, thousands of Israelites
died for their cultic infidelity to Yahweh: the deaths of Nadab
and Abihu would have been a reminder to P's first readers of
the crucial necessity for reform. It was the Law – not the old
cultic dramas of the Sacred Marriage that had tempted so many
Israelites from the covenant – which would ensure the fertility
of the devastated land:

> If you live according to my laws, if you keep my com-
> mandments, I will give you the rain you need at the right
> time; the earth shall give its produce and the trees of the
> countryside their fruits. You shall thresh until vintage
> time and gather grapes until sowing time. You shall eat
> your fill of bread and live secure on your land.[26]

Above all, the laws of separation would restore the Israelites to
the old union with God that Adam and Eve had enjoyed when
Yahweh walked with them in the cool of the evening. God

would now dwell among them in the newly built Temple: 'I will set up my dwelling among you, and I will not cast you off. I will walk among you and will be your God and you shall be my people.'[27] The separation from the other nations would lead to a new kind of exile but, paradoxically, it would also return Israel to man's primal home.

P believes that the old judicial functions of the priests have ended. Their new task is to approach God in the rituals that make this possible. There is, of course, no question of Aaron and his descendants re-presenting God like the old pagan priests: God is beyond any human representation and soon Jews will not even be able to pronounce his name. The Aaronic priesthood could simply represent the people. The various spheres of holiness were now carefully 'separated' and marked off from one another. Only Aaron and his sons could enter the Holy of Holies but they were always to be mindful of the dangers, performing the symbolic actions of purification, sacrifice and the changing of garments as a reminder of the terrifying Otherness of God. Every time priests approached the Sanctuary, they faced potential danger and death on behalf of their people. As such, they were 'set aside' for this service in the rite of Ordination, which stressed the crossing of boundaries since it takes place on the threshold between the courtyard and the Sanctuary. P emphasizes the perils and responsibilities of priesthood rather than its privileges, yet for him Aaron has become the holiest of beings, symbolically separated from his fellow Israelites by his special clothes: 'They must not wear tonsures, shave the edges of their beards, or gash their bodies,' God says of his priests, 'they must be consecrated to their God.' They may have no blemish – another symbol of the ritual purity required to approach God. Priests are hedged around with extra purity regulations, forbidden as in Ezekiel to have any contact with dead bodies, and subject to special marriage laws. Even though God's presence is once again available in the Temple, the priestly order is necessary to protect the people from God's holiness and to protect God's holiness from profanation. There is no room for democracy in P's vision. When Korah leads a party of Levites to rebel against Aaron's special status, God destroys him as ruthlessly as he did Nadab and

Abihu. Korah and his allies had protested to Moses and Aaron: 'You take too much upon yourselves! The whole community and all its members are consecrated and Yahweh lives among them. Why set yourselves higher than the Community?'[28] Not only does the ground split open to swallow Korah but 250 rebellious Levites who dare to carry incense into the Sanctuary are consumed by fire. As Yahweh says to Aaron: any layman who 'comes near' shall die; it is only Aaron and his family who can 'bear the burden' of priesthood.[29]

Consequently all other Israelites can only enter the courtyard of the Sanctuary and gentiles may not even go into the courtyard. The new separations were ruthlessly observed. There were no women priests in the new order. Not only were they a painful reminder of the priestesses of Asherah who had polluted the old Temple, but there were new purity laws about women. In the old dispensation before the exile, women had sometimes been religious leaders. Moses's sister Miriam was an accredited prophetess; Deborah was a judge who had led her people into battle; Huldah the Prophetess had been involved in Josiah's reforms, and even during the exile, Israelites had revered the memory of valiant women such as Judith and Esther. P has a positive vision of the female sex in one important respect. In his Creation account, he insists that both male and female were created in God's image – something which the earlier version, in the second chapter of Genesis, does not emphasize in the same way. There the author known as the 'Yahwist' (who may have written in about the tenth century BCE) says that Eve was created almost as an afterthought from Adam's rib. P's careful insistence that 'male and female he created them'[30] is a vital text for those who support the ordination of women today, but there was no question of ordaining women to the Aaronic priesthood.

One of the new major separations of the Law was that women were now put into a separate ritual category. Menstruation and the 'impurity' of childbirth excluded women from the realm of the sacred. The new purity laws decreed that a woman was unclean not only during the week of her period but for a further seven days afterwards. During this half of the month:

Anyone who touches her will be unclean until evening.
Any bed she lies on in this state will be unclean; any seat
she sits on will be unclean. Anyone who touches her bed
must wash his clothing and wash himself and be unclean
until evening.[31]

A man who sleeps with a menstruating woman will be contaminated and unclean himself for seven days. Only after the
fifteen days of seclusion and isolation can a woman present
herself to a priest at the door of the Tent of Meeting to make a
ritual offering of two doves or pigeons. In the same way, the
blood discharged by a woman during childbirth renders her
unclean thereafter for forty days in the case of a boy child and
eighty days for a girl. True, men are rendered unclean by a
discharge caused by venereal disease, but this is an abnormal
sickness and does not exclude all men *qua* men from normal
contact with others. Again, nocturnal emissions not ejaculated
into a woman's vagina also make a man unclean, but the Law
was designed to prevent men 'wasting their seed' in this way.
They were not regarded as intrinsically unclean in the same
way as a woman, whose normal female cycle made her incompatible with the holiness of the cult.

There are several theories about this new priestly ruling.
Mary Douglas has suggested that in a time of social crisis, a lack
of physical integrity is threatening and people suddenly become concerned about the orifices of the body. Others have
seen a woman's involuntary bleeding as a disturbing lack of
control, which would have placed her in the realm of unor-
dered, unsanctified nature. The man, on the other hand, who
was not subject to this unstoppable cycle, would have seemed
to have belonged to the realm of culture, the re-creation of
nature which was so important to P. Others have noted that it
was the priestly tradition which emphasized the rite of male
circumcision as *the* official rite of entry into Judaism.[32] Where P
sees the blood of a woman as excluding her from holiness, the
blood shed by a Jewish man at his circumcision included him in
the sacred community. Indeed, menstruation was equated
metaphorically with the impurity acquired by carrying idols.[33]

Taken to its logical conclusion, these purity laws almost dis-
qualified women from the Jewish nation. This was graphically
clear in the Temple which had just been completed by King
Herod in the time of Christ. This Temple depicted the various
grades of holiness in a series of concentric circles. On the inside
was the Holy of Holies which could only be entered by the High
Priest once a year on the Day of Atonement. In front of the
Temple was the court of the priests, inaccessible to laymen.
Surrounding this was a courtyard for the laymen of Israel; next
came the court of women and after that the court of the *goyim*,
the gentiles. When a woman was menstruating or ritually
impure after childbirth, she was not even allowed to enter the
court of women and was officially in the same category as the
gentiles.

Recently the Jewish feminist writer Judith Plaskow has noted
that this perception of women virtually makes them 'the gentile
within' the holy nation of Israel. As Plaskow points out, when
Moses was preparing the Israelites for the revelation of Sinai, he
ordered them 'do not go near any woman'.[34] The holiness of
God was deemed incompatible with a woman's presence, just
at the moment when the people of Israel were covenanted to
their God. Have Jewish women never truly been included in the
covenant at all?[35] But these purity regulations have also been a
problem for Christian women and have played an important, if
unstated, role in the recent debate about the feasibility of
women priests. As we shall see, these ancient blood taboos
have affected the Christian as well as the Jewish perception of
women and their relation to the sacred. It is no accident that
those bishops who are opposed to the ordination of women
today are at the time of writing concerned about the 'taint' they
will incur if they give women Holy Orders.

The priestly tradition was a product of its time. It was a
creative answer to many profound anxieties about the nature of
God, the identity of Israel and the trauma of the exile. In the
book of Numbers, P constantly depicts the people of Israel
bemoaning 'the fleshpots of Egypt' during their forty years in
the wilderness. Clearly, there was worry about the temptation
to remain in the Diaspora, as many Jews did after the exile,
where they could live a more comfortable life. Instead, P

preaches a new exile from the *mores* of the gentiles and from the easy access that pagans enjoyed to the divine world. The reward would be a symbolic and hard-won closeness to God. But there were other strands in the Bible, which had a more egalitarian view of holiness. The early tenth- or ninth-century author known as the 'Elohist' seems to share the rebellious Korah's view of the holiness of the whole of Israel. He makes God tell the Israelites, 'I will count you a kingdom of priests, a consecrated nation.'[36] Later generations would turn back to this perception to find a message for their own times, which had developed different needs and a view of God that was less transcendent than the terrifying God of P. Five hundred years after the exile, some Jews were less than enthusiastic about King Herod's magnificent new Temple. As a Nabatean, Herod was a foreigner who had collaborated with the *goyim*: how could his Temple be 'holy'? Other Jews had begun to experience God as an immanent presence, who could be freely approached by every single Israelite. They tended to prefer the simpler worship in the synagogue, the meeting place which had sprung up all over the Jewish world – in the Diaspora as well as in Palestine. Originally, the synagogue had been tied to the worship in the Temple, answering the need for a local shrine which the reforms of Josiah had abolished. In order that a local area should feel that they had some share in the Jerusalem cult, a group of laymen (known as the *ma'amad* or 'post') would accompany their priest when it was his turn to officiate in the Temple for a week. While the priests performed the sacrificial ritual, the 'post' of laymen would pray together in the synagogue situated in the Temple precincts, while back home another group would hold a similar meeting in the local synagogue. It was a symbolic way of synchronizing the prayers of the laity with their priest, but by the first century CE the synagogue was acquiring an independent identity. By this time, various Jewish movements felt the need for change and some were beginning to feel disenchanted with the institution of priesthood. One of these would ultimately take the holy God of Israel into the gentile world.

— 2 —

Jesus, Women and the Twelve

JESUS OF Nazareth began his mission during the second decade of the first century CE. After his baptism at the hands of John the Baptist, who proclaimed him as the long-awaited Messiah, he began to preach in the small lakeside towns of Galilee in northern Palestine, announcing the arrival of the Kingdom of God. Perhaps he was a charismatic *hasid*, a devout man of a type that was common in Galilee but rather scorned by the establishment in Jerusalem. In any event, Jesus made good his Messianic claim by healing the sick, exorcizing demons and forgiving sins – activities that properly belonged to God alone. His mission, he said, was to the sinners and lost sheep of the House of Israel. He had come to liberate the poor and oppressed and in the New Israel the last would be first, the proud and complacent cast down, and the humble, marginalized people would take precedence. Crowds flocked to hear him speak, and to further his mission he chose an inner circle of disciples. Fishermen left their nets, a despised tax collector abandoned his disreputable trade, and even women left their homes and families to follow Jesus. He inspired such faith that although he was crucified by the Roman authorities, his followers could not abandon their Messianic expectations. They believed that he had risen from the dead and would shortly return in glory to establish God's rule definitively on earth.

The four Gospels, which tell Jesus's story, are not the earliest Christian writings. Mark's account was probably written in about 70 CE, some forty years after Jesus's crucifixion. Matthew and Luke are usually dated from the 80s and John's account could be as late as 100. Their perceptions are often coloured by the preoccupations and experiences of the Churches in their own day. The very first Christian documents are the epistles of St Paul, which he began to write during the 50s. But Paul is not primarily interested in Jesus's earthly life. Instead, he concentrates on the religious significance of his death and Resurrection. It is important, therefore, to begin our investigation of Christian priesthood with the Gospel stories, since much of the debate about the ordination of women has centred on the person and ministry of Jesus. For two thousand years people have meditated on the Gospels and interpreted them in many different ways. Jesus has been seen as wholly human and as a divine figure, as a Jewish nationalist, an anarchist, a defender of the *status quo*, a Pharisee, the founder of a wholly Jewish sect, the founder of a universal religion and the enemy of traditional Judaism. It is not possible to find a picture of Jesus that will please everybody or to reconcile these conflicting interpretations, but had the Gospel portrait been less enigmatic and flexible it would not have inspired so many people in so many different cultures and circumstances. Similarly in the current dispute about the ordination of women, Jesus has been described as both the champion and the opponent of women priests. It may not be possible to find a definitive solution, but the four Gospels do display an underlying consistency which may provide important principles to guide us in forming an opinion of the role of women in Christian ministry today.

Throughout Christian history, people have been selective in their reading of the Gospels, emphasizing those aspects that have seemed relevant to their particular situation. One of the things that Christians have tended to overlook until relatively recently has been the essentially Jewish nature of Jesus's message. In the second half of our own century, Jewish and Christian scholars have done valuable work to show the interrelation of these two monotheistic traditions. Whatever our view of Jesus's divinity, we cannot escape the fact that he was also a man of his time, born into a specific historical situation. His teaching was not especially original: many of his words, as they have come down to us in the Gospels, are remarkably similar to the rabbinic traditions enshrined in the Talmud and other contemporary Jewish texts. Thus Jesus's view of women and priesthood must be seen against this Jewish background. Again, the first Christians were primarily concerned with the apocalyptic content of Jesus's message. People like Paul did not believe that they were legislating for two thousand years of Church history because they were convinced that they were living in the Last Days and that Jesus would return in their own lifetime. But when this did not happen, Christians had to rethink their faith. One of the ways in which they expressed their new perception of Christianity was by making provision for Church order, by establishing offices and institutions that would preserve the Gospel values and take the Church safely into the future.

The Gospels tell us that Jesus chose twelve of his disciples to form an inner circle. They are usually known as the Apostles and they figure largely in any discussion of Church ministry. It has been claimed that the validity of Christian priesthood depends on what is known as the apostolic succession. Priests are supposed to have received their powers in an unbroken tradition that can be traced right back to the Twelve and to the ministers they ordained to succeed them. As neither Jesus nor the Twelve chose to ordain women, it has been argued that to do so now would break this tradition. The Church would no longer be apostolic.

In the first century, however, the word 'apostle' did not yet have the hallowed significance that it has acquired since. The noun *apostolos* ([one] sent out) was not common in written Greek. Originally used as an adjective, it had the neutral meaning of 'dispatched' and then came to mean the thing or person dispatched, such as a fleet or a messenger. The word often carries this neutral meaning in the New Testament but it acquired a particular importance when applied to the people whom Jesus had 'sent out' or commissioned to preach the good news of the Kingdom.

Matthew, Mark and Luke, the three Synoptic Gospels, all record the commission of the Twelve. When they were ready, Luke says, Jesus 'called the Twelve together and gave them power and authority over all devils and to cure diseases, and he sent them out to proclaim the Kingdom of God and to heal'.[1] But Luke also tells us that Jesus gave another commission to seventy-two other disciples and sent them out as *apostoloi* or plenipotentiary messengers who represented himself. He tells the Seventy-two: 'Anyone who listens to you listens to me; anyone who rejects you rejects me, and those who reject me reject the one who sent me [*ton aposteilanta me*],'[2] using exactly the same formula with which Matthew makes him dispatch the Twelve in his Gospel. Elsewhere in the New Testament we find that other people who were not among the original Twelve are called 'apostles'. Some of these had not even been disciples of Jesus during his lifetime but had received their commission after the Resurrection. Thus James, the brother of Jesus, who had not believed in him while he was on earth but who had had a vision of the risen Christ, was the leader of the Jerusalem congregation until his death in 66 CE.[3] The last and most famous of the specially commissioned envoys was the Apostle Paul, who had never even met Jesus and had once been a bitter opponent of Christianity. He had been converted by an over-powering vision of the risen Jesus on the road to Damascus. As he explained:

> I am the least of the Apostles; in fact, since I persecuted the Church of God, I hardly deserve the name Apostle; but by God's grace that is what I am, and the grace that he gave me has not been fruitless.[4]

The term 'apostle', therefore, was not confined to the Twelve. These Apostles were leaders of the primitive Church, but since the chief qualification of apostleship was to have been directly commissioned by the Lord himself, the office was not communicable to the next generation. The Apostles cannot be said to have appointed successors.

But the Twelve did appoint somebody to take the place of Judas Iscariot, one of their number who had betrayed Jesus and after his arrest had committed suicide out of remorse. After Jesus had ascended to Heaven, Peter emerged as the leader of the Twelve and announced that they must fill the vacancy that Judas had left behind him. Judas's successor must be somebody who had been with them from the beginning of Jesus's mission and could bear witness to his Resurrection. The lot fell upon Matthias who was thenceforth listed as one of the Twelve.[5]

Why was it so important to keep the numbers up in this way? What was the significance of the inner circle of twelve disciples? The Gospels make it clear that the Twelve were a crucial element in Jesus's Messianic vision: in the new dispensation of the Kingdom, they were to represent the Twelve Tribes of Israel and would judge them on the Day of the Lord.[6] Jesus does not seem to have envisaged a future Church with a long history. His message is shot through with an acute consciousness of the End of Days. He had come to bring a fire upon the earth and was impatient for it to blaze; the Judgement which would destroy the old order was approaching: those found unworthy would be cast into flames or into outer darkness where there would be weeping and gnashing of teeth. His disciples were to be alert and continuously on the watch. There were people living now who would not taste death before the End came. We must see the appointment of the Twelve in this apocalyptic light: when the Judgement came, they would flank Jesus on his right and left – a powerful sign of a reconstituted Israel. The primitive Church shared this vision of an imminent apocalypse, seeing itself as the New Israel and as the culmination of Jewish history. The author of the book of Revelation saw the Twelve in apocalyptic rather than administrative terms: they were the foundation-stones of the New Jerusalem, juxtaposing the Twelve Tribes of the old dispensation.[7]

The Twelve were undoubtedly all men. Is it true, therefore, as many claim, that women should not be ordained to the priest-hood since Jesus, whose decisions were infallible, chose only men? Such a view assumes that we can take Jesus's ministry as a model for discipleship in the late twentieth century. It was essential that the Twelve Apostles should all be male since they were to represent the twelve sons of the patriarch Jacob, the ancestors of the Jewish people. Had women been included, the symbolism would not have worked. In the synagogues at that time, only men could constitute the quorum necessary for an official meeting. But we should also reflect that the Twelve were not only all men, they were also all Jewish. This was equally essential to Jesus's Messianic vision. People never argue that because Jesus chose only Jews, gentiles should be debarred from the priesthood. The Churches have all been selective about their interpretations of discipleship, as of so many other elements of the gospel message. The ideal of an apostolic succession is indeed important, but not because it enshrines an exclusively male priesthood. The symbolism of the Twelve reminds Christians of their continuity with the people and religion of Israel: in the late twentieth century it would be more productive to use the imagery of the Twelve Apostles to repair the Churches' links with the Jewish people than as a weapon against women priests.

Jesus made other stringent demands of his disciples, which are not regarded as necessary qualifications for ministry today. Because Jesus and the first Christians believed that they were living in the Last Days, they required all or nothing. A disciple had to be ready to abandon his wife and family, leave the dead to bury the dead and renounce all their possessions. At the end of Mark's Gospel, the list of the signs which were to character-ize the true disciples reflects this apocalyptic extremity:

> In my name they will cast out devils; they will have the gift
> of tongues; they will pick up snakes in their hands, and
> they will be unharmed should they drink deadly poison;
> they will lay their hands on the sick who will recover.[8]

Some radical sects believe that these charisms are essential, but the vast majority of church-goers today would be disconcerted, not to say appalled, if their pastors went in for these kinds of activities. Times have changed and what seemed necessary in the first century is no longer a priority. Again, most Churches today do not make celibacy obligatory for ordained ministers, despite Paul's recommendations in this regard, and few expect the absolute renunciation of worldly goods that Jesus demanded of his disciples as a *sine qua non*.[9] Over the centuries,

Christians have tempered Jesus's demands, adapting them to meet their changed and changing circumstances.

We must also understand that Jesus did not envisage either the Twelve or the other disciples as priests. In fact, as we shall see, the Christian priesthood was a much later development, another of those adaptations that were deemed necessary as Christianity spread into a very different world. We know that Jesus attended services in the Temple and that after the Resurrection his Apostles and their disciples did the same.[10] The only priesthood they would have recognized was the Temple priestly caste, represented at that time by the party of the Sadducees. They had no ambitions to usurp these liturgical functions but worshipped in the Temple as lay folk. Indeed, Jesus and his followers seem to have been more in sympathy with those Jewish movements that were beginning to distance themselves from the Jerusalem Temple and the conventional priesthood.

Thus in first-century Palestine, the Essenes and the Qumran group, who had settled in a monastic-style community beside the Dead Sea, had both withdrawn from Jerusalem and the Temple cult – not because they were indifferent to the Holy City and its ancient rites but, on the contrary, because they cared so deeply about them. The Essenes had cut themselves off from ordinary society in a way that was unusual for Jews, in order to form their own communities. They held all goods in common, abhorred all forms of war and violence, opposed slavery and commerce and avoided marriage (although the contemporary Jewish historian Josephus tells us that one branch did consist of married people). The Essenes were convinced that the Temple had become corrupt, and they lived as priests – they may have been of the Levitical caste – taking great care to live in a state of ritual purity. Their communities would constitute the new Temple, a new centre of holiness: they expressed this commitment in sacred, communal meals that celebrated the new covenant that God had forged with a New Israel.

The Qumran sect had similar ideals. In about 90 BCE, a group of priests and laymen had quarrelled with the official Temple priesthood, accusing the establishment of corruption. Led by their own 'Teacher of Righteousness', they migrated first to

48 THE END OF SILENCE

Damascus and eventually to Qumran by the Dead Sea where they lived a monastic life. They were not pacifists like the Essenes, however, but like Jesus had a fiercely apocalyptic vision, looking forward to the advent of a Messiah who would also be a Priest. Their holy books, known today as the Dead Sea Scrolls, describe the holy war that the Priest would fight with his colleague the Kingly Messiah, a descendant of King David, against the Romans and the other *goyim*. Eventually the forces of light would triumph and would build a new Temple, establishing a strict regime in which the whole of Jerusalem would become a sacred area and the laws of ritual purity would be obligatory for all its inhabitants. Originally élitist, the ideology of Qumran had an ultimately more democratic vision in which the whole of the New Israel would become a nation of priests and a holy people.

The Pharisees, who are so frequently mentioned in the Gospels, shared this vision of a transformed priestly nation. They formed the majority party in Palestine in the first century, though they were sometimes referred to as Sages or Scribes. They get a bad press in the Gospels, which often depict them as blatant hypocrites who concentrated obsessively on external observance of the Law of Moses but neglected its inward dimension. This is an inaccurate portrayal, which reflects the tensions between Jews and Christians in the 70s and 80s. In fact, the Pharisees were devoutly religious men and their brand of Judaism would become normative. They were principally concerned with the revision of the Law to make it relevant to contemporary circumstances. They instituted some important and humane reforms, many of them positive for women, who were given rights of inheritance and divorce that would not become common in the Christian world until the nineteenth century. The Pharisees were also concerned to cultivate a sense of God's presence in the smallest details of daily life and emphasized the importance of charity and respect for the inalienable rights of others. There is a story that one day a pagan approached the great sage Hillel the Elder and told him that he would be willing to convert to Judaism if the Master could recite the whole of the Torah to him while he stood on one leg. Hillel replied: 'Do not do unto others as you would not have done unto you. That is the whole of Torah: go and learn it.'[11]

It has been argued that Jesus himself was a Pharisee of Hillel's school. Certainly many of his teachings resemble those of the Pharisees which were later included in the Talmud, particularly those which emphasize the duty of charity and loving kindness as the most important *mitzvot* of the Torah. Like Jesus, the Pharisees also worshipped in the Temple, although the synagogue was their main field of operation. By the first century, the synagogue had become a unique religious institution: since it had no cult, liturgy or priesthood, many of the pagans in the Diaspora regarded it more as a school of philosophy than as a conventional religious centre. It was simply a place where Jews could meet to pray and study together. It will be recalled that originally the synagogue had been tied to the Temple cultus, but by the first century it was acquiring an independent identity which was largely shaped by the Pharisees. A synagogue service consisted of the recitation of the *Shema*, the profession of faith in God's unity, and of the blessings and prayers which stressed the Pharisaic commitment to the love of God and neighbour, the Messianic Kingdom and the religious mission of Israel as a priestly nation, that was set apart or consecrated to Yahweh. The Pharisees did not regard themselves as priests in the old sense, however, but took part in the synagogue services as ordinary members of the congregation (though the chief sages were usually allotted a place of honour). Every synagogue had its own sage, who did not mediate with God on behalf of the community but was simply a counsellor or a judge of disputes, with no liturgical or sacramental function. The Pharisees were populists, who had a profoundly democratic vision of Judaism; they were beginning to find the notion of a priestly caste unhelpful. Instead they envisaged every Jew approaching God independently, without a priestly representative.

This gradual movement away from the Temple was acted out more dramatically by some of the Pharisees who formed what were known as *haberim* (table fellowships) in order to practise a strict ritual purity. Since the whole of Israel was called to be a holy nation of priests, God was present in the humblest home as well as in the Temple. Consequently the members of the *haburah* lived as though they were priests themselves, eating their meals, for example, in accordance with the purity laws. They considered that the table of every Jewish household could be as sacred as the altar in the Temple. Thus, like the Essenes who used to bathe before their communal meals, the members of the *haberim* would immerse themselves in the ritual pool (*mikveh*) before they came to the table. Even though they were not going to eat the special Temple food of the official priests, they believed that the produce of the holy land of Israel should be eaten with as much reverence as the conventionally sacred provisions. They did not regard their concern for ritual purity as binding on all Jews: this was a voluntary form of piety that aimed to break down the distinction between priest and laity. When Jesus is made to inveigh against the Pharisaic concern for ritual purity at meal-times,[12] he accuses them virulently of being exclusive, hypocritical and élitist in their behaviour, but the opposite may have been the case.

It appears that not all the Pharisees went to these lengths, though many shared the underlying idealism, but they did attempt to sanctify the Jewish home as a new sort of Temple. They instituted the *kiddush* (sanctification ceremony) which the head of every household performed over the wine at Sabbath and other festive repasts, and taught him to pronounce a blessing over the bread at every meal. Women had a special responsibility for ensuring the sanctity and purity of the home, and this sphere of influence was often expressed in priestly terms. When they spoke of the woman's role, the sages liked to use the language of the Temple. Thus the first-century sage Rabbi Jacob said: 'One who has no wife remains without good, or help or joy or blessing or atonement',[13] while Rabbi Phineas ben Hannah went so far as to say that provided a wife remained in domestic seclusion, she had an atoning power that was not inferior to that of the altar in the Temple. Clearly the Jewish woman's place was in the home but at this date she was not excluded from a more public religious role. In theory, the wife or daughter of a rabbi was allowed to study the Torah, although some sages disagreed with this.[14] There were even cases of first-century Jewish women being sufficiently learned to be consulted about the Law: Imma Shalom, the wife of Rabbi Gamaliel

II, had some of her sayings recorded in the Talmud. Women could not be priests but they were permitted to take part in some of the Temple rituals, bringing sacrifices there and offering the wheat oblations alongside the official priests. Women prayed in the synagogues alongside men and were not forced to sit in a separate section until the second century CE. The Talmud says that women could be called upon to read the Torah during the services,[15] although it seems that by Jesus's time they were expected to refuse. Inscriptions have even been unearthed which describe certain women as *archisynagogissa* (head of synagogue) or *presbutera* (elder or member of the council). Even though these were probably mere honorary titles, they do show how highly women could be respected within the synagogue.

The synagogue had become so well established in Palestine and the Diaspora that it was able to replace the Temple after it had been burned to the ground by the Romans in 70 CE. This meant the end of the Jewish priesthood, since the sacrificial ritual could only be performed in the Jerusalem Sanctuary, but the Pharisees had prepared their people for the catastrophe. Charity and love of neighbour would replace the old animal holocausts, as this Talmudic story of the great sage Johannan ben Zakkai, a contemporary of Jesus, shows:

> Once as Rabbi Johannan ben Zakkai was coming forth from Jerusalem, Rabbi Joshua followed after him and beheld the Temple in ruins.
>
> 'Woe unto us!' Rabbi Joshua said, 'that this, the place where the iniquities of Israel were atoned for, is laid waste!'
>
> 'My son,' Rabbi Johannan said, 'be not grieved. We have another atonement as effective as this. And what is it? It is acts of loving kindness, as it is said: "For I desire mercy and not sacrifice."'[16]

Jews would not replace the Temple priesthood. Instead they would attempt to sanctify their homes, their tables and their daily lives by observing the purity regulations in exile. They would build a new Temple in the rabbinical legislation and commentary upon the Torah and sacred study would replace the ancient sacrificial liturgy. The destruction of the Temple in 70 was a tragedy but it had slowly been receding from the religious consciousness of many Jews in Palestine, and their brethren in the Diaspora had long regarded its rituals as rather embarrassing and barbaric. Judaism was able to accommodate and even to profit from its loss and would replace the old priestly caste with a more egalitarian style of leadership.

From the little we know of Jesus, it seems likely that he would have been in sympathy with this strain in Judaism. Many of the themes of the Essenes, the Qumran sect and the Pharisees would also characterize Christianity: the communal meals, the ritual baptisms or immersions, the new spiritual Temple and the ideal of loving kindness. Although the Gospels suggest that Jesus was frequently in conflict with the Pharisees, this could reflect a later polemic against the Jews. Certainly Jesus should have been sympathetic to the egalitarian ideal of Pharisaism. When James and John, the sons of Zebedee and prominent members of the Twelve, asked if they could have privileged seats beside Jesus on the Last Day when they judged the Twelve Tribes, Jesus made it clear that Christian ministry meant service not status:

> You must know that among the pagans their so-called rulers lord it over them, and their great men make their authority felt. This is not to happen among you. No; anyone who wants to become great among you must be your servant [*diakonos*], and anyone who wants to be first among you must be slave [*doulos*] of all. For the Son of Man himself did not come to be served [*diakonethanai*] but to serve [*diakonesai*] and to give his life as a ransom for many.[17]

Later, a 'deacon' would become a Christian official and the diaconate would be a step up the ladder to the exalted state of the priesthood. But the Greek word as used in the Gospels simply signified a personal servant who waited at table and performed other household duties.

Paul often referred to his apostolic mission as *diakonia*, a word which is often translated 'ministry' but which had humbler connotations when he used it. Paul also liked to refer to himself as the 'slave' (*doulos*) of his converts.[18] In the Greco-Roman world, where freedom was a crucial value and slavery incompatible with happiness, this would have made a strong impact. One of the most menial and demeaning of a slave's tasks was to wash the feet of his master and his guests. In his Gospel, John gives us a memorable picture of Jesus assuming this servile status and washing his disciples' feet. When he had finished, Jesus laid the same duty on them: 'You call me Master and Lord, and rightly; so I am. If I, then, the Lord and Master, have washed your feet, you should wash each other's feet.'[19] In the New Testament there is a profound distrust of honorific titles and offices. As Jesus tells his Apostles: 'You must not allow yourselves to be called Rabbi, since you have only one Master, and you are all brothers. . . . Nor must you allow yourselves to be called teachers, for you have only one Teacher, the Christ. The greatest among you must be your servant [*diakonos*].'[20] Christians have not always been true to the ideal of *diakonia*. When the Churches discuss the best ways of implementing the ideals of Jesus's ministry, they might do well to remember it, since the acrimonious disputes about ministry and office – about who can become a 'deacon', a 'teacher' or a 'priest' in the Church – seem far from the humble and fraternal spirit of the Gospels.

Indeed, the Twelve themselves found it very difficult to grasp this principle. The Gospels show that they seem to have envisaged a far more glorious and glamorous mission for their Master and themselves. This critical portrait of the men who were revered as leaders in the early Church is remarkable: the obtuseness of the Twelve frequently drives Jesus to distraction and on one occasion he calls Peter, their leader, a Satan who is tempting him from the path of God. His women disciples, however, seem to have had a much clearer idea of *diakonia*. Luke tells us that when Jesus began to travel through the towns and villages of Galilee, preaching and proclaiming the Kingdom, he was accompanied not only by the Twelve but by certain women who had been cured of evil spirits and ailments; Mary surnamed the Magdalene, from whom seven demons had gone out, Joanna, the wife of Herod's steward Chusa, Susanna and several others, who served [*diakonoun*] him out of their own resources.[21]

In later years, Churchmen would use such passages to remind women of their subordinate and ancillary status, but when we read them in the light of Jesus's admonitions about the nature of Christian 'ministry', the *diakonia* of these women takes on a new meaning. When Jesus's women disciples are depicted in the Gospels waiting at table, ministering to Jesus's needs or washing his feet, they are shown to be much closer to Jesus's conception of ministry than the male disciples who squabble about status and rewards.

The four Evangelists all have very different attitudes towards women. Matthew is perhaps the most conventional and patriarchal: when he tells the story of Jesus's miraculous conception and birth, he focuses on Joseph rather than on Mary and traces Jesus's Davidic ancestry through his foster-father, even though Mary is the only true parent. It is to Joseph not Mary that the angel comes with the glad tidings of the Virgin Birth, Joseph whose male susceptibilities have to be soothed, Joseph who makes all the decisions. Mary is not consulted about this divine invasion of her body and remains submissive and silent. Luke, however, who is by far the most positive of the Evangelists in his view of women, takes the opposite perspective. The Angel Gabriel appears to Mary to ask for her cooperation; she is the 'highly favoured one' and it is Joseph who is silent. When – on her own initiative – Mary goes to visit her cousin Elizabeth (who has miraculously become pregnant with John the Baptist), she becomes a prophetess, proclaiming the advent of the Messianic Kingdom where the proud are pulled down from their thrones and the lowly exalted. In this way, perhaps, Luke suggests at the very beginning of his Gospel the power and effectiveness that have come to women in the Christian dispensation.

But even though they were themselves differently disposed, the Evangelists all paint a remarkably consistent portrait of Jesus's behaviour towards the female sex. In the Gospels he persistently overturns the conventions, sometimes in a way that must have seemed shocking to a first-century reader. Thus even chauvinist Matthew, who is especially interested in Peter and in the male leadership of the primitive Church, makes Jesus constantly berate the Twelve for being 'of little faith'. He only says 'Your faith is great'[22] to one person in the entire Gospel: a woman who is not even Jewish. Again, Mark, who is not particularly interested in women, shows Jesus castigating the Twelve for their lack of belief, while praising the faith of a poor widow, a Syro-Phoenician woman and a woman with an unclean issue of blood.[23] Luke shows over and over again that women were among the poor and oppressed whom Jesus had come to redeem. He is fond of arranging his material to compare and contrast the male and female responses to Christ. Thus in his account of Jesus's childhood, it is Elizabeth who believes that she will conceive a son and her husband Zacharias, a priest of the Lord, who doubts; it is Elizabeth who cries aloud with joyful recognition when Mary comes to visit her carrying the unborn Messiah, while Zacharias is struck dumb. When the child Jesus is presented in the Temple, Simeon and Anna, a prophetess, both recognize that he is the Christ, but when Simeon sings his quietus, Anna, one of the very first evangelists, goes out to spread the good news. Of all four Evangelists, Luke is particularly close in spirit to the Apostle Paul. It is worth remembering this. Paul, who has subsequently been regarded as an arch-misogynist and held responsible for the long oppression of women, may in fact be better represented by the third Evangelist, whose women are far from silent and passive. Finally, John is extremely interested in women: he shows Jesus defying convention by speaking alone to a despised Samaritan woman of dubious morals. It is she who gives Jesus truly spiritual nourishment by her faith and eagerness to listen to him, while the male disciples lamely offer him ordinary bread from the village.

But women were not simply objects of Jesus's interest and benevolence. Some, as we have seen, played a more active role in his ministry, leaving their homes and travelling with him and the Twelve. In his book *Jesus and the World of Judaism*, the Jewish scholar Geza Vermes has pointed out that the charismatic

hasidim of Galilee often had women disciples, as had the prophets Elijah and Elishah, who operated in the same region. But
many more conventional Jews would have been shocked by a
prophet who had women as travelling companions. They were
not remaining in their homes, as the Pharisees urged, but were
abandoning the traditional domestic vocation for a more active
life. The three Synoptic Gospels all give lists of the most
prominent of these women which differ slightly but which all
begin with Mary of Magdala. Some of these women seem to
have been relatives of either Jesus or his male disciples, such as
his mother, her sister and the mother of the sons of Zebedee.[24]
They must have been well known to the early Churches, since
the Evangelists give few details about them and some, such as
Joanna or Susanna, are not mentioned in the New Testament
again.

It seems that there were other women disciples who were
very close to Jesus but did not travel about with him. Both Luke
and John tell us of Mary and Martha, the sisters of Lazarus, who
lived in the village of Bethany near Jerusalem. Luke's story is
especially interesting, as it presents a very different view of the
role of women from that which would later be current in either
Judaism or Christianity:

> In the course of their journey he came to a village and a
> woman named Martha welcomed him into her house. She
> had a sister called Mary, who sat down at the Lord's feet
> and listened to him speaking. Now Martha who was
> distracted with all the serving said, 'Lord, do you not care
> that my sister is leaving me to do the serving all by myself?
> Please tell her to help me.' But the Lord answered,
> 'Martha, Martha,' he said, 'you worry and fret about so
> many things, and yet few are needed, indeed only one. It
> is Mary who has chosen the better part; it is not to be taken
> from her.'[25]

Here Martha objects to humble *diakonia*, though we shall see a
different attitude in John's portrayal of the sisters. Luke focuses
on Mary. The phrase 'to sit at the feet of' then, as now, was
synonymous with 'to be a disciple of'. Later in both Judaism and

Christianity, women would not be encouraged to study – indeed they would be expressly forbidden to do so. In this story, however, Jesus yet again overturns traditional expectations, indicating that women need not be confined to the domestic sphere. The 'one thing necessary' – for both men and women – is faith and attention. Jesus may not have seen either men or women as priests in a future Church but he may have envisaged women as potential rabbis, studying the Torah and the Word of God at the feet of a master.

John goes further in his account of the raising of Lazarus, the brother of Martha and Mary, from the dead. He introduces the Bethany family by saying that 'Jesus loved Martha and her sister and Lazarus', reversing the conventional order by mentioning the women first. Later, we shall see Paul greeting a famous woman evangelist before her husband. Perhaps Martha and Mary were especially important people for John's first readers. In this story, it is Martha who shows the greater faith. The sisters have asked Jesus to come to their brother who is mortally ill, but when he finally arrives, Lazarus has already died. Martha greets Jesus with the news: if he had come in time, she says, Lazarus would not have died but 'I know that even now, whatever you ask of God, he will grant you.' She has perfect confidence that Lazarus will rise on the Last Day, but when Jesus asks if she believes that *he* is the Resurrection and the Life, Martha affirms her faith in his Messiahship – in the face of personal bereavement and disappointment: 'Yes, Lord, I believe that you are the Christ, the Son of God, the one who was to come into this world.'[26] This is arguably the fullest profession of faith made to Jesus during his lifetime in the whole of the fourth Gospel. It is similar to the one made by Peter, leader of the Twelve, in Matthew's Gospel, and fuller than the declaration that John puts on Peter's lips earlier: 'We know that you are the Holy One of God.'[27] In the Gospels, women are not required to be silent or to keep in the background. They frequently voice their opinions and come nearer to the truth than the male disciples.

John tells us that six days before Passover, at the beginning of the last week of his life, Jesus dined with the family at Bethany. This time Martha 'waited on them' willingly, like a true *diakonos*,

while Mary anointed Jesus's feet with a very expensive per-
fume. Judas Iscariot objected that the money should have been
given to the poor, but Jesus rebuked him. Mary, he said, had
anointed his body in preparation for his burial. Mark and
Matthew both give versions of this story, though they do not
attribute this symbolic action to Mary of Bethany but locate it in
the house of one Simon the Leper. Both tell us that the Apostles
failed to understand the significance of the woman's action and
both record Jesus's rebuke: 'She has done what was in her
power to do: she has anointed my body beforehand for its
burial. I tell you solemnly, wherever throughout all the world
the Good News is proclaimed, what she has done will be told
also, in remembrance of her.'[28] Yet again, a woman has understood the deeper meaning of Jesus's mission, accepting his
death, while the male disciples refuse to listen to Jesus when he
prophesies his passion.

Jesus's final warning of his approaching death was issued
during the last supper he ate with his disciples shortly before
his arrest. Mark tells us that this happened to be the ceremonial
seder or Passover Meal, which Jews still celebrate annually in
remembrance of the exodus led by Moses of the Israelites from
Egypt and their liberation from slavery. Mark also indicates that
only the Twelve were present. During the meal, Jesus told them
that one of their number was about to betray him and that he
would, therefore, go to his appointed fate. Then he took a piece
of bread, blessed it, broke it and distributed it to the Twelve,
saying that the bread was, in some sense, his body. Next he
picked up a cup of wine, telling the Twelve that it was 'the blood
of the covenant, which is to be poured out for many'.[29] In his
account of this last supper, Matthew adds that Jesus explained
that he was about to shed his blood 'for many for the remission
of sins'.[30] Jesus is thus presented in the Synoptic Gospels as
using this solemn Jewish festival with its overtones of salvation
and liberation as an opportunity to lay bare his own inner
purpose in approaching and accepting a shameful death: he has
interpreted his coming suffering as a sacrificial offering that
would provide the blood for a new alliance between God and
Israel.

Luke's account of this last supper is fuller and rather more complex but all three of the Synoptics recall the Elohist's story of the original covenant between God and his chosen people in Exodus. Moses, the Elohist says, had built an altar at the foot of Mount Sinai, surrounded by twelve standing stones to represent the Twelve Tribes of Israel. He had then directed some young men to sacrifice bullocks to Yahweh, had collected the blood, placed half of it on the altar and sprinkled the rest on the assembled people, after he had read the Law to them. '"This," he said, "is the blood of the Covenant that Yahweh has made with you, containing all these rules."'[31] Now, surrounded by the Twelve, as Moses had been surrounded by the twelve standing stones, Jesus is shown symbolically instituting a new covenant with the New Israel, looking forward, as all three Synoptics emphasize, beyond his death to his final vindication and glorification in the Messianic Kingdom, when he would drink new wine with his disciples.

These gospel accounts of Jesus's last supper probably reflect the commemorative meals that Christians would eat together in honour of this new covenant in the churches of the three Synoptic Evangelists during the second half of the first century CE. Paul tells us that it was a very early practice, begun by Jesus himself. Ultimately the Lord's Supper would become the Christian Eucharist or thanksgiving service. It would take many forms and be interpreted in many ways by future generations – in the elaborate Roman Catholic Mass or in the simpler services of the various Protestant Churches and sects. Traditionally a male priest or minister has re-presented Christ. We should note, however, that the early gospel accounts of what would become a distinctively Christian celebration stress its profoundly Jewish origin. The fact that only the Twelve were present certainly does not indicate that the Eucharist could only be celebrated by men – as has been argued – but merely emphasizes this Jewish context. As the representatives of the Twelve Tribes of the New Israel, these Twelve Apostles were standing in for the 'many' who would be saved by Jesus's sacrificial death. They were the representatives of the people (*laos*) of God, not priests. The only person with anything like a priestly role in this ritual enactment of the covenant was Jesus himself – an important point, as we shall see. The Twelve Apostles thus represent future Christian congregations. To exclude women from the Christian priesthood (that would not develop until some three hundred years after Jesus's death) on the grounds that there is no mention of women at the last supper is not logical: such a literalistic interpretation would mean that women should not be present at the Eucharist at all. It is ironic that this Jewish meal should eventually have inspired the formation of a Christian hierarchy, since it was, Luke and John both tell us, at the last supper that Jesus told the disciples that there should be no privileged élite and that all Christians were equal and humble servants.

We shall see that some of the early Christians assumed that women such as Martha and Mary had in fact been present at the last supper. If, however, women were absent on that occasion, it seems that the male disciples were conspicuously and shamefully absent when Jesus died by the hideous Roman punishment of crucifixion on the following day. All four Evangelists tell us that the male disciples proved to be woefully inadequate when the crisis came: Judas betrayed Jesus and Peter denied him, after he, James and John had slept all through the Agony in the Garden of Gethsemane. Only in John's Gospel is there mention of a 'beloved disciple' who made it to the foot of the Cross. It was the women who had the courage to stand by Jesus at the end. The chief witnesses to the crucifixion, death and burial of Jesus, all accounts agree, were women.[32] All four Evangelists tell us that Mary of Magdala was present, but differ about the other women witnesses: in various combinations they list the mother of the sons of Zebedee, Mary of Clopas, Jesus's mother and her sister, the mother of James the Apostle, the mother of James and Joseph, and Salome. Luke gives no names at this point but simply tells us that the women beside the Cross were those who had travelled with Jesus from Galilee. These women were of great importance, since they alone witnessed the events that were crucial to the gospel message. Later some Christians would deny that Jesus had actually died on the Cross; some said that what had seemed to die had only been a phantom. Obviously this would affect Christian faith in the Resurrection. Indeed, it has been suggested that these gospel lists of the women witnesses were as important as the list of witnesses to the Resurrection that Paul gave to his Corinthian converts and which seems to have been an essential part of the earliest proclamation or *kerygma*.[33] Without the women's witness, the truth of the gospel was incomplete. These women were the only believers who actually saw what happened on Golgotha on the first Good Friday; they passed on what they had seen and heard to the men.

Women thus made a vital contribution to the Christian *kerygma*. It is important to emphasize this point, since later Christians would forbid women to take part in spreading the gospel, in formulating its doctrines or contributing to the ongoing theological interpretation of the Christian message. They would be told to keep silent. But this does not seem to have been the case in the very beginning.

When Paul gives his long list of people who had seen the risen Christ, he does not mention any of the women. But the Evangelists all agreed that the women disciples were the first to discover the empty tomb and to receive the good news of the Resurrection. Again, they differ about details but they all agree that Mary of Magdala had accompanied the women who had bravely gone to the tomb to anoint Jesus's body, while the male disciples were skulking in hiding. In Mark's and Luke's accounts, the women see the empty tomb and hear the good news from the angel but they do not themselves see the risen Christ. However, Matthew and John both tell us that the women did see Jesus and greeted him eagerly. All four accounts agree that these women were given a divine commission to take the gospel to the men. They were to be the *apostoloi* to the Twelve and impart the *kerygma* to them. Again, there is a contrast between the faith of the male and female disciples, since in general, the men respond with typical male prejudice against a woman's testimony. As Luke says: 'this story of [the women] seemed pure nonsense, and they did not believe them'.[34]

Later generations of Christians would argue that Jesus had not given the women disciples permission to teach and evangelize the world: their commission ended when they gave the *kerygma* to the Twelve. *Apostoloi* only for an hour, they were then told to keep silent and retire to the margins of the Christian mission. It is true that we cannot find a clear gospel statement to support a permanent active ministry for women after the Resurrection. But such an approach can seem pettifogging, given the freedom with which later generations have ignored or edited some very clear directives of Jesus about the nature of discipleship and ministry. One thing on which all four Evangelists are agreed is that Jesus did not respond to women in a conventional way, and in a world that was less sexually egalitarian than our own his behaviour would have seemed shocking and disturbing. How would the early Church respond to the women in their midst?

— 3 —

Paul and the Ministry of the Primitive Church

T HERE WERE no priests in the primitive Church. The
priestly spirituality with its emphasis on caste, elaborate
ritual, mysterious symbolism and minute adherence to
past tradition was alien to the spirit of the first Christians. We
can see a glimpse of the early Christian ethos in Luke's account
of the descent of the Holy Spirit in the Acts of the Apostles, the
sequel to his Gospel. He tells us that a group of Jesus's disciples
had gathered together on the Jewish feast of Pentecost, which
celebrated God's gift of the Torah to Moses on Mount Sinai.

> Suddenly they heard what sounded like a powerful wind
> from heaven, the noise of which filled the entire house in
> which they were sitting; and something appeared to them
> that seemed like tongues of fire; these separated and came
> to rest on the head of each one of them. They were all filled
> with the Holy Spirit and began to speak foreign languages
> as the Spirit gave them the gift of speech.[1]

The New Israel born that day was to be a charismatic community. It relied on direct inspiration from the Spirit, on dreams,
visions and prophecy rather than on a tradition of Law.
Prophets had sometimes criticized the cult of the Temple in the
past and these Christian prophets were not interested in

administration, institutional office or time-honoured and elaborate cultic ministry, even though they all worshipped daily in the Temple as devout and observant Jews.

The Church was also strongly egalitarian, whereas the priesthood presupposed a caste of ministers who had been set aside from the laity. The early Church, as we see it in the Acts or in the letters of St Paul, was not interested in such distinctions. From the very beginning, for example, women received the inspiration of the Spirit alongside the men. Thus, Luke tells us, the inner circle of disciples who were seized by the Spirit at Pentecost consisted of the Twelve 'together with several women, including Mary, the mother of Jesus, and his brothers'.[2] After the descent of the Spirit, Peter explained to the crowds that they were witnessing the birth of the new dispensation foretold long ago by the Prophet Joel:

> In the days to come – it is the Lord who speaks –
> I will pour out my spirit on all mankind.
> Their sons and daughters shall prophesy,
> your young men shall see visions,
> your old men shall dream dreams.
> Even on my slaves, men and women,
> in those days I will pour out my spirit.[3]

The old distinctions had been abolished: in the Messianic era sexual and social equality would be the rule.

The Spirit could be downright frightening. Acts is written in beautiful Greek but in some ways it presents the crudest picture of Christianity in the New Testament. Miracles abound which, unlike the miracles of Jesus, were not always beneficent: people were struck blind, struck dead. But Luke is at pains to show the solidarity of the early Christian community, giving an idealistic picture of the brethren sharing everything in common and united, heart and soul. The Spirit had descended in a Jewish setting and the first Christians still lived as fully observant Jews, going in a body every day to worship in the Temple but meeting in one another's houses to share a meal together – perhaps not

dissimilar to the 'table fellowships' that other Jews were forming at this time. Probably the only thing that radically distinguished these first Christians from their fellow Jews was
their belief that Jesus of Nazareth, who had died the death of a
common criminal, had been the long-awaited Messiah. He
would shortly return in glory to inaugurate the Kingdom of
God. These 'Nazarenes', as they were called, were approved by
the Sanhedrin, the Jewish governing council, as an authentic
Jewish sect.[4] It would not have occurred to any of them to
ordain a Christian as a priest. Even though, like other Jews at
this time, the Temple was no longer central to their religious
life, they were loyal to its cultus and priesthood and saw their
own ministry as something quite different.

We often call this Christian community the Jerusalem Church
but it is probably more accurate to call it the synagogue of the
Nazarenes. It was common then – as it is today – for various
groups or nationalities to have their own synagogue in Jerusalem. The word *ecclesia*, which is translated as 'church', was, like
the Hebrew *qahal*, an assembly or gathering. The Nazarenes
broke bread together like other Jews but, like Jesus at the last
supper, they also looked forward to the Messianic banquet that
they would soon share with him in the Kingdom. It does not
seem as though anybody with special 'priestly' functions presided at this meal. These were not full-blown liturgies but
intimate gatherings in one another's houses, and, presumably,
the host would break and bless the bread as was customary at a
Jewish festive meal. These 'house-churches' were crucial and
formative. The Christians called their assembly the House of
God or the Temple of God because the Spirit was present but, as
we have seen, other Jews were evolving similarly exalted views
of a new Temple and a sacred community. In their synagogues,
the Christians, like other Jews, appointed 'elders' (*presbuteroi*) to
deal with administration and order. Later the word 'presbyter'
would acquire sacerdotal overtones in Christianity and would
give us our term 'priest', but the *presbuteros* was not a new
official and bore no relation to the later Christian presbyterate.
These *presbuteroi* simply showed that the early Church was still
functioning within Judaism.

Luke also tells us that in the very early stages, the Nazarenes found that they needed to create a new office. The numbers of converts had increased to include a significant number of Greek-speaking Jews from the Diaspora. These 'Hellenic' Jews complained that their widows were being overlooked when the food was being distributed, so Peter urged them to appoint seven of their own number to take care of this problem and 'wait at table' (*diakonein*).[5] It is often assumed that this marked the beginning of the diaconate, properly so called; the Seven were not new ministers, however, but were simply performing a humble but necessary service. Two of them – Stephen and Philip – were important preachers, yet they were ready to undertake tasks usually performed by a servant or, in the Greco-Roman world, by a woman. This was not the start of a new Christian order, in the later sense, but a sign that the primitive Church was still committed to the *diakonia* and its role reversals which Luke had previously described in his Gospel.

The little Nazarene community might have remained a purely Jewish sect had it not been for the conversion of one of its principal opponents. Saul of Tarsus, whose Roman name was Paul, was a Pharisee and a Roman citizen who had conceived a loathing for Christianity. He had set out to Damascus at the behest of the High Priest (for reasons that are not at all clear) in order to arrest the Christians there – both men and women, Luke tells us, another sign that women must have been prominent members of the early Church. Before he reached the city, however, Paul had a vision of the risen Jesus which hit him with such devastating impact that he was thrown from his horse and temporarily blinded. Luke gives us no fewer than three descriptions of this vision in the Acts of the Apostles. Paul's account was terser in his letter to his converts in Galatia: 'God, who had specially chosen me while I was still in my mother's womb, called me through his grace and chose to reveal his Son in me, so that I might preach the Good News about him to the pagans.'[6] By quoting the prophet Jeremiah, Paul shows that he regarded this vision as similar to the terrifying revelations of God to the Hebrew prophets, except that he had been commissioned not by Yahweh but by Jesus, the Messiah, and dispatched with a message not to other Jews but to the gentile world. Jesus henceforth became the sole source of Paul's religious experience. He now believed that Jesus was the Christ, the Greek translation of the Hebrew *Massiach*, Anointed One. But Paul had also become convinced that Jesus had not come for the Jews alone but to found a New Israel which would include the *goyim*.

Accordingly, for the next thirty years of his life, he travelled tirelessly in what is now Turkey, Macedonia and Greece to spread the gospel. His determination to admit gentiles into the Jewish sect without forcing them to submit to circumcision and the whole of the Torah brought him into conflict with the Twelve and with James, Jesus's brother, who was now a prominent Christian. Luke describes the dispute in polite terms but Paul's letters show that it was very bitter and heated.[7] The decision to admit gentiles was a momentous one and, as we shall see in Chapter 8, may be regarded as similar to the conflict about the ordination of women to the priesthood. It involved a complete break with Jewish tradition, which many of the original Apostles found impossible and painful to contemplate. Yet while the earliest disciples of Jesus and the mother Church of Jerusalem hung back in the name of the sacred past, the younger Diaspora Churches founded by St Paul were ready for the new vision and went ahead. In our own day, it has been the daughter Churches of the Church of England abroad which have proved able to lead the way in ordaining women priests.

It was Paul's vision that prevailed. The Nazarene sect petered out in the Jewish world and Christianity became a predominantly gentile religion. Paul was convinced that Jesus had 'died for our sins'[8] and by his Resurrection had given new life to the world. The Easter event had given birth to a new type of humanity into which Jews and gentiles alike could be incorporated – in Christ – by the rite of baptism. Christians had died to sin and now lived a new kind of life for God in Jesus, the Messiah. But Paul had no intention of founding an institution. He was convinced that Christ would return, even within his own lifetime. The things of this world were passing away.[9] He was not building administrative structures for the future, therefore; he certainly had no intention of founding a new Christian priesthood. The very notion of the sacerdotal office, in both

Judaism and paganism, was associated with notions of status and privilege that were quite alien to Paul's vision of the New Israel. Priesthood was part of the old order, which would soon be abrogated when Christ returned to establish his presence (*parousia*) on earth. Like Jesus, Paul saw Christian ministry as a humble service, a *diakonia*, and himself as a slave (*doulos*) of both Christ and his converts. Christians, he said, quoting an early hymn, were not to lord it over one another but were to adopt the same attitude as Christ, who had voluntarily assumed 'the condition of a slave' for their sakes.[10] He could not give them orders but could only point to the Christian tradition handed down from the Lord Himself;[11] when Paul did give advice, he was always careful to say that it was simply his own personal opinion.[12]

Consequently the idea of a Church hierarchy was alien to Paul. He and his fellow apostles and evangelists were simply co-workers, co-strivers.[13] There was no organized ritual and nobody presiding over the *ecclesia* in a cultic capacity. When Christians ate the Lord's Supper, they were simply to wait for one another before beginning:[14] there was no question of waiting for a priest to officiate. Paul saw the New Israel as a charismatic community: every baptized person had a call to *diakonia*, a ministry in the Kingdom. Everybody had a gift given to him or her by the Spirit of God and every gift was valuable. Naturally there were different levels of service, but that did not mean that the community should be split up into different ranks, some superior to others:

> There is a variety of gifts but always the same Spirit; there are all sorts of service to be done, but always to the same Lord; working in all sorts of different ways in different people, it is the same God who is working in all of them.[15]

He explained his vision of community in the metaphor of the body, made up of many parts which are entirely interdependent. The body could not be identified with any one of its parts and, in the same way, the *ecclesia*, the body of Christ, is not to be identified with its leaders. Some Christians were inspired to be apostles or prophets or teachers; some were healers, others performed miracles or spoke in tongues. But no one group formed a separate priestly caste, consecrated and sacralized by special clothes and laws. All the charismatic gifts were valuable but the most vital of all was the gift of love which alone ensured that there was no discord in the body of Christ.

In the Nazarene synagogues, the *presbuteroi* had formed a governing council, but in Antioch, where Paul had begun his mission, there was no mention of 'elders', only of teachers and prophets.[16] As Peter had explained at Pentecost, the New Israel was characterized by a revival of prophecy, and Paul esteemed this charism highly. He was less enthusiastic about the gift of tongues, the ecstatic babbling of some inspired Christians, because nobody could benefit from what they were saying. He could speak in tongues himself, he wrote to the Corinthians, better than any of them, but 'when I am in the presence of the community I would rather say five words that mean something than a thousand words in a tongue'.[17] Church services do not seem to have been orderly or decorous: people extemporised, standing up to receive an oracle, to recite a psalm, to speak in tongues – sometimes two or three people would speak at once. Others delivered spontaneous sermons.[18] There was no presiding 'priest': each Christian was a minister (*diakonos*) and exercised this ministry as he or she chose.

For women were certainly not marginal figures; rather, they were fully active in Paul's Churches. He takes it for granted that women would pray and prophesy in the meetings of the *ecclesia* along with the men. In Acts, Luke tells us that Paul's first European convert was Lydia, a gentile business woman of Macedonia, where women had long been influential members of society. She opened her home to Paul and this became the first house-church in Philippi. Just as Jesus had relied on the *diakonia* and hospitality of disciples such as Martha, so Paul depended on women like Lydia. Always anxious to advance the cause of sexual equality in Christ, Luke goes out of his way to emphasize that Paul was ready to found a Church with a woman convert in a way that marked a new departure.[19] In Judaism, no woman would have been allowed to found an embryonic synagogue. Other women also had an active, important ministry. In the sixteenth chapter of the letter to the Romans, Paul sends greetings to thirty-six of his 'co-workers' (*synergeoi*): of these, eighteen were women. There is no hint of patronage, no suggestion that these women colleagues were in any way dependent upon a male ministry. Thus Phoebe, who may have been the bearer of the letter, is called a *diakonos* of the Church at Cenchrae, the port of Corinth. This is often translated 'deaconess', as though there were already a separate and inferior order of women in the primitive Church. But this is simply a projection of subsequent practice back on to the Pauline era which knew of no distinction between 'deacon' and 'deaconess'. The Greek *diakonos* can be either masculine or feminine. Paul uses it of himself and of his male missionaries and there is nothing in this passage to suggest that there is anything different about Phoebe's *diakonia*.[20] Similarly, later in the chapter a woman called Junia is actually called an 'outstanding apostle'. She and Andronicus, who may have been her husband, had been Christians before Paul, so there was no suggestion that Phoebe was subservient to him in any way. He calls the pair his 'compatriots and co-prisoners'.[21] He also sends greetings to other women, to Euodia and Syntache, Mary, Tryphema, Tryphosa and Persis, who have all 'contended' side by side with him like athletes or 'toiled' (*kopian*) beside him – words that Paul also applies to his own ministry. Just as John mentioned Martha and Mary before Lazarus, so Paul sends greetings to Prisca before her husband Aquila when he praises this famous missionary couple. They had also been converted before him and seem to have had a quite separate apostolate. Luke also mentions Prisca first when he speaks of the couple in Acts, so she may well have been the most important and famous of the two.[22] It seems that Prisca had instructed the distinguished Alexandrian convert Apollos, who became an influential minister in his own right. This appears to have been an egalitarian period of Christianity: women worked valiantly alongside men as equals.

This would have been startling in the first century, where in both Judaism and the Greco-Roman world women were generally confined to the home. As we have seen, Macedonian women enjoyed considerable liberty and influence, and Jewish women were at this stage honoured in the synagogues, theoretically able to read the Torah in services and to study with their husbands and fathers. But their main sphere of influence was the home. In the pagan world, women were perpetual minors. In about 400 BCE the Greek philosopher Thales expressed gratitude that he 'was born a human being not a beast, next that he was a man and not a woman and, thirdly, a Greek and not a barbarian'.[23] The position of women had improved somewhat, largely due to the influence of Rome, but the attitude was still prevalent. Jewish men were already beginning to thank God in their morning prayers for making them a Jew not a gentile, free not a slave, and a man rather than a woman. Many men today would not find this position strange.

Consequently the Christian principle enunciated by Paul in his letter to the Galatians was revolutionary and deeply challenging:

> All baptized in Christ, you have all clothed yourselves in Christ, and there are no more distinctions between Jew and Greek, slave and free, male and female, but all of you are one in Christ Jesus.[24]

A considerable body of scholarly opinion believes that this statement was not Paul's own but a baptismal formula already in use. It had nothing to do with ministry but marked the convert's entry into the Christian community. It expressed the New Testament ethos perfectly and would be constantly quoted by those who support the equality of the sexes. Paul himself concentrated on abolishing the distinction between Jew and Greek, working all his life to ensure that gentiles were accepted into the New Israel. But, as we have seen, he admitted the essential equality of Christian women, permitting them to pray and prophesy during meetings and regarding them as co-workers and fellow *diakonoi*. He viewed this radical abolition of racial, social and sexual discrimination as a practical ideal to be worked out in this world, not as an aspiration for the eschatological future. Christianity in his view was a new way of being human while waiting for the Lord's return; to belong to the *ecclesia* was to become a member of the 'assembling' of a community in which people should try to live together in love and service, similar to the sacred communities envisaged by other Jews at this time.

Inevitably this would bring the *ecclesia* into conflict with conventional *mores*. In Paul's terms, being part of 'the age to come' in the midst of 'this present age' would involve opposition from the powers that be. It would mean 'martyrdom' in the literal sense of the word, a 'witness' (*martyrion*) to the belief that the old things of the unredeemed world were indeed passing away. A community in which the women would do everything that men did as Christians – preaching, praying, prophesying and – later – becoming martyrs by dying for Christ – was in the context of the first century a dramatic sign that something new had come into existence, that the Kingdom was already a going concern. But Christian men like Paul were only human and on at least one occasion he fell back into the old chauvinist attitudes. Thus in his first letter to the Corinthian converts, the same epistle in which he had articulated the metaphor of the body of Christ, Paul insists rather stridently that when women are praying or prophesying during meetings they must cover their heads with a veil.[25] His tone is not pleasant – a woman who refuses to wear a veil, he says, might as well have all her hair cut off! – and his theology dubious. But we should still give him credit, even in this much-disputed passage, for taking it for granted that there were women prophets. There was no question in his mind but that women were allowed to preach and prophesy aloud during the services. Prophets were extremely important people in Paul's eyes, second only to the Apostles themselves. They played a crucial role during the Lord's Supper and were venerated throughout the Church. But Paul still insists that when women utter an inspired oracle during a meeting, they must be veiled. Why was this so important to him?

It appears that Paul was very concerned with what was 'proper'.[26] He was attempting to spread a religion that was potentially subversive, which in late antiquity was almost a contradiction in terms. In the Greco-Roman world, *religio* was not expected to provide a radical answer to the essential questions of life: people looked to philosophy for that. *Religio* was more about preserving old sanctities and a continuity with the values and traditions of the past. In the early second century, the Roman biographer Gaius Suetonius would condemn Christianity as *superstitio nova et prava*, a 'fanaticism' that was 'depraved' precisely because it was 'new'. Innovation was not prized as it is today and Christians would be persecuted for failing to give the ancestral gods their due – an impiety which could bring disaster on the Empire. Nothing arouses such ire – even in our own day – as a threat to 'family values', and Christianity was beginning to evolve shocking doctrines at this time. In the same letter, Paul had just recommended celibacy for both men and women while they were waiting for Christ's return. He made it clear that this was one of those occasions when he was simply citing his own opinions: it was not part of the official teaching of Christ and the gospel that he had received from Jesus's friends. Nevertheless, it seemed more sensible not to get bedded down in a permanent family relationship when the things of this world were passing away. Paul was emphatic, however, that anybody who wished to find a husband for his daughter was perfectly within his rights: there was no sin in marriage.[27] Yet pagans would have found even this heavily qualified recommendation of celibacy profoundly disturbing. In the Greco-Roman world, which was heavily conscious of mortality, marriage and procreation were the chief weapons against death, the only way in which human beings could ensure the continuity of their fragile society into the next generation. After Paul's death, more radical Christians known as the Encratists believed that it was their duty to bring the world to an end by preaching obligatory celibacy, and this filled their pagan neighbours with fear and dread.

The relative freedom given to women by Paul's converts would have been equally distressing to most people of late antiquity. In the Greek world, where wives were the property of their husbands, women had to be specially careful not to dishonour them by appearing to resemble an adulteress or a courtesan. The situation was particularly delicate in Corinth, which was famous for its courtesans and prostitutes throughout the Mediterranean world. Consequently married women were forced to be extra discreet. They tended not to speak in public and never appeared outside their homes unless shrouded by a veil. The veiled or kerchiefed women seen in Greece or North Africa today preserve this old Mediterranean habit. Paul may have been anxious that Christian wives, who were already provocative because they prayed and prophesied in public and even travelled around openly as evangelists, could bring unnecessary scandal on the Church by appearing unveiled like prostitutes. This was especially important in Corinth, where some Christians, believing that they were already fully redeemed, claimed that they could do anything they wanted, such as taking part in idolatrous services and sleeping with prostitutes.[28] In an age where a person's appearance was a very important emblem of his or her position or status, a woman who appeared in the Christian assembly unveiled or with her hair flowing loosely around her instead of being confined in the usual coiffure of a matron was giving an ambiguous message to the pagan world.

Most Churches no longer require women to cover their heads during services, though some did until recently. In my own childhood, it was impossible for a woman to enter a Roman Catholic church without a hat or scarf: if caught without a hat while visiting historic cathedrals, we used to put handkerchieves over our heads. This no longer applies today and in most denominations Christians have been happy to 'forget' this stern teaching of Paul. But, with the selectiveness that we have already noted, many Christians still adhere to the theological reason that Paul gives for this regulation of the veil. He argues in a way that is clearly not compatible with the egalitarian doctrine that he has promoted elsewhere: women should veil themselves as a sign of their subordinate status. This doctrine of 'headship' has played an extremely important part in the debate about the ordination of women, so it is important to look at it here in some detail. Those who are against women priests believe that this teaching is so fundamental to the faith that the whole of Christianity will be fatally undermined if the Churches abandon it and put women in positions of authority. 'Christ is the head (*kephale*) of every man,' Paul wrote to the Corinthians, 'man is the head of woman, and God is the head of Christ':[29]

A man should certainly not cover his head, since he is the image of God and reflects God's glory; but woman is the reflection of man's glory. For man did not come from woman; no, woman came from man; and man was not created for the sake of woman, but woman was created for the sake of man.[30]

This simply will not do. Paul comes perilously close to suggesting that woman was not made in God's image at all but only reflects it in man, a doctrine which contradicts the priestly doctrine of Creation in the first chapter of Genesis: 'God created man (*adam*) in the image of himself; in the image of God he created him; male and female he created them.'[31] This account of the Creation of the world was probably composed in the sixth century BCE. Paul, however, has made use of the older myth, written down in the ninth or eighth centuries and found in the second and third chapters of Genesis. In this more figurative and anthropomorphic account, God creates woman almost as an afterthought from Adam's rib. Thus, Paul seems to say, she was only created in the image of Adam, not in the image of God himself. These ill-considered verses have inspired a great deal of patriarchal theology over the centuries, receiving perhaps its most memorable expression in John Milton's *Paradise Lost*. Adam and Eve, Milton says, were

> Not equal, as thir sex not equal seemd;
> For contemplation hee and valour formd,
> For softness shee and sweet attractive grace,
> Hee for God onely, shee for God in him:
> His fair large Front and Eye sublime declar'd
> Absolute rule.[32]

It is very difficult to square this view of the inequality of the sexes with the teaching of either Christ or Paul in most of his writings.

Indeed, Paul himself does not seem happy with his argument. We can almost sense him flailing around, aware that he is on dubious ground. Instead of resting content with his graded hierarchy of 'headship', he produces more reasons, trying them out, as it were. 'That is the argument for women's covering their heads with a symbol of authority,' he explains, but then adds a complete *non sequitur*: the veil is worn 'out of respect for the angels'[33] – an obscure argument that nobody has satisfactorily explained. Were the angels the guardians of public order in the liturgy? Is this a reference to the 'Sons of God' who mated with mortal women in mythical times,[34] as the North African theologian Tertullian believed? Paul then changes tack altogether, appealing to the Corinthians' 'natural' sense of decency, hoping, perhaps, that it would be more convincing than his exegesis of Genesis: 'Ask yourselves if it is fitting for a woman to pray to God without a veil,' he asks his converts man to man, 'and whether nature itself does not tell you that long hair on a man is nothing to be admired, while a woman, who was given her hair as a covering, thinks her long hair a glory.'[35] At one point, he seems to go back on the whole thrust of the passage and, in verses that are seldom quoted by the more patriarchal theologians, speaks of the profound interdependence of the sexes: 'However, though woman cannot do without man, neither can man do without woman, in the Lord: woman may come from man, but man is born of woman – both come from God.'[36] Finally, Paul seems to give up. Floundering hopelessly and clearly aware that not everybody will be convinced by all this, he concludes: 'To anyone who might still want to argue: it is not the custom with us, nor in the Churches of God'[37] – a rather lame argument which seems to show Paul's unease with everything he has said on the subject. Paul did not teach the inferiority of women because he had found the doctrine in Genesis. Like many men today who are basically in favour of the liberation of women but who sometimes fall back into the traditional chauvinism, Paul simply voiced the normal prejudice of his time and then found a text which seemed to support it.

There is a similar inconsistency in Paul's bad-tempered remarks later in the same letter to the Christians of Corinth:

> As in all the Churches of the saints, women are to remain quiet at meetings since they have no permission to speak; they must keep in the background as the Law itself lays

down. If they have any questions to ask, they should ask
their husbands at home: it does not seem right for a
woman to raise her voice at meetings.[38]

This is puzzling, since Paul had just made it quite clear that
women *are* permitted to pray and prophesy aloud in church,
provided that they wear their veils. The reference to the Law
presumably refers to the story of the Fall of Adam and Eve in
Genesis: God decrees that because of her sin, Eve must henceforth be subject to her husband, who 'will lord it over you'.[39]
But this does not cohere with the rest of Paul's theology: time
and again he makes it clear that Christ's death has changed this
sad situation. Christians have now been incorporated into a
new, redeemed humanity and a new Creation.

Many serious scholars believe that these verses are so incon-
sistent, both thematically and stylistically, with the rest of the
epistle that they were not written by Paul himself but must
have been added later. If this is so, it was a very early addition,
since the verses appear in all the manuscripts but not, signifi-
cantly, in the same place. Sometimes they are found at the very
end of Chapter 14. Indeed, these verses (34 and 35) do interrupt
the flow of the argument. If we examine the passage, it becomes
obvious that verses 36–8 follow verse 33 quite naturally, continuing the discussion of prophecy. Scholars have also found
the vocabulary and style, such as the formula 'as even the Law
says', to be uncharacteristic. The reference to the Torah here
suggests that these interpolated verses might have come from
the Jewish-Christian milieu at a later date, when women had
been completely silenced in the synagogues too. It may be that
they derived from the Jewish Churches that produced the so-
called pastoral epistles to Timothy and Titus, attributed to Paul
but not written by him, and which take a very similar line on the
position of women, as we shall see later in this chapter. Unfortunately these sentences imposing a silence upon Christian
women have done great harm over the centuries. They have
also damaged Paul's reputation. Paul was certainly not perfect:
he was a hot-headed, irascible man with a lot of insecurities and
phobias. But he was also a genius and largely responsible for

the survival of Christianity and its transplantation into the gentile world. Apart from these two passages from one epistle, he was usually well disposed towards women and would probably have been horrified to see his words – if they truly are his – used to justify later oppression.

The first fine charismatic rapture of the Pauline Church was too intense to last. Such violent delights come to a speedy end, since human beings cannot keep up that level of fervour indefinitely. In his later epistles, written in the 60s, Paul indicates that offices and an embryonic Church hierarchy were beginning to emerge in the Churches he had founded. Thus he addresses his letter to the Church at Philippi to their *episkopoi* and *diakonoi*, usually translated 'bishops' and 'deacons'.[40] It would be a mistake to imagine that bishops and deacons, as we know them today, were ruling the community in an official capacity. A more accurate rendering of *episkopoi* and *diakonoi* would be 'overseers' and 'servants'. But the Jewish-Christian communities not founded by Paul still retained the synagogue leadership of *presbuteroi* or 'elders'. In the epistle attributed to Peter, which comes from a strongly Jewish Church, the author sends a message to his fellow 'elders': the 'younger' Christians there are to 'do what the *presbuteroi* tell you'.[41] This Jewish-Christian epistle is important, since it mentions the word 'priest' for the first time in a Christian context: it is therefore of the utmost importance to note that the 'priest' is not the *presbuteros* but the whole community. In this crucial text, which refers to the words God addressed to the ancient Israelites on Mount Sinai, the Jewish author tells the New Israel: 'You are a chosen race, a royal priesthood, a consecrated nation, a people set apart to sing the praises of God.'[42] He was looking back to the early 'Elohist' tradition which had seen the whole of Israel as holy and had not envisaged a priestly caste which approached God on behalf of the people. The days of the Aaronic priesthood celebrated by P were over. In these Jewish branches of the Church, there was no such thing as a lay man or woman. All the baptized were priests, all had been consecrated and made ready for sacred action. This was dramatically demonstrated by the Jewish author of the book of Revelation. It will be recalled that the Jerusalem Temple consisted of a series of concentric circles, which reflected the different grades of holiness: in the inner and most sacred spot was the Holy of Holies, which only the High Priest could enter; next came the court of the Priests, then courts for lay men, for women and, finally, the court of the gentiles. Now that the whole of the New Israel was a nation of priests, there was no further need for these old barriers. When the author of Revelation describes the New Temple in the New Jerusalem that will descend from Heaven when Christ returns in glory, he notes that the court of lay men had been abandoned, since there was no further need for it.

But this was not just an eschatological hope for the future but a present reality. The epistle to the Ephesians may have been written by St Paul but some scholars believe that it was penned some fifty years after his death. The author ascribed his epistle to Paul as a sign of discipleship and certainly he shared many of Paul's ideas. He (or St Paul) reminds the Church at Ephesus that before the coming of Christ they had been pagans, excluded from membership of Israel. They had no part in the covenant with God: 'you were immersed in this world, without hope and without God'.[43] But Christ's death had broken down these old barriers and had reconciled Jews and pagans with one another:

> But now in Christ Jesus, you that used to be so far apart from us have been brought very close by the blood of Christ. For he is the peace between us, and has made the two into one and broken down the barrier which used to keep them apart, actually destroying in his own person the hostility caused by the rules and decrees of the Law.[44]

Jesus's death had been a sacrifice of reconciliation, therefore, which had broken down the walls dividing the court of the gentiles from the rest of Israel. The blood of Christ had created a 'New Man'[45] and, like the animal sacrifices of the old Temple priesthood, it had enabled human beings to approach God. Now, however, it was not just the High Priest who could 'come to the Father', but the whole of mankind.[46] Even gentiles, who had been on the outermost circle of holiness, had been integrated so that they were 'no longer aliens or foreign visitors'.[47]

Just as there was no longer any need for a priesthood to re-present the laity to God, the old Temple itself, the sign of God's presence on earth, had been superseded. 'You are a part of a building that has the apostles and prophets for its foundations, and Christ Jesus himself for its main cornerstone,' the author tells these pagan converts. 'As every structure is aligned on him, all grow into one holy temple in the Lord; and you too, in him, are being built into a house where God lives, in the Spirit.'[48]

In this perspective, the priesthood of mere men had become redundant. This theme is most fully explored by the author of the epistle to the Hebrews, another later book of the New Testament attributed to Paul. The old Aaronic and Levitical priesthood had simply been a type or symbol, the author argued. It had encouraged Jews to look forward to a more perfect reconciliation effected by a Messiah who was also a High Priest, entering the Tent of Meeting on our behalf:

> Now Christ has come, as the high priest of all the blessings that were to come. He has passed through the greater, the more perfect tent, which is better than the one made by men's hands because it is not of this created order; and he has entered the sanctuary once and for all, taking with him not the blood of goats and bull calves, but his own blood, having won an eternal redemption for us.[49]

Christ had not taken the priesthood upon himself, any more than Aaron had. He had been given the title of priest by God himself. In the old dispensation, there had had to be a whole succession of priests, since death had brought an end to their priesthood. But Christ's priesthood was eternal: he 'would not need to offer sacrifices every day, as the other high priests do for their own sins and then for those of the people, because he has done this once for all by offering himself'.[50] His blood had achieved a far more effective purification than the old animal sacrifices; he had not entered a man-made Sanctuary but that which the old Tent of Meeting had symbolized: 'Heaven itself, so that he could appear in the actual presence of God on our behalf'.[51] Christ was the High Priest *par excellence*, therefore:

there would be no need for a human priesthood; temples and a sacrificial liturgy were now otiose. The necessity for a mediator like Aaron had gone now that all Christians could approach God directly: 'In other words, brothers, through the blood of Jesus we have the right to enter the Sanctuary', the author concludes, 'by a new way which he has opened for us, a living opening through the curtain, that is to say, his body. And we have the supreme high priest over all the house of God.'[52]

For the author of the epistle to Peter, the whole community was priestly; for the author of the epistle to the Hebrews, Christ was the only priest. In a Pauline perspective, there was no contradiction here, since all Christians constituted the body of Christ and shared his High Priesthood. In the early Church, therefore, the idea of ordaining Christians to act as priests would have seemed both wrong and foolish. Yet in the epistle to the Hebrews we can see that the fervour of the primitive Church was beginning to flag. The author actually feels it necessary to exhort the Christians to attend Church services regularly, something that would have been unthinkable in Paul's day. He is also worried about apostasy and the danger of persecution. There are similar signs of disaffection in the short treatise known as the *Didache*, or 'The Teaching [*didache*] of the Lord to the Gentiles through the Twelve Apostles'. The date of this text is uncertain. Some scholars believe that it was written in the primitive Church, during the apostolic period; others would give it a later date in the early second century. The *Didache* was not included in the canon but was regarded as an authoritative scripture by many of the early Christians. The author is clearly worried about the possibility of losing the faith and teaching of Christ, hence his concern to stress that he is repeating the teaching of the Apostles, who had been directly commissioned by the Lord himself. He is already beginning to conceive of the necessity of an 'apostolic succession' to ensure a true continuity of doctrine. But his treatise makes it clear that the Church was still a highly charismatic community: the most important members are the 'prophets' who had been so prominent in Paul's day. Some of these charismatics were abusing their position, however. They were moving around from place to place and trying to make a living out of their ministry.

Consequently the author urges the Christians to introduce a more stable type of leadership. With the air of somebody who is about to urge a novel course of action, he advises the various communities:

> You must choose for yourselves overseers [*episkopoi*] and assistants [*diakonoi*] who are worthy of the Lord: men who are humble and not eager for money, but sincere and approved; for they are carrying out the ministry of the prophets and teachers for you. Do not esteem them lightly; for they take an honourable rank among you along with the prophets and teachers.[53]

Yet the idea of such local officials was clearly controversial. The author feels that it has to be justified: he concedes that those charismatic prophets who do not abuse their calling are still the natural heirs of the Apostles who had actually seen the Lord. The author compares them to the 'High Priest' of the old dispensation; they have the right to recite the prayers over the offerings at the celebration of the Lord's Supper and, speaking as inspired people in a trance, they are not bound by any liturgical formula but can extemporize. We are still far from a decorous Eucharist in the parish church. There is no question of an official, permanent priesthood which alone can preside at the Supper and consecrate the bread and wine. The charismatics are still the most authoritative leaders and the *episkopoi* and *diakonoi* are secondary figures: they may only officiate at the Eucharist if no apostles or prophets are present.[54]

The author of the *Didache* also speaks of *presbuteroi* or elders. The system of Paul's Churches, with their 'overseers' and 'assistants', was beginning to be fused with the synagogue system of 'elders' used by the more Jewish communities. Writing in the late 90s, Clement, the *episkopos* of Rome, remarks that certain elders had been appointed by the Apostles to preside at the Eucharist. For the first time in Christian history, Clement writes as though Jesus himself had founded a cult and liturgy similar to the Temple cultus of the Old Israel. Clement sees this ordered liturgy as essential to the life of the Church: he describes the strict rules that Jesus had prescribed and suggests that the *episkopos* or overseer should be equated with the High Priest of the Levitical caste.

> The High Priest, for example, has his own proper services [*leitourgai*] assigned to him, the priesthood has its own status, there are no particular ministries laid down for Levites; and the layman [*laos*] is bound by the regulations affecting the laity.[55]

This is a new departure indeed. By this time, the Jewish Temple had been in ruins for over twenty years and the High Priest and the Levites must have been shadowy, literary figures to a Western Christian such as Clement. The old ideal of service (*diakonia*) is beginning to become the exclusive right of certain Christian officials. Soon the 'liturgy' will require a special caste of 'priests', in a way that would have been alien to the very first Christians who had simply blessed bread in their homes in memory of the Lord. In Clement we have the origins of the Roman Catholic tradition: a divinely appointed liturgy and priesthood with an apostolic succession of bishops.

If the Church was going to survive it had to adapt and change to meet the new circumstances. Clement's Roman solution was not the only innovation. Writing in the early years of the second century as he made his way to Rome to die for his faith, Ignatius, *episkopos* of Antioch, also speaks of a clearly graded hierarchy of Christians. The elders or presbyters comprise the bishop's council and below them are the deacons, servants of the Church of God. But in Ignatius's letters, Church order is not valued for its own sake, as in Clement's Roman Church. The unity of the episcopate, presbyterate and diaconate were a sign of the unity of the whole Church with Christ, a sacrament of holy fellowship. In this blending of the spiritual with the official we can discern the beginnings of the Greek Orthodox tradition.

Yet another solution appears in the 'pastoral epistles' that were supposedly written to Paul's old missionary companions Timothy and Titus. In fact they were written long after Paul's death in about 67, and may even be as late as the middle of the second century. As we saw earlier, they probably derive from the Jewish-Christian tradition of Peter rather than from the

Pauline Church. The literary device of ascribing authorship to an historical personality was quite common and these pastoral epistles are in no way forgeries. They show a desire to preserve a continuity with the apostolic period and to preserve the spirit of the primitive Church as far as possible in a very different world. Other late texts attributed to Paul in this way but not actually written by the Apostle himself are the epistle to the Colossians and, some would say, the letter to the Ephesians. In the epistles to Timothy and Titus, a Church order is now taken for granted. The *episkopos* or bishop as we may now call him has risen to a position of authority over his fellow elders or *presbuteroi*. Yet unlike the situation in Clement's Roman Church, the emphasis here is not on cult and liturgy but on the teaching mission of the Church. Here the pastoral epistles betray their Jewish origin: their Churches were in line with the rabbinic Judaism which had become normative throughout the Jewish world after the destruction of the Temple and its priesthood.

By this date, rival forms of Christianity had arisen in the various Christian communities. In particular the author is concerned about the Gnostic 'myths and genealogies' which encourage distracting and useless speculation. The duty of all the clergy is to promote 'sound teaching'.[56] For the first time we hear of the qualities that people should seek in a candidate for the ministry: sobriety, moderation and common sense are the new Christian virtues. These are very different from Paul's list of charismata. Further, the bishop is to be a good family man who keeps his own household in order. There is no mention of celibacy here, no suggestion that the true minister will abandon his wife and children and live as a mendicant with nowhere to lay his head. The author also refers to a rite of ordination, a laying on of hands, as in the ordination of a Jewish elder, which confers the Holy Spirit on the members of the clergy.[57]

There is no question of women being ordained to this ministry. The author takes it for granted that bishops, elders and deacons are all men, since women are expressly forbidden to take part in the teaching ministry of the Church:

During instruction, a woman should be quiet and respectful. I am not giving permission for a woman to teach or to tell a man what to do. A woman ought not to speak, because Adam was formed first and Eve afterwards, and it was not Adam who was led astray but the woman who was led astray and fell into sin.[58]

There is no hint of Paul's hesitations about the doctrine of 'headship'. The author has reformulated and merged the two passages from the first epistle to the Corinthians to produce a categorical relegation of women to an inferior position. Eve was second in order of Creation and first in order of sin. There were to be no more Phoebes or Priscas in the Church. It is notable that in this first Christian scripture to forbid the ordination of women, the only argument raised is the 'headship' doctrine, which sees the subordination of women to be essential to the God-given order of Creation. Later Christians would bring forward other arguments: that God was conceived in masculine terms, had become incarnate in a man, that Jesus had chosen only male Apostles. In this one scriptural rebuttal of a Christian ministry for women, none of these reasons is adduced. The author of the first epistle to Timothy only uses the 'headship' doctrine to silence women in the Churches. It has been suggested that in the pastoral epistles we have the beginning of the reformed Protestant tradition. Certainly his picture of meek, submissive women in quiet clothes and with neatly braided hair looks forward to the women of Calvin's Geneva and of Puritan New England. The author totally ignores the fact that in Genesis Adam is also rebuked and punished for his sin. Woman's only Christian role, in his view, is childbearing: that is where she will find salvation, provided that she lives a modest and holy life.[59]

There is, however, just a hint that some women were rebelling against this new Christian chauvinism. The author speaks slightingly of 'silly women who are obsessed with their sins and follow one craze after another in the attempt to educate themselves but can never come to the knowledge of the truth'. We shall see in the next chapter that women did not let their old Christian freedoms disappear without a struggle. In this male author's contempt for these women we can unfortunately hear the first of later clerical sneers at the piety of women. By this time Christianity had settled down in the world. The Second Coming of Christ had obviously been postponed indefinitely and accommodation with the world was now the order of the day. The late epistles attributed to Paul, such as Colossians and Ephesians, contain what are called 'household codes' which make it clear that women were now to express their Christianity by fitting in to the prevailing male domination of the secular world. Thus the author of the letter to the Colossians:

> Wives, give way to your husbands, as you should in the Lord. Husbands, love your wives and treat them with gentleness. Children, be obedient to your parents always, because that is what will please the Lord. Parents, never drive your children to resentment or you will make them feel frustrated. Slaves, be obedient to the men who are called your masters in this world.[60]

The egalitarianism of Paul's letter to the Galatians – neither male nor female, slave nor free – seems to have given way to an ethic of submission. Such 'household codes' were common in Greek and Roman writings at this time. Christians were beginning to sacrifice the active women of the early charismatic period, who had been an eloquent and shocking sign of a new dispensation. Instead, they were starting to assimilate with the respectable *mores* of the dominant culture in order to survive: by this time, some Christians had died for their faith at the hands of the Roman Empire.

Yet by including these later texts in the official canon, the Churches had expressed an important principle. Jesus had told his disciples that after his death and glorification he would send them his Spirit to make his will plain in the new circumstances when they would no longer have him as a guide. Ascribing such texts as the pastoral epistles to Paul only draws attention to their radical difference. The people who compiled the New Testament seemed to be giving later generations of Christians a message: it was not obligatory to follow the past slavishly. Each generation had to create its own form of Christianity and meet the challenge of modernity. Today many of the opponents of the ordination of women argue that the Church must not submit to the *mores* of the day; it must be ready to fly in the face of prevailing feminism, in order to uphold primitive values. But after the early period of charismatic fervour, the Churches had already begun the process of accommodation and assimilation with the world. Some of the texts that have been used against the innovation of women priests were themselves the product of this kind of adaptation and departure from primitive Christianity. If the Churches had not had this flexibility, they would have vanished – as did the Jewish-Christian sect of the Nazarenes which refused to accommodate gentiles. The New Testament was tacitly indicating that the Churches must always be open to change and respond to the needs of the day.

— 4 —

The Patristic Age: Silent Women and Eloquent Fathers

IT WAS NOT surprising that most Christians were anxious not
to offend the prevailing values of late antiquity unneces-
sarily, since, by the second century, their position was
perilous. Seen as enemies of the State, they were subjected to
periods of severe persecution at the hands of the Roman
authorities: thousands of men and women died in the stadiums
during the second and third centuries, until the Romans realized that persecution was counter-productive, since the crowds
were edified by the courage and dedication of the Christian
martyrs. This long period of persecution and insecurity made
an indelible impression on the Christian spirit, especially in the
West. There martyrs and confessors (people who had been
imprisoned and suffered for the faith but who had not actually
died) were frequently regarded as superior to officials such as
bishops or presbyters. Some of the more radical Christians
believed that there could be no accommodation with the world
but the majority decided that it was better not to appear
subversive and confrontational. We have also seen that there
was conflict and division within the Christian ranks. During the
second century, Gnostic teachers attempted to mythologize
Christianity, divorce it from its historical roots in Judaism and
transform it into a purely psychic, interior drama. They
attracted an impressive number of enthusiastic disciples in

major Christian centres such as Rome and Alexandria. It had been to counter this internal threat that the authors of the pastoral epistles had urged the bishop to become the leader of the flock in order to preserve 'sound doctrine'.

These various pressures, from without and from within, contributed to the development of a Christian hierarchy of clergy. Not all the far-flung Churches developed in the same way. We have already noted a considerable difference in emphasis between the Roman Church of Clement, the Eastern Church of Ignatius of Antioch and the Jewish-Christian communities. But gradually the various Churches began to move away from a charismatic style of leadership, which depended upon the inspiration of the Spirit, towards a more settled, prosaic establishment. An increasing number of Christians came to see that the very survival of their faith depended upon finding some *modus vivendi* with Greco-Roman culture. During the second century, Christian apologists tried to reach out towards the pagan world to show that their faith was not a disreputable novelty but was deeply in tune with its own traditions. Thus Justin of Caesarea, who eventually died a martyr, wrote his first Apologia in about 155, stressing the continuity of the Jewish-Christian teaching with that of the ancient Greek philosophers, who had also believed in only one God. At the beginning of the third century, Clement of Alexandria, one of the first highly educated men to convert to Christianity, preached a Platonized version of the faith.

During the centuries of persecution, the Churches still had a remarkably unofficial lifestyle. Members had no special buildings for worship but continued to meet in one another's houses – a fact which the pagans found extraordinary and suspect. 'We have no temples and no altars,' wrote the Christian apologist Minucius Felix in about 200. Their bishops, presbyters and deacons do not seem to have worn distinctive dress to mark their status and there was no great divide between them and the rest of the community. The Greek word *laos* still applied to the whole people of God rather than to those Christians who did not belong to the clergy. Christians did not see their clergy as 'priests' in our sense of the word: they may have sought an accommodation with Greek philosophy but would have no truck with pagan worship and ritual. For the Christians of the second and third century, the institution of priesthood was associated with idolatry on the one hand and with Judaism on the other. They were struggling to be independent of both.

Yet the orthodox were increasingly unwilling to trust their faith to charismatic leaders. The Gnostics posed too serious a threat, as did the followers of the Christian prophet Montanus, who began to preach a fiercely apocalyptic version of the gospel in the 170s. The End was nigh, he declared, and Christians should withdraw from the world, from sexuality and pleasure, hastening the Second Coming by willingly accepting martyrdom. His rigorist creed spread like wildfire in Asia Minor, Gaul and North Africa – provinces which had a tradition of disaffection from Rome. Montanus and his two female colleagues Priscilla and Maximilla believed that they had been directly inspired by the Holy Spirit: some of their followers considered that Montanus was the Spirit Incarnate and Priscilla was said to have had a vision of Christ in the form of a woman. The inspired oracles of Maximilla and Priscilla were collected in book form and revered as new Gospels. The more conventional Christians found all this extremity profoundly disturbing – not least the prominence of the two prophetesses. Where was the philosophic calm which was supposed to characterize the rational mind? By the end of the century, rapture, ecstasy and inspired frenzy had become suspect to bishops such as Irenaeus of Lyons, who had a Montanist group in his own diocese. Even though the early Church had been highly charismatic, the orthodox now preferred the more tranquil piety of a teacher like Clement of Alexandria. Direct inspiration of the Spirit had given women a certain freedom and status in the Pauline Church. The Holy Spirit blew where it willed; the approaching End had made conventional distinctions between the sexes irrelevant. By the end of the second century, however, when most Christians were yearning for calm and acceptance, the cause of women's liberation was damaged by the high profile of the Montanist prophetesses.

To counter the rival versions of their faith, Christians developed still further the ideal of an apostolic succession, borrowing the notion from the secular, pagan world. The concept of a tradition (*paradosis*) and a succession (*diadoche*) of teachers which could be traced back to the original Master derived from the Greek philosophical schools of antiquity. At first some Christians were unenthusiastic about the idea: the authors of the pastoral epistles preferred to speak of a 'deposited trust' rather than of a line of succession. But people who claimed to belong to the Greater, Catholic or Universal Church (as opposed to the 'heretical' sects) wanted to establish their teaching as orthodox or correct against their rivals'. Consequently they began to emphasize the teaching role of the bishop as guardian of 'orthodoxy', a teaching that he had inherited from the Apostles. Originally, therefore, the 'apostolic succession', about which we hear so much today, did not refer to a succession of persons but to the continuity of doctrine. This notion of a 'succession' was itself an innovation, however, specially designed to meet the needs of second-century Christians. As such, it was a success since it gave a sense of cohesion and identity to the scattered Christian communities which were struggling to stay alive in a hostile world. At the end of Irenaeus's life in 200, he could speak of a 'Great Church' with a single rule of faith.

But the idea hardened, as does most 'orthodoxy', and the apostolic succession came to mean a chain of bishops whose teaching could be trusted because it derived, as it were, from the horse's mouth. Thus in his *Ecclesiastical History*, Eusebius (d. 340) favoured Irenaeus because he had been instructed in the faith by Polycarp, Bishop of Smyrna, who had in turn been a disciple of the Apostle John. As early as 180, the Christian man of letters Hegesippus had wanted to present the 'undisturbed tradition of apostolic preaching'. Approving of what he had seen in Rome and Corinth, he had tried to justify this view by compiling a list of bishops of Rome which could be traced back to the Apostle Peter. This was a largely fictional exercise, since there is no historical evidence, only a strong oral tradition, of Peter's residence in Rome. Did the Twelve preach exactly the same doctrine as Irenaeus, Hegesippus and Eusebius? It seems unlikely, since according to the New Testament the Twelve had continued to see themselves as observant Jews. Nevertheless the idea of *diadoche* or succession came to signify a line of bishops who reassured the faithful that they – and not the people who were dubbed as 'heretics' – held the one, true faith.

Despite this vaunted continuity with the Apostles, Jesus, Paul and the Twelve would all have been surprised by the Church of the third century. Circumstances had made the old egalitarian ideal impracticable and a gap was beginning to separate the clergy from the 'laity' in a way that was alien to most of the New Testament. One highly significant change was the application of Roman imperial words, which denoted power, influence and authority, to the Church which Christ had declared to be not of this world. The highly influential North African theologian Tertullian (160–220) was the first to speak of the *ordo* of the clergy. In Roman society, the term signified class or rank: the upper *ordines* consisted of senators (*senatores*) and knights (*equites*), while the *plebs* comprised the lower 'orders'. A man was admitted to one of the higher ranks in a ceremony known as *ordinatio*. Consequently, Latin-speaking Christians quite naturally began to apply the term 'ordination' to the consecration of a bishop or presbyter. There was no conscious betrayal of gospel principles in this use of words, even though it associated the clergy with the language of privilege which Christ had told them to avoid. He had said that nobody was to be given honorific titles, such as Rabbi, Lord and Master. But, as always, Christians spontaneously explained their faith and the organization of their community in terms of the surrounding culture. It could be seen as a way of incarnating the divine imperative in the mundane world, a process that nearly always involves paradox and difficulty. Later the Roman words 'province', 'diocese' and 'vicar' would also be used. When opponents of major change in the Christian tradition object to the abandonment of early values, it is perhaps salutary to reflect that the very idea of clerical ordination, which has acquired such sacred associations over the centuries and which, when applied to women, arouses such complex emotions, does not derive from either Christ or his Apostles but from the secular institutions of the powerful Roman Empire.

Another major innovation of this period involved the use of the word 'priest' (in Latin *sacerdos* and in Greek *hiereus*). In the early third century, Christians began to apply priestly imagery to Christian institutions in an entirely new way. Tertullian applies the symbols and language of priesthood to the bishop as does the historian Hippolytus, who had worked with Irenaeus in Gaul during the 190s and had become embroiled in clerical politics in Rome at the beginning of the third century. In his important treatise *The Apostolic Tradition*, he has recorded the rite for the ordination of a bishop. Here, for the first time, we see the episcopal office conceived principally in terms of the bishop's liturgical role, which Hippolytus describes, again for the first time, in priestly language. The presbyters are to stand silently round the candidate, while the presiding bishop lays his hands upon him, praying that the Holy Spirit may help him to 'feed thy flock and serve as thine High Priest . . . and offer to thee the gifts of thy holy Church. And that by the high-priestly Spirit, he may have the authority to forgive sins, according to thy command.'[1] Hitherto the bishop's main job had been to protect the orthodox doctrines of the Church. Now, in Hippolytus's rite of ordination, he has emerged as superior to the other presbyters by virtue of the liturgical powers vested in him alone. Other bishops from neighbouring dioceses are to be present at the ceremony to show that this is not just a local event but concerns the universal Church. The setting of the ordination is still humble: the ceremony will take place in a house-church, and provision for the ordination of confessors shows that Christians were still highly conscious of themselves as a persecuted minority. But already the Church was beginning to mirror the structures of the Roman Empire, with vicars ruling each province, and was also taking on the mantle of the long-dead Levitical priesthood.

In *The Apostolic Tradition*, the ordination of a presbyter shows that his position is quite different. Hippolytus tells us that when the bishop lays his hands upon the candidate, the other local presbyters also touch him. Where the bishop had, as it were, risen above his fellow presbyters to a position of eminence as the sole ruler of the local community, the presbyterate is still

seen as a corporate body, primarily concerned with administration. The presbyter is not called *sacerdos* or *hiereus*. The prayer
asks that the candidate may share the spirit of grace and
counsel with the other presbyters in order to govern the people
of God. His job is still analogous to that of the elder of a Jewish
synagogue. Gradually, however, the presbyter would also become a 'priest' during the third century, as he began to share
some of the liturgical privileges of the bishop. When a bishop
was unable to preside at the Eucharist, he would delegate this
liturgical function to one of the presbyters. Thus the presbyter
shared the 'priesthood' of the bishop by association with his
ministry but would not himself be called 'priest' in his own
right until the fifth century.

The ordination to the 'diaconate', the third *ordo* of the
Church, was also described by Hippolytus. The deacon was
ordained by the bishop alone, not by the presbyterate, since he
was primarily the bishop's assistant. His function was 'not for
the presbyterate but for the service of the bishop'.[2] He did have
an important liturgical function, however, albeit an ancillary
one, since it was his job to carry the offerings of the congregation up to the altar, or, as Hippolytus explained, 'to bring up in
holiness to thy holiness that which is offered to thee by thine
ordained high priest'. But his chief role was administrative: 'to
take charge of property and report to the bishop what is
necessary'.[3]

There was as yet no notion of a body of priests and clergy
acting as intermediaries and approaching God on behalf of
others. Nor was the bishop, who had begun to officiate at the
Eucharist, yet perceived to be standing in for Christ as his
representative. The notion of the priest as *alter Christus*, another
Christ, which has been so crucial in the current debate about
the ordination of women, would not emerge until the Middle
Ages. In the theology of the Lord's Supper, the emphasis was
still on the priesthood of Christ. These Eucharistic meetings, at
which bread and wine were offered to God and then shared by
everybody, still stressed the union of the whole *laos*. Together
the whole community, who had been incorporated by baptism
into Christ, offered the bloodless sacrifice of the Last Age. The
stress was on the priesthood of the whole people of God rather

than on their human representative: the High Priesthood of the bishop was at this stage more of a literary image than a sacramental reality. In the same spirit, Justin the Apologist had described the work of Christ as involving, among other things, teaching us how to offer such sacrifices – quite distinct from the animal sacrifices of the priests of old. But Hippolytus's use of priestly imagery together with the imperial terminology which, in effect, equated the bishop with the city magistrate, did mark the beginning of a major change.

In the writings of Cyprian, who became Bishop of Carthage in 249 – just three years after his conversion to Christianity – we see quite a different conception. Here we find a clear assumption of a clerical hierarchy with the 'laity' at the bottom and the bishop at the top. Cyprian assumed a division between clergy and laity that is far clearer than anything we have encountered hitherto. He has no hesitation whatever in calling the bishop a High Priest and is convinced that, like Aaron, the bishop has been through a rite of ordination which gives him the powers to perform liturgical tasks that are impossible for a layman. The bishop has also become an absolute monarch in his 'diocese'. When he first became a bishop, Cyprian had tried to preserve something of the old egalitarianism and had made it a rule not to act without the permission of the presbyterate. But the internal disputes of the North African Church, which was suffering severely from persecution and did not know how to deal with apostates, caused him to act on his own responsibility.

Cyprian did not seem to see the bishop's power as deriving from the priesthood of the whole people of God; rather, it was the other way around. Without a bishop there was no Church: 'For not only is the bishop in the Church but the Church is in the bishop, and if anyone is not with the bishop, he is not with the Church.'[4] The laity is no longer to have the freedom in the Spirit to act on their own initiative. They have to be obedient to the human institution which is personified in the bishop and the clergy who assist him. The bishop alone has the authority to teach. Cyprian had no concept of freelance lay teachers such as Tertullian and Clement of Alexandria. In his rite of ordination, Hippolytus had envisaged a collegiality or solidarity of bishop and presbyters but in Cyprian's writings this has been replaced by the collegiality of bishops with one another. Cyprian liked to use the Old Testament categories of High Priest, Priest and Levite to refer to the three Christian *ordines* of episcopate, presbyterate and diaconate. Other groups, such as the confessors and the ascetics, were now relegated to 'minor orders'. From this point in the Western Church people would start to think in careerist terms of 'rising through the ranks' and ascending the ladder of episcopal power.

The tendency towards the hierarchical and imperial style of Church government inevitably accelerated when the Emperor Constantine legalized Christianity in 312, enabling Christians to own property, build their own places of worship and take a full part in public life. When Church and State went into partnership, the Emperor persuaded the bishops to take over some of the prerogatives of the civil power. He granted them privileges, such as the right to a throne, to be accompanied by lights and incense and being greeted by a kiss on the hand. Bishops began to wear some of the insignia worn by civil dignitaries, such as the *pallium* (a woollen cloak worn over the shoulders), the *campagi* (special shoes) and a golden ring. Like the Emperor, the Bishop of Rome could expect to be greeted by choristers on his arrival at a church, to be waited on at the altar with covered hands and to have the people genuflect before him and kiss his feet. The ceremonial of the papal Mass became similar to that of the imperial court. We are clearly a long way from the *diakonia* of the New Testament which saw the minister as the humble slave of Christ and the people. It was the people who now bowed and knelt before the bishop like slaves. Indeed Jesus himself began to be depicted in Byzantine art as a great emperor: frescoes and mosaics depicted Christ as Pantocrator, ruler of Creation, seated on a throne, adorned with jewels and surrounded by a heavenly retinue of apostles and angels. The Church had begun to build grand basilicas, modelled on the secular basilicas or state meeting halls, where a statue of Christ stood in place of the imperial effigy. Some bishops, such as Hilary of Poitiers, Martin of Tours and Augustine of Hippo, were uneasy about this development, but it persisted apace and has survived in the

liturgy of the Roman Catholic and Greek Orthodox Churches to
the present day.

We have seen that in the later books of the New Testament
women had been excluded from the active teaching ministry
even before the humble *diakonia* had been transformed into a
High Priesthood. By the second century, the memory of women
apostles and teachers such as Prisca, Phoebe and Junia survived
but had faded into a romantic, nostalgic dream. In the second
century, the apocryphal *Acts of Paul and Thecla* recounted the
legend of one of Paul's women disciples. It was regarded as a
canonical book for centuries and Thecla was revered as one of
the most important women saints. But this tale, written in the
genre of a popular romance, shows that by the second century,
the idea of independent women preaching and baptizing converts was a vague memory, gilded over with fictional glamour.
Thecla, we are told, fell in love not with Jesus but with Paul
when she heard him preach in her home town of Iconium in
modern Turkey. She immediately threw over her fiancé, vowed
perpetual virginity and followed Paul slavishly, begging for
baptism. Fearing that she would become 'mad after men', Paul
contemptuously refused to admit her to the Church. In this
legendary account of his mission, Paul is made to live up to his
reputation as an arch-male chauvinist. The author tells us that
he callously abandoned Thecla to her fate, even though on two
occasions she was flung into the arena to face death. To the
astonishment and edification of the spectators, however, her
virginal body could not be killed: it remained unconsumed by
the flames and untouched by the wild beasts. Eventually,
Thecla took matters into her own hands, baptized herself (in a
trough of man-eating seals in the arena) and set off once again
in pursuit of Paul, clad, as befits the liberated woman, in a
man's cloak. When she finally caught up with him, Thecla's
deference was gone: she coolly told Paul that she was now his
equal and had a divine sanction for her ministry: 'He who
wrought along with thee for the gospel, has wrought in me also
for baptism.' Greatly wondering, Paul was forced to confirm her
mission and Thecla went back home to Iconium to preach and
baptize.

In some of the manuscripts, the story has a rather instructive epilogue. By the time she was ninety years old, Thecla had acquired a marvellous reputation as a faith healer but she was taking custom away from the local doctors. In their fury, the physicians came together to her cave, to violate her virginal body which they saw as the source of her powers. Not surprisingly, perhaps, they discovered that they were incapable of ravishing the aged virgin and Thecla melted miraculously into the mountainside. Even in the second century, romantic writers could see that it was extremely dangerous for women to step outside their proper sphere and invade male territory: this could arouse irrational, unChristian and atavistic violence that was every bit as inimical to women as the hatred that made the Romans cry out for Christian blood.

It is perhaps significant that Thecla cast aside her dependency in the arena when facing martyrdom. It is this that causes Paul to recognize her right to an active ministry. Martyrdom was indeed a great leveller, since women faced the same agony as men and sometimes behaved more courageously. One of the earliest accounts of persecution in the Western Church tells the story of the martyrs of Lyons, who died in 177. Conspicuous among them was a young slave girl called Blandina, who, the author says, proved the truth of St Paul's words 'that the things that men think cheap, ugly and contemptuous are deemed worthy of glory before God'.[5] Her companions – men and women alike – were understandably terrified, but Blandina's fearlessness astonished her torturers. The author compares her to a noble athlete and to the mother of the Maccabees, who in 165 BCE had cheered her seven sons on to martyrdom in the persecution of Antiochus Epiphanes. In the same way, Blandina encouraged her companions and helped them to die bravely. 'Tiny, weak and insignificant as she was', Blandina became an icon of Christ:

Blandina was hung on a post and exposed as bait for the wild animals that were let loose on her. She seemed to hang there in the form of a cross, and by her fervent prayer she aroused intense enthusiasm in those who were undergoing their ordeal, for in their torment with their physical

eyes they saw in the person of their sister Him who was
crucified for them.[6]

In the discussion about the ordination of women in our own
day, many people have doubted the ability of a woman to act as
the representative of the male Christ. The early Church had no
doubt that a woman could fulfil this role. In 177 there were still
no Christian priests. It was the martyr, not a member of the
regular clergy, who became the *alter Christus* (another Christ)
and a woman could represent him as well as a man.

Perpetua, the young matron who died in Carthage in 203
during the persecution of Severus, showed how martyrdom
enabled a woman to transcend the limitations usually imposed
upon her sex. She kept a diary while she was in prison and after
her death this was edited and completed. Most scholars believe
that this quite remarkable document is authentic. In her diary
we see that Perpetua was a sensitive and fearful young woman.
In the early days she was terrified, depressed, grief-stricken by
the pain she had caused her aged father and heartbroken about
her little boy. But she managed to prepare herself for her
horrible fate by means of a series of dreams. In late antiquity,
people still believed that the barriers between the divine and
the human worlds were lowered during sleep, and because
Perpetua had such a rich dream life her companions in prison
believed that she was *in dignitate,* in a specially distinguished
relationship with God. Her sex did not enter into this at all.
They asked her to see if they really were going to be martyred
and Perpetua had some fascinating dreams in rather the same
way as analysands today are able to produce significant dreams
for their therapist, coming to terms thereby with buried fears
and anxieties that can be expressed in no other way. In the end
Perpetua was able to die bravely and serenely, having prepared
herself for martyrdom at a profound level, and also ministering
to her companions and enabling them to do the same. There
was no question of Perpetua's being commanded to be silent
and submissive: she was the leader and spiritual director of the
men and women in the group.

In one of her most interesting dreams, Perpetua felt that she
had transcended her gender and become the 'new creation'

described by St Paul. She dreamed that one of the deacons in her Church led her into the arena, where she was stripped naked and rubbed with oil, as for a wrestling match. Her opponent was a massive Egyptian, whose foul appearance she identified with 'the Fiend'. With the complete lack of astonishment which characterizes dream life, Perpetua found that she had become a man, yet she also mysteriously remained female, since the adjudicator still addresses her as 'daughter', 'she' and 'her'. It is a powerful depiction of Paul's assertion that in Christ there is no longer male and female. Perpetua felt exhilarated and free. In her struggle with the Egyptian, she 'felt airborne . . . as if I were not touching the ground'. She defeats him, the crowd cheers joyfully and triumphantly Perpetua walked towards the Gate of Life. Then, she records, 'I awoke. And I knew that I should have to fight not against the wild beasts but against the Fiend; but I knew the victory would be mine.'[7]

Some have said that Perpetua and her companions were Montanists; some have argued that the editor of Perpetua's diary who added the account of her death was none other than Tertullian, who eventually abandoned orthodoxy and became a Montanist. Yet Tertullian had extremely repressive views about women. While still a Catholic, he had condemned the way that heretics like the Gnostics allowed women such a high profile: 'And the women of the heretics, how wanton they are!' he had exclaimed. 'For they are bold enough to teach, to dispute, to enact exorcism, to undertake cures – maybe even to baptize.'[8] Tertullian was horrified to hear of a Carthaginian woman who belonged to the Cainite sect (which rejected baptism) actually daring to teach and quoting Thecla as her model. This was unprecedented, Tertullian complained, conveniently forgetting such important evangelists as Prisca. *The Acts of Paul and Thecla* were known to be a forgery, he argued; the presbyter responsible had confessed his crime. Women would next be claiming that they had the power to baptize, if they took this false document seriously:

How could we believe that Paul should give a female power to teach and to baptize, when he did not allow a woman even to learn by her own right? 'Let them keep silence,' he says, 'and ask their husbands at home.'[9]

In this treatise on the subject of baptism, Tertullian put women in an entirely separate category from the rest of the *laos*. The right to confer baptism belongs to the bishop but, if he is not available, presbyters and deacons or – at worst – even a layman had a right to baptize. Since this priestly power comes from God, anybody could perform the ceremony in an emergency. But not a woman. 'No woman is allowed to speak in Church,' Tertullian argued in another treatise, 'or even to teach, to baptize, or to discharge any man's function, much less to take upon herself the priestly office.'[10] Tertullian knew that the whole people of God was a priestly people and shared in the royal priesthood of Christ, but women could not participate in this priestly function.

There was, therefore, a basic inconsistency in Tertullian's attitude, a flaw that would characterize many of the arguments against women's active ministry in the Churches. Indeed, when they complained about the ministry of the heretical women, the arguments of the orthodox were not theologically based but centred on the 'wantonness' or 'brashness' of the women concerned. We know very little about the actual status of women in Gnostic or Montanist groups, since most of our information comes from the writings of their opponents. It was said, for example, that Marcion, who preached a Gnostic-style dualism and who founded a rival Church in Rome, appointed women to all its major offices alongside the men. But it would be mistaken to romanticize the attitudes of the heretics, who shared many of the patriarchal assumptions of the orthodox. In Marcion's theology, femaleness belongs to the earthly, unre- deemed sphere of Creation, and maleness was the attribute of heavenly, transcendent values. All Gnostics regarded maleness as the ultimately desirable norm and, whatever their sex, saw themselves as 'female' until their final redemption. Neverthe- less, the heretics' reputation for allowing women to take such an active role in their Churches seems to have hardened the chauvinism of the orthodox, reinforcing the social customs that were endemic to Greco-Roman culture where, in general, women could be seen but not heard. Silent, submissive women were becoming one of the hallmarks of orthodoxy, even though this had little to do with the egalitarian ethos of the New Testament.

Indeed, an unhealthy misogyny was also creeping into some forms of Western Christianity. Thus Tertullian followed the example of the first epistle to Timothy in blaming women for the fall of man. Writing to his 'best beloved sisters', he suddenly launches into an astonishing attack in his treatise *On Female Dress*:

> Do you not know that you are each an Eve? The sentence of God on this sex of yours lives in this age: the guilt of necessity lives too. You are the devil's gateway: you are the unsealer of that forbidden tree: you are the first deserter of the divine law. . . . You destroyed so easily God's image, man. On account of your desert – that is death – even the Son of God had to die.[11]

Tertullian believed that even without their realizing it, women could tempt men to sexual sin. Consequently they should hide their bodies, shrouding them in veils and making themselves as unattractive as possible.

It is ironic that Christians were beginning to turn away from the physical with such revulsion, since at the Council of Nicea in May 325, the bishops of the Universal Church decided that Jesus the man had also been the uncreated and unbegotten Son of God. In other words, God had been revealed in human flesh. This doctrine is now considered fundamental to Christianity but the decision of Nicea was regarded as extremely controversial at the time. Christians had always believed that Jesus had been the Son of God and was, somehow, divine, but they were not sure what this meant. How could the sublime God, who was beyond time and change, have been a weak, puling baby? For about two hundred years, Christians argued passionately about the precise meaning of the Incarnation. The decision of Nicea proved to be as divisive as the more recent decision of the Church of England Synod in November 1992. The unity of Christendom was irrevocably split into warring sects as Arians,

Nestorians, Monophysites, Monothelites and Apollinarians all refused to submit to the teaching of the Orthodox Church about the divinity of Christ. They were particularly concerned – as well they might be – about the unity of God. Was Jesus, the Son of God, a second divine being? To answer these difficult questions, three brilliant theologians of Cappadocia in eastern Turkey formulated the doctrine of the Trinity. Basil, Bishop of Caesarea (329–79), his younger brother Gregory, Bishop of Nyssa (335–95), and best friend Gregory of Nazianzus (329–91) stressed the mystery and the ineffability of God. We should not think about Him in simplistic terms as 'Father', 'Son' or 'Spirit': these were simply terms that human beings used to describe a reality which could never be defined. The mysteriousness of the Trinity was meant to be a reminder that the indescribable God could only reveal Himself to us in an incomprehensible manner. The doctrine of the Trinity was always difficult for Western theologians, who did not fully understand the Greek terms used by the Cappadocians, but it has remained central to the spirituality of the Orthodox Churches. It should remind us, in the current dispute about the male God and the feasibility of women priests, that the reality that we call 'God' should not be conceived as a male personality but transcends such human categories. The Greek theologians did not envisage the Son of God, the second person of the Trinity, becoming man in any simplistic way: rather, they envisaged humanity being absorbed into the divinity. Maximus the Confessor (580-662), who has been called the Father of Byzantine Theology, formulated the doctrine of the Incarnation in a way that eventually satisfied the Christians of the Eastern Orthodox Church. He saw Jesus as a deified human being, his human flesh transfigured by the divine, in rather the same way as Buddhists see Gautama, their Buddha, as 'the enlightened one' who has become identified with Nirvana. The Greek Fathers of the Church constantly stressed the distinction between 'maleness' and 'humanity' when they attempted to describe the mystery of the Incarnation. When the Word had been made flesh, it had not become a male human being (*aner*); the Word had become humanity or Man (*anthropos*). One day we should all become what Jesus had been: the deified Man whose radiant humanity had been transfigured on Mount Tabor as the first fruits of a universal redemption. St Paul had spoken in this sense when he had talked about Jesus being the New Man and a New Creation.

Because of this important distinction between *aner* and *anthropos*, Greek theologians like Basil of Caesarea or Gregory of Nyssa had no problem about seeing a woman as the re-presentative of Christ or the image of God. Thus Gregory had written the biography of their sister Macrina, who was a consecrated virgin and had lived with a community of like-minded women at Averni in Cappadocia. For Gregory, Macrina and her companions had been liberated from the immense emotional and physical toil of childbirth and managing a huge Cappadocian household. They represented a new type of womanhood, which approached the original perfection of Adam. Macrina had yearned wholeheartedly towards God, in the way that was natural to humanity, and seemed to stand on the threshold of the invisible world. Far from regarding her as an inferior, Gregory used to consult her as his spiritual adviser, as had Basil when he had made his important monastic reforms. In Gregory's dialogue *On the Soul and Resurrection*, Macrina played the role of Socrates in a Platonic dialogue. She was an *alter Christus* for Gregory, a mirror in which human beings could glimpse the image of God. In his *Life of Macrina*, Gregory tells us that on the night she died, he had dreamed that he held a relic in his hand, which had caught the flash of the sun's light like a mirror. The next day, when he took the body of his sister into his arms to carry her into the grave, the glow of her skin against her black robe reminded Gregory of his dream and he realized that Macrina's body had become a holy thing. In death as in life, Macrina's soul had reflected the blinding purity of God, rather as the divinity of Christ had shone through his transfigured humanity on Mount Tabor. In our own day those Greek Orthodox Christians who deny that a woman can be a true icon or image of God seem to have lost sight of this patristic vision.

In the West, however, the great theologians followed Tertullian in seeing the male as normative and the female as a pale shadow of his humanity. At this time, Western Europe faced the prospect of being overrun by the barbarian hordes and was developing a fearful, defensive theology. For Ambrose, Bishop of Milan, *integritas* (wholeness) became the crucial Christian virtue. Like the virginal body of Mary, the mother of Jesus, the true faith must remain whole and unpenetrated by the errors of the heretical barbarians, many of whom had converted to Arianism, a form of Christianity which denied the divinity of Christ. Like Gregory of Nyssa, Ambrose extolled the glories of a virginal life, but not because it revealed a new type of humanity. For Ambrose, all women should aspire to the condition of men.

> She who does not believe is a woman and should be designated by the name of her sex, whereas she who believes progresses to perfect manhood, to the measure of adulthood of Christ. She then dispenses with the name of her sex, the seductiveness of youth and the garrulousness of old age.[12]

Virginity could make a woman an honorary man but this did not mean that a virgin could share in the clerical ministry. Ambrose insisted that the virgins of his diocese should withdraw from the world into a separate sphere. They should not even visit their closest relatives but would find Christ in the seclusion of their cells.

Western theologians were confusing humanity with maleness; in Greek terms, they did not see the distinction between *aner* and *anthropos*. This bias against the female is especially clear in Ambrose's disciple Augustine, Bishop of Hippo (343–420), who can be described as the father of the Western spirit. Apart from St Paul, no other theologian would have such an influence on Western Christendom: not only did he affect the thought of formative Roman Catholic thinkers such as Thomas Aquinas, but Luther and Calvin also owed him a profound debt. It was Augustine who formulated the terrifying doctrine of Original Sin, which is unique to the West and has had a profound influence on our view of human nature. Because of the sin of Adam, all mankind was doomed to eternal damnation. Until the coming of Christ, the 'damned lump of humanity was lying prostrate, no, was wallowing in evil, it was falling headlong from one wickedness to another'.[13] Even though we had been redeemed by Jesus's death, the Original Sin of Adam is still evident in each one of us in the concupiscence which makes us take pleasure, against all reason, in a mere creature instead of in God. It forces us to sin, even when we know that what we desire is forbidden. When do we experience concupiscence more acutely than in the sexual act, when two creatures revel shamelessly in one another and forget all about God? Because it springs from concupiscence, the sexual act transmits Original Sin to the next generation like a venereal disease. Each flicker of desire for a woman, therefore, reminds a man of his chronically sinful nature. Sin, sex and woman were bound together in an unholy Trinity in the Western Christian imagination by the powerful theology of Augustine.

Because Eve had been responsible for the sin of Adam, all women were dangerous. Even though he loved his own mother Monica, this did not affect Augustine's theology: 'What is the difference,' he asked a friend, 'whether it is in a wife or a mother? It is still Eve the temptress that we must beware of in every woman.'[14] Indeed, woman was not physically created in God's image. Her sexual organs, the 'concupiscential parts', made her an imperfect copy of the man who, as St Paul had taught, was her 'head':

> The woman together with her husband is the image of God, so that her whole substance may be one image; but when she is referred to separately in her quality of help-mate, which regards the woman herself alone, then she is not the image of God; but as regards the man alone, he is the image of God as fully and completely as when the woman too is joined with him.[15]

Augustine would have fully shared the opinion of those Christians today who argue that a woman cannot re-present the male God and the male Christ at the altar. The Greek Fathers did not share this view since they had no similar theology of Original Sin. Maximus the Confessor taught that the Incarnation would still have occurred, even if Adam had not sinned. But Augustine's theology of sin and concupiscence oversexualized

women in the Western imagination, making Christians highly
conscious of their physical difference from men. In the recent
debate about women priests, some have argued that it is
impossible for a woman to be a priest because she cannot lay
aside her sexuality as a man is able to do. Since Augustine's
time, Western Christians have been made hyper-conscious of a
woman's 'concupiscential parts'.

Virginity became the prime vocation for a woman. Because
the Western doctrine of Original Sin saw motherhood as a way
of passing on the taint of Adam, Christian women would not be
honoured as wives and mothers in the way that Jewish or
Muslim women would be, until the seventeenth century. The
ordo of Virgins became a minor order in the Church, so that a
celibate woman, who had nothing whatever to do with men,
could rank among the clergy as a kind of honorary man. But
virginity was possible only for the few, élite women who could
manage to support themselves.

The other *ordo* open to women was the Order of Widows. In
the New Testament, Christians are constantly exhorted to take
care of widows whose position was vulnerable. For their part,
widows were to be shining examples of virtue to the rest of the
faithful. They were to engage in practical works, pray cease-
lessly and live entirely chaste lives. They were to busy themselves with the education of young girls. Gradually, the Church
in the West made a special *ordo* for those specially virtuous
widows who lived up to their Christian calling and were
determined never to marry again. In Carthage, they had special
seats in the church, and penitents seeking readmission into the
community had to prostrate themselves before the widows as
well as the presbyters. Widows were honoured, but had no
power and no active ministry, and theirs was a very minor
order indeed. In *The Apostolic Tradition*, Hippolytus carefully
distinguished the widows from the male clergy. They were only
'appointed' (*kathistasthai*) and not 'ordained' (*cheirotonein*).
There was no laying on of hands and the candidate was simply
'named' like a subdeacon, and declared to be among the officially designated widows. They had no liturgical role but were
simply appointed to pray, rather like nuns in the Middle Ages.

In Egypt, widows were not even an *ordo*, though they had prominent seats in the Church of Alexandria. Origen, the brilliant theologian who succeeded Clement as the head of its catechetical school, was as fiercely opposed to the idea of women exercising a teaching ministry as Tertullian. Women were to remain silent in the churches. Quoting Paul, Origen declared: 'It is improper for a woman to speak in an assembly, no matter what she says; even if she says admirable things, even saintly things, that is of little consequence, since they come from the mouth of a woman.'[16] Widows must limit their activities to the instruction of young women, training them to be good chaste wives and housekeepers.[17] Both Origen and Clement clearly found it surprising that Paul had had female disciples and Clement managed to account for this apparent eccentricity on the part of the Apostle by deciding that it had been necessary to prevent scandal: through women such as Phoebe 'the Lord's teaching penetrated also the women's quarters without any scandal being aroused'.[18]

In Syria, however, there were more varied opportunities for women. The *Didascalia Apostolorum*, an ecclesiastical constitution composed during the first half of the third century, shows that 'appointed widows' occupied an *ordo* separate from that of the laity, as in the West. To be admitted to the order, a widow must have had only one husband and be no younger than fifty. But, as in the West, widows were required to stay at home and pray: they were not to be like the merry widows in the community who bustled around gossiping and causing trouble. They were to be like 'the altar of God', fixed in one place, and must obey the bishop and his deacons, doing nothing on their own initiative. They were certainly not to teach anybody but should refer unbelievers who asked them questions to the male clergy. A widow could only answer incompetently and no pagan would take the faith seriously if expounded by a mere woman.

The author mentions another ministry, however: that of the woman deacon (*gyne diakonos*) who was to be specially 'appointed' by the bishop to minister to other women. He seems aware that this is a rather controversial notion, an idea that needs some justification: 'For our Lord and Saviour also was ministered unto by women ministers, Mary Magdalene, and Mary, the sister of James and daughter of Josepas, and the mother of the sons of Zebedee, with other women besides.'[19] He also suggests that while the bishop is in the image of God the Father, and the deacon of Christ and the college of presbyters represent the Apostles, the woman deacon should be honoured as a symbol of the Holy Spirit.[20] But her functions are far more limited than those of the male deacons. The deacon is called God's right-hand man, 'his ear and his mouth'; he assists at the Eucharist; but the ministry of the woman deacon is confined to an apostolate to other women: she is to look after the sick women, since she can enter the women's quarters without giving offence to the pagans, and, in the interests of modesty, takes care of the women catechumens when they come out of the baptismal waters. A society which secluded its women, as in the Christian East, felt the need to enhance that segregation by giving those women female ministers. In the West, where women were not secluded in quite the same way, the office of a woman deacon was never so important.

In the fourth-century *Apostolic Constitutions*, another Syrian text, the woman deacon is called a *diakonissa*, a deaconess, for the first time. Her ministry was still limited to the care of women. Her sole liturgical function was to welcome the women as they entered the church at the same time as the deacons welcomed the men. 'A deaconess does not bless, nor perform anything proper to the office of the presbyters or deacons.'[21] She certainly did not assist at the altar or distribute communion. While the diaconate was now seen as a step on the royal road to the presbyterate and a rung on the clerical ladder, the deaconess had reached the end of her clerical road. Although hers was the highest of the women's *ordines*, ranking above the orders of widows and virgins, she was definitely inferior to the male clergy. Surprisingly, the author draws on the earlier comparison of the women deacons to the Holy Spirit to make this point: in the Gospels, the Paraclete cannot do anything on its own authority but simply glorifies Christ by doing his will. In the same way, the deaconess, a type of the Holy Spirit, cannot do anything without the permission of the deacon, who is in the image of Christ. Just as nobody can have faith in Jesus without the Holy Spirit, no woman is allowed to visit the bishop or one of the deacons without taking a deaconess along as a chaperone.[22] The author's Trinitarian theology is rather shaky here. There is great irony in the Spirit of freedom, which had originally descended upon men and women together at Pentecost, being used here to marginalize and relegate women to a subordinate and separate role.

Nevertheless the deaconess had taken a significant step forward, since she had now been given a proper ordination in *The Apostolic Constitutions*. The prayer follows the pattern of ordination petitions for the male clergy, calling upon figures from the Old Testament and asking for the descent of the Holy Spirit:

> O Eternal God, the Father of our Lord Jesus Christ, the creator of man and of woman, who replenished with the Spirit Miriam and Deborah and Anna and Huldah; who didst not disdain that thy only begotten Son should be born of a woman; who also in the tabernacle of the testimony, and in the Temple, did ordain women to be keepers of thy holy gates – do thou now look down upon this thy servant who is to be ordained to the office of a deaconess, and grant her thy Spirit, that she may worthily discharge the work which is committed to her by thy glory, and the promise of thy Christ, with whom be glory and adoration to thee and the Holy Spirit for ever.[23]

The office remained somewhat vague and confused, however. In the sixth century, the legislation of Justinian included deaconesses among the clergy, assigned forty of them (some 10 per cent of the assigned clerics) to the new basilica of Hagia Sophia in Constantinople and acknowledged the validity of their ordination by a laying on of hands. But it remains rather noncommittal about their liturgical duties, apart from assisting the women catechumens, saying only that deaconesses 'attend to other sacred functions which they habitually perform in the most venerable mysteries'.

Several wealthy deaconesses were very powerful figures, however, largely because they had independent means. In

Constantinople Olympias (b. 368) and her friend Pentadia were
staunch supporters of their Bishop John Chrysostom, protesting vigorously against his banishment and supporting the
faithful during his absence. Olympias in particular was famous
for her austerity, lavish hospitality and ministry to the poor and
sick. Chrysostom himself valued her counsel. But, again, the
power exercised by an autocratic heiress is a far cry from the
diakonia of the New Testament. In the West, Christians opposed
the ordination of women to any ministry at all, although we still
hear of some deaconesses, such as Hilaria, the daughter of
Bishop Remegius of Rheims, and Radegund, the wife of King
Clothaire I, who fled from her husband, was ordained a deaconess and founded a convent in Poitiers. She ended her days as an
enclosed nun, renowned for her learning.

It is likely that such women wanted to go further up the
clerical ladder, for we find in our texts buried references to a
vigorous dispute about the ordination of women. Some of the
scriptures used by the Gnostic groups of the second and third
centuries, for example, emphasized the role of the women in
Jesus's life more strongly than the gospels that were finally
declared canonical by the Orthodox Church. Thus in the
second-century *Gospel of Mary*, the male disciples appear reluctant to preach the gospel after Jesus had ascended into Heaven
because they were afraid of suffering the same fate as he. It is
Mary Magdalene who urges them 'to be men', promising that
the grace (*charis*) of the Lord will be with them. The Gnostic
gospels often speak of a special intimacy between Mary of
Magdala and Jesus and, after he has left them, they want to hear
the private teaching he gave her. But Peter and Andrew are
openly contemptuous and jealous of these extra doctrines,
since, as Peter says, they show that 'He preferred her over
against us.' The Apostle Levi, also known as Matthew, however, comes to Mary's defence:

> Peter, thou hast ever been of a hasty temper. Now I see
> thou dost exercise thyself against the woman like the
> enemies. But if the Saviour hath made her worthy, who
> then art thou to reject her? Certainly, the Saviour knows
> her surely enough. Therefore did he love her more than

us. Let us rather be ashamed, put on the Perfect Man, as the Lord has charged us, and proclaim the gospel.[24]

Whatever the truth of the *Gospel of Mary*, this argument shows that there had been discussion in the Christian communities about the role of women in the Churches and sects.

Similarly, the *Pistis Sophia* (The Teaching of Wisdom), a third-century text, gives the Apostle John and Mary of Magdala leading roles. Jesus says that they will both 'surpass all my disciples and all who shall receive mysteries of the Ineffable. They will be on my right and on my left and I am they and they are I.'[25] Some of the Gnostic Churches used this text in their ordination of women as prophets and teachers. As Mary of Magdala is the chief teacher in this text, asking thirty-nine out of the forty-six questions, Peter resents her: 'She takes our opportunity,' he complains to Jesus, 'and has not let any of us speak but talks all the time herself.' It was the reverse of the Pauline injunction to silence, which meant that men would see only themselves as entitled to do the talking. Mary complains that Peter 'hates the female race' but is told that people who receive a revelation of the truth have a duty to speak, whatever their sex.[26] In these ancient disputes, which, it has to be said, have a strong resemblance to some recent exchanges on the topic of the ministry of women, we can hear some of the arguments that may have been employed by the Gnostics and their opponents about women's vocation. Had they received an apostolic revelation and commission like the male disciples? Could they be allowed to teach? The Gnostics seem to have taken the view that to reject the ministry of women because of contempt for 'the female race' is an attitude unworthy of the Gospels.

The Gnostics, Marcionites and Montanists were defeated by the Great Church and their doctrines were suppressed, but some of the arguments about the role of women seem to have continued. Thus in *The Apostolic Constitutions*, which we examined earlier, the author forbids widows and deaconesses to teach because Jesus had not given a teaching mandate to the women disciples when he commissioned the Twelve. He makes the Apostles argue that Jesus had a significant number of women about him and that 'if it had been necessary for women to teach, he himself would have commanded these to instruct the people with us'.[27] Some women must have been asking for the right to administer baptism, because the author also embarks on a long argument against it. For a woman to baptize, he says, citing Paul's argument of 'headship', is 'dangerous or, rather, impious and wicked'. Women priests are, moreover, a relic of paganism: 'For this is one of the ignorant practices of Gentile atheism, to ordain women to the female deities.'[28] If women had been allowed to baptize, Jesus would surely have let his mother baptize him rather than having recourse to John the Baptist. But, as the Creator of the Universe, he knew the correct and decent thing to do.

It seems likely that in Egypt some women may have been asking why they could not celebrate the Eucharist, for the *Apostolic Church Order*, a fourth-century Egyptian text, includes a debate about this question between Jesus's male and female disciples. The author makes John point out that at the last supper Jesus did not let the women stand up with the men when he blessed the bread and wine (a comment that shows that the Eucharist was beginning to acquire hieratic rituals and was no longer a simple meal). Martha, however, is made to disagree. Jesus had forbidden the women to stand simply because he had seen Mary of Magdala laughing, he said, not because he was making a point about the unsuitability of women as Eucharistic presidents. But the author comes out strongly against a Eucharistic ministry for women by making Mary herself argue against it. Had not Jesus said, 'The weak shall be served through the strong?' That is, women should be redeemed by men and not vice versa. Finally, James is made to conclude that the only valid ministry for women is to care for needy members of their own sex.

At a time when the Orthodox Churches were gradually introducing the order of the priesthood into Christianity, it seems that women were asking why they should be excluded from an active Church ministry. These disputes which are attributed to Jesus and his disciples are found in Gnostic gospels like the *Pistis Sophia* and orthodox texts like *The Apostolic*

Constitutions. The authors may have been quoting oral traditions that were still current in the Churches but which had not
been included in the canonical Gospels. Or these disputes may
be an attempt to portray what Jesus and the Apostles would
have said about this issue, if they had been alive and able to
contribute.

The arguments for and against the ministry of women in
these early writings are far from brilliant. They display no great
theological insight on either side. The evidence will seem trivial
to a modern reader, who has his or her own questions to ask
about this vexed matter. The point is that the issue was still
being debated three hundred years after the death of Christ in
both orthodox and heretical circles. The New Testament had in
the main been positive about the position of women; ordination
itself was an innovation which could be called a betrayal of the
egalitarian tradition of the primitive Church, and the introduction of a Christian priesthood could be seen as an even greater
departure from apostolic practice. During the Middle Ages, the
gap between clergy and laity, men and women, would grow
still wider.

The Middle Ages and the End of Diakonia

B Y THE EARLY medieval period, there had been a major change in the concept of Christian priesthood. The Fathers of the Church had come to take it for granted that a lay person could not officiate at the Eucharist but they had all stressed that priesthood resided with the people of God as a whole. The bishop may have been called a High Priest but he derived his powers from the *laos*, which was a royal priesthood. Augustine had disliked the clericalization of Christianity that he had discerned in some of the heretical sects, insisting that lay people were also called to God's service and that the entire body of the Church had a priestly vocation.[1] In the Eastern Church, Gregory of Nazianzus, the friend of Basil of Caesarea and Gregory of Nyssa, had emphasized not the privileges but the appalling responsibilities of the priesthood, suggesting that it was almost impossible for a bishop to serve as teacher, preacher and shepherd of his congregation unless he developed extraordinary spiritual resources.[2] John Chrysostom took the same line in his treatise *On the Priesthood*: it was a fearful prospect to be the person who gave new life to Christians at baptism and to have the responsibility of making the Lord present in the Eucharist:

When you see the Lord sacrificed and lying before you

and the high priest standing over the sacrifice and praying, and all who partake being tinctured with that pre-
cious blood, can you think that you are still standing on
earth?[3]

But by the beginning of the Middle Ages, Western Catholics
were starting to stress the powers and privileges of the priest,
who was becoming an increasingly remote figure to his
congregation.

Other monotheists had rejected the whole idea of having a
priestly caste to mediate between God and the masses. The idea
of a priest re-presenting God to his congregation would have
seemed downright pagan and blasphemous to Jews and Muslims at this period. The idea offended the egalitarianism that
characterized the religion of the One God. Christians, as we
have seen, had drawn upon the sacrificial imagery of the Jewish
scriptures and had spoken of their ministry in terms of the old
Temple priesthood, so it was rather ironic that Jews themselves
had turned away from priesthood and sacrifice at this time. We
have seen that even before their Temple had been destroyed by
the Romans in 70 CE, some Jews had already been cultivating
alternative forms of worship, almost as though they had out-
grown the need for that kind of mediatory cultic ritual. Indeed,
when the Emperor Julian (331–63), who was known as 'the
Apostate' because he had wanted to replace the new Christian
religion with the old paganism, offered to rebuild their Temple,
the rabbis refused. They spoke of the ancient priesthood with
reverence but, so to speak, kicked it upstairs by saying that it
was no longer for this world: the priesthood and Temple could
only be rebuilt by the Messiah. In Islam, the youngest of the
three monotheistic religions which had come to birth in Arabia
during the lifetime of its Prophet Muhammad (c. 570–632), the
idea of priesthood was entirely alien. Like the Jews, Muslims
insisted that each individual must approach God directly, without an intermediary. Like the rabbis, the Muslim ulema were
distinguished by their knowledge of scripture and law: their
leadership was based on learning, not on exclusive cultic
powers. The imam might lead the prayers in the mosque but

that was all he did: he did not stand alone as the people's representative or intercede with God on their behalf.

Christians, therefore, were alone in their decision to revive the priestly ministry. It was Cyprian, Bishop of Carthage, who had been the first to speak of a full-blown Christian hierarchy and who first used sacrificial language to describe the role of the bishop, the High Priest, at the Eucharist:

> Certainly that priest truly discharges the office of Christ who imitates that which Christ did; and then offers a true and full sacrifice in the Church to God the Father when he proceeds to offer it according to what he sees Christ himself to have offered.[4]

Cyprian had been trying to insist that this was really Christ's offering, not that of the bishop, in the spirit of the epistle to the Hebrews. But his High Priest was beginning to stand on his own in his imitation of Christ: he was re-presenting him rather than immersing himself in Christ's priesthood and that of the entire *laos*. By the end of the eighth century, the use of the word 'priest' was no longer controversial in the Western Church. The notion of priesthood had lost its associations with paganism and had been absorbed into the Christian world view. In much the same way, the insignia which the bishops had borrowed from the Roman-Byzantine Empire had also lost their secular connotations and had assumed an entirely religious significance. When the newly ordained bishop donned the pallium and the other special garments, this vesting had become a liturgical and sacred act which set him apart from the laity. The robes of his office marked him out as holy and separate, as had the divinely ordained vestments of Aaron.

During the eighth century the northern European countries of France, Germany and Britain were also being drawn more closely into Christendom by the Roman Church. Hitherto these countries had been distant outposts of Empire and, since the fall of Rome in the fifth century, predominantly pagan in outlook. But as the Bishop of Rome began to assume the leadership of the Western Church and became increasingly estranged from the Greek Orthodox Patriarch in the Eastern

Church, he turned to these countries north of the Alps for a support that they were eager to give. On Christmas Day 800, the Frankish Emperor Charlemagne was crowned Holy Roman Emperor of the West in Rome – an act which the Byzantines found provocative and offensive. From the eastern provinces of the Empire, where Rome had never fallen, it was horrifying to see an ignorant, illiterate barbarian assume the imperial purple. Determined to implement the Roman liturgy in his domain, Charlemagne was given a copy of the Roman Sacramentary and attempted to implement its directives in Gaul and Germany. But where the Romans had understood that 'the dew of heavenly unction' in the prayer for the ordination of a bishop was a symbol of heavenly grace, northern Christians interpreted it literally. Since Frankish kings were anointed with oil, in conscious imitation of King David, the new bishop was anointed too. He was now king and priest, assuming a prerogative which would have horrified the early Christians.

The feudal system of Western Europe was deeply hierarchical and this inevitably influenced the Church there, which, once again, had to express itself in terms of the prevailing culture. Feudalism also affected the Western view of God and Christ. Anselm, Archbishop of Canterbury (1033–1109), evolved what would become the standard view of the redemption wrought by Christ in the West, in which the notions of sacrifice and representation were crucial. He believed that the Original Sin of Adam, which had been transmitted to the whole of humanity, had been so dire that it was very difficult for a God who was wholly just as well as wholly merciful to pardon the human race, which was therefore destined for Hell. The only solution had been the Incarnation. In his treatise *Why God Became Man*, Anselm argued that the gravity of Adam's sin meant that only a divine being could atone for it, but since the offence had been committed by a man, the redeemer also had to be human. The result was the God–Man Jesus, who had died on the Cross in our stead. This unpleasant portrait of a God who demanded the human sacrifice of his only Son was highly anthropomorphic. It envisaged the deity acting and weighing things up as though he were a feudal overlord dealing with a recalcitrant vassal and deciding the type of retribution that would be appropriate. In the East, the Greek Orthodox had developed a conception of Christ's divinity closer to Buddhism: Jesus had been the first example of a new type of deified humanity. All baptized Christians could share his divinity. The Greeks did not see the redemption in such sacrificial and representational terms: Maximus the Confessor (580–662), known as the Father of Byzantine theology, had taught that the Incarnation would have occurred even if Adam had not sinned. The notion of a priestly, representative sacrifice was becoming central to Western Christianity, however, and in the Middle Ages that would inevitably have an effect on its concept of priesthood.

Thus the ordination of a bishop or a presbyter was now interpreted in the light of the feudal system. Consequently it was seen as a referral of powers, which were transmitted from above, as from an overlord to one of his representatives – not, as it were, from below, as in the early Church when ministers received their mandate from the *laos*. Indeed, ordinands did not think of themselves as humble servants of their people in quite the same way. They now tended to be men who had embarked on an ecclesiastical career and were climbing towards the episcopal ladder. They started with 'minor orders', progressed through the diaconate to the presbyterate and, if they were lucky and had powerful friends, they might even make it to the episcopate. It was an ascent that took them away from the rest of the *laos*, and the word 'laity' now referred to the *plebs* who had no *ordo* at all. This separation of the clergy from the rest of the community was symbolized by the increasing custom of the absentee priest. It was no longer necessary to work and serve the congregation which had called him to the ministry. A presbyter was chosen by his superiors, and the community to which he had a 'title' simply gave him an income; it was not necessary for him to live and minister within it.

Laity were also separated from their clergy ideologically. During the twelfth and thirteenth centuries, the theology of ordination was developed in such a way that the rite itself became a *sacramentum*, a symbolic outward sign of an inner transformation. Increasingly the ordained minister was held to have become spiritually different from other Christians.

Ordination became one of the seven sacraments listed by the theologian Peter Lombard (1100–1164), whose *Sentences* were a standard text-book right up to the Reformation. Like baptism, ordination was seen as conferring an indelible 'character', which marked the ordinand with a 'seal' that made him qualitatively different from the layman. Ordination, Lombard declared, was 'a seal of the Church by means of which spiritual power is conferred upon the person ordained'.[5] In the New Testament, the minister had thought of himself as a slave, as one without power and privilege. Now the emphasis was on power rather than on *diakonia*. The 'seal' of ordination would even separate the clergy from lay folk in the next world: Thomas Aquinas (1225–74) believed that it would still mark them after death. Thus grew the adage: 'Once a priest, always a priest'. Even if a priest fell into deadly sin, his powers never left him. He could not resign his office and there was no question of his being deposed: he retained the power to celebrate the Eucharist, baptize and confer the forgiveness of God in the sacrament of confession, whatever he did.

By this time, ministry in the West was being conceived almost exclusively in terms of priesthood: it was now assumed that bishops and presbyters shared the same order rather than two different *ordines*. Both had received what was now considered to be the highest priestly power of all, that of celebrating the Eucharist. Yet an ordinary priest could only exercise this power with the permission of his High Priest, the bishop. Despite the egalitarian teaching of the New Testament, the priesthood had become as exclusive as the Aaronic and Levitical priesthood of the Old Israel. In a society where Church membership had become compulsory, only men in orders had the benefit of the advanced education which was necessary for government. The clergy also enjoyed exemption from secular law courts and taxation. They were governed by their own canon law that was completed and in place by 1300, and the Pope, head of the rigid hierarchy, ruled Christendom in secular as well as in spiritual ways. The Church had become a clerical institution in Europe with graded privileges that the ordinary lay people could not share unless they were rich or members of the aristocracy. There were more priests in Europe than ever before. In England alone there were 40,000 secular clergy, not counting priests who were members of religious orders, out of a total population of three million.

The increase in numbers led to a liturgical practice which isolated the laity from their clergy even further. During the eighth century, when monks had begun to be ordained as priests, the practice of the private Mass had developed in the monasteries. These monk–priests naturally wanted to exercise their power to celebrate the Eucharist, so pressures of numbers meant that Masses had to be said by the monks at side-altars without a congregation. This would have been an incomprehensible practice to the early Christians, since the emphasis had then been on the priesthood of the whole community. Without a congregation, a 'communion service' made no sense. Naturally, without a congregation, there was no offertory procession for the laity to bring their gifts to the altar, thereby becoming personally involved in the rite; there was no need to read the lessons from scripture aloud and, since other priests were likely to be celebrating their own Mass nearby, the celebrant was expected to whisper the words of the liturgy inaudibly. These practices gradually spread to the High Episcopal Mass and meant that the Eucharist was perforce becoming a purely private priestly devotion. In the first Christian basilicas, it had been customary for the altar to be positioned in the centre of the room and the celebrant to stand facing the congregation behind the altar. But in the parish churches of Europe, the altar had been placed against a rear wall as early as the sixth century. This meant that the priest had been forced to say Mass with his back to the congregation. Now that the service was also conducted in a whisper, the people could not even hear the Canon, the great Eucharistic prayer. Gradually they were reduced to silent spectators gazing at the priest's back. Furthermore, as the vernacular languages gained respectability during the Middle Ages, knowledge of Latin became a purely clerical accomplishment, an exclusively priestly lingo. This meant that the few words that were audible to the congregation were often incomprehensible to a significant number of them. Distanced from their liturgy, the laity occupied themselves in private devotions, a state of affairs that persisted in the Roman Catholic Church until the long-overdue liturgical reforms of the 1950s and 1960s.

As the Mass receded, its various ceremonies acquired an allegorical significance for those lay people who valiantly tried to make sense of these increasingly obscure rites. Thus when the priest made the sign of the Cross three times at the start of the Canon, this came to stand for the three times that Jesus had endured mockery during his Passion: before the Sanhedrin, Herod and Pilate. The three great silences of the 'Secret' prayer, the Canon and the Lord's Prayer (which were mouthed inaudibly by the priest) came to represent Jesus's three days in the Tomb. When the celebrant turned five times to greet the people with the words 'Dominus vobiscum!' ('The Lord be with you!'), this symbolized the five appearances of the risen Jesus to his disciples. The priest had become the representative of Christ in an entirely new way. In the old days, he and the people together had simply participated in Christ's priesthood. Now the priest had become the sole actor in a stylized drama which reproduced Christ's Passion and Resurrection, a role which it would obviously have been much more difficult for a woman to fulfil – even if she had been allowed to do so. The faithful had come to see the elevation of the consecrated host as the high point of the Mass: a bell would be rung to call their attention from their private prayers at this point, so that they could bow together in silent worship when the priest held the bread and wine aloft. People would strain to catch a glimpse of it and venerate the elements as divine. During the Middle Ages, the feast of Corpus Christi (the Body of Christ) was instituted. The body of Christ no longer signified the Christian community as in Paul's epistles, but the presence of Christ in the Eucharist: the sacred host was now venerated outside the context of the Mass. Not surprisingly, some people would come to see this adulation of a piece of bread as rank idolatry.

Women were even more outcast than lay men. During the thirteenth century, the popes finally managed to impose celibacy on the reluctant secular clergy so that women were distanced physically and seen as entirely incompatible with the priesthood. Oversexualized as they were in the Christian imagination, they were now regarded as a tainting, polluting presence. Some of the old Jewish purity laws had been applied in such a way as to reinforce this. Couples were told not to communicate after sexual intercourse, as were women who were menstruating and men who had had a nocturnal emission. Sex and women were more incompatible with priesthood in Christendom than in ancient Israel, where priests had been expected to marry and had simply refrained from sex during their turn in the Sanctuary.

Thomas Aquinas attempted to find some more rational explanations of women's exclusion from the Orders of the Church. He followed the teaching of Aristotle, who had seen women as biologically inferior. Men possessed reason and self-sufficiency, the highest human virtues, but women were an aberration from this norm. As 'misbegotten males', embryos which had not quite made it at the moment of conception, they lacked these superior human qualities and were innately irrational. They were only capable of a nurturing role in the house, the private sphere, since social order should reproduce the hierarchy of mind over body. Perpetual minors, women must be subservient to the freeborn Greek males who represented the dominion of the rational over the material world. St Paul had attempted to replace this Greek prejudice by stating that there was neither male nor female in Christ. Aquinas, however, endorsed Aristotle. He also saw woman as *mas occasionatus*, a failed man. Generically women were human, but as individuals every woman was a botched conception:

> As regards the individual nature, woman is defective and misbegotten, for the active force in the male seed tends to the production of a perfect likeness in the masculine sex; while the production of a woman comes from a defect in the active force or from some material indisposition or even from some external influence.[6]

Hence women were by nature inferior and should be subservient to men, who were more reasoning and discerning. Since it was therefore impossible for a woman to signify eminence and superiority, she could not incarnate leadership. Because women lacked full rationality, they could not represent God's *logos*, the divine Word or Reason which, according to St John, had become incarnate in Christ.[7] For the same reason they were incapable of receiving the character or seal of ordination. It followed that women must be debarred from Holy Orders, along with murderers, slaves and bastards. This was impeccable Aristotelianism but had nothing to do with the New Testament. If such remarks were taken to their logical conclusion, women did not really qualify for human status, let alone the priesthood. Aquinas's biology may be out of date but his views about the priesthood have persisted. In Chapter 8 we shall see that theologians of both the Roman Catholic Church and the Church of England would argue that women could not re-present the divine Logos at the altar, since the divine rationality was basically a masculine principle. It is also surely significant that Aquinas saw the priesthood not so much as a *diakonia* but an 'eminence' and mastery.

Christian women were not the only ones to suffer in this way. Jewish women, as we have seen, were debarred from the rabbinate because they were not permitted to study the Talmud; cut off from learning, they were excluded from the source of leadership and power. Over the years, they had been excluded from the liturgy of the synagogue, though they had important ritual duties in the home. The practice of calling them to read the Torah during the service had been abandoned, because of the 'honour' of the community.[8] Although women were obligated to say a grace at meals, the Talmud stated that a man whose wife recited the blessings for him was 'cursed' in the eyes of the community.[9] It was said that the reason why women and men had been separated in the Temple, and, later, in the synagogue, was because women's presence led to frivolity.[10] Over the centuries, Jewish women were seen as incompatible with liturgy and were declared unfit for the liturgical responsibility incumbent upon Jewish men. The legal principle from which this exclusion derives is that women were exempt from those commandments of the Torah which had to be performed within a given time limit, such as, for example, the wearing of ritual fringes (*zizit*) which men were obliged to wear during the daytime. It was impossible to make this up by donning the *zizit* at night. Because the ritual prayers had to be recited at particular times, it followed that women did not have to say them. It is not entirely clear why the rabbis who compiled the Talmud exempted women in this way, but the ruling yielded a negative image of women, as we see in the maxim: 'Women, slaves and children are exempt.'[11] This suggested that women shared a lower status than the adult free male and that they were in fact in a worse position than slaves and children who could change or grow out of these exempt categories, while women were perpetually unaccountable and – by extension – not seen as capable of leading a full Jewish life.

Later generations interpreted this ruling according to the ethos of the time. Thus a thirteenth-century midrash explains that women, children and slaves were mentally limited. Women could only concentrate on serving their menfolk, just as 'a child has foolishness in his mind and a slave is slavishly bound up with his master'.[12] Another medieval rabbi quoted the view, still shared by many Christians, that a woman was naturally subservient and her place was in the home:

> Women were exempt from time imperatives because a woman is subservient to her husband and should be free to tend to his needs as they arise. So as to eliminate possible time conflicts between serving God and serving her husband, and in order to foster harmony in the home, God exempts women from certain of his commandments that had to be performed at a specific time.[13]

Certain prayers in the synagogue are only valid if they are performed communally – a ruling designed to enhance the sense of community, which is so crucial in all three monotheistic religions. Consequently, there has to be a quorum, a *minyan*, of ten Jews in order to recite the official prayers, but women, because of their time-exemption, do not count as members of a *minyan*. It has been suggested that the reason for this particular exclusion is that women's menstrual periods mean that they cannot be counted upon to be in a state of ritual purity. Whatever the reason, some Orthodox women today find it demeaning. If 'all Jews' are said to be obliged to wear *zizit* and 'ten Jews' are required for a *minyan*, the fact that women's presence will not do implies that they are not really Jewish at all.

Today Jewish feminists argue that these laws are outmoded and should be changed in order to preserve the Jewish commitment to justice and equality. Muslim feminists have a similar agenda. Despite the image of Islam as a fiercely misogynistic religion, which is often taken for granted in the West, it was originally very positive for women. Many of the Prophet Muhammad's first converts were women, who found in his religion a message of hope. Muhammad himself was committed to the cause of women's emancipation. It is nonsense to expect this seventh-century prophet to have been a feminist in the twentieth-century sense, but what he achieved for women was extraordinary in the context of his time. In pre-Islamic Arabia all but the most privileged women had no human rights and were treated little better than slaves or animals. Unwanted girl babies were often destroyed mercilessly at birth. The Koran, the inspired scripture that Muhammad brought to the Arabs, gave Muslim women rights of inheritance and divorce that women in Christendom would not receive until the nineteenth century. Muhammad himself loved and needed women. His very first convert and spiritual adviser was his wife Khadija and he was deeply dependent upon her in the difficult early years. He often bewildered his male companions, who had traditionally chauvinist views, by his respect for women. He regularly helped with the housework and mended his own clothes. Islam was a passionately egalitarian faith and like the New Testament the Koran has no time for hierarchy and privileged élites.

Contrary to popular Western belief, the Koran does not prescribe the veiling of all women or their seclusion in harems. This only came into Islam three or four generations after Muhammad, possibly due to the influence of Byzantium and Persia: we have seen how the veiling and seclusion of women in the Greek world affected the status of Christian women. Muhammad himself only required his wives to be veiled for reasons that are not at all clear. He was adamant that in Islam women were the equal of the men, however. On one occasion in Medina, the home of the first Muslim community, the women asked the Prophet to give them special instruction in the Koran to enable them to catch up with the men, who were gaining an unfair advantage. This Muhammad did and shortly afterwards included those verses in the Koran which insist that women and men have equal rights and responsibility in Islam: there was only one law for both sexes. We can see this as the Muslim equivalent of St Paul's maxim in Galatians 3:28:

> Verily, for all men and women who have surrendered themselves unto God, and all believing men and believing women, and all truly devout men and truly devout women, and all men and women who are true to their word, and all men and women who are patient in adversity, and all men and women who humble themselves [before God], and all men and women who give in charity, and all self-denying men and self-denying women, and all men and women who are mindful of their chastity, and all men and women who remember God unceasingly: for [all of] them God has readied forgiveness of sins and a mighty reward.[14]

The Koran thereafter frequently addressed women specifically – something that very rarely happens in the Bible.

In the early years after the Prophet's death in 632, many of the Muslim women played a vital part in the political and religious life of the community, revered as custodians of knowledge and approached for instruction by the Prophet's male companions. Some of Muhammad's wives, such as Hafsa, Umm Habibah, Maymunah, Umm Salamah and Aisha, were outstanding transmitters of *ahadith*, the oral traditions which preserved the maxims and religious practices of Muhammad and which, with the Koran, became the source of Muslim Law. Aisha was one of the most important figures in the history of *hadith* literature and was also renowned for her accurate interpretation of these traditions. Unfortunately, as in Christianity, there was a retreat from this early acceptance of women, and men hijacked the religion. But women continued to work on the *hadith* literature alongside men. During the medieval period, when both Jewish and Christian women were excluded from leadership roles, liturgy and scholarship, some Muslim women were important teachers. Thus Karima al-Marwaziyyah (d. 1070), Fatima bint Muhammad (d. 1144) and Shuldah, known as 'the Writer' (d. 1178), were revered as eminent scholars, traditionists and calligraphers. Other women, such as Sitt al-Wazam (d. 1316) and Zayneb bint Ahmad (d. 1322), delivered lectures which drew large crowds of serious students, as did Karima the Syrian (d. 1218), who was described as the leading *hadith* scholar of Syria. Ibn Hajan, one of her biographers, tells us that about 170 prominent scholars consulted her, under many of whom he had studied himself. Other male scholars speak of equally large numbers of prominent women *hadith* teachers in the fourteenth and fifteenth centuries, including, for example, Umm Hani Maryam (1376–1466) who had learned the whole of the Koran by heart as a child, studied theology, law, history and grammar, and then travelled to Cairo and Mecca to study *hadith* under the best traditionists of the day. Although it is true that many women in the Islamic world were marginalized and housebound, during the medieval period not all were doomed to silence and anonymity simply because of their sex.

The few women who were able to become serious scholars in Western Christendom were often acutely conscious of its negative image of women. Thus Heloise, the brilliant student and lover of the philosopher Peter Abelard (1079–1142), had been able to acquire an education that was normally reserved for those in orders. She was the niece of Fulbert, one of the canons of Notre-Dame Cathedral in Paris, in whose house Abelard had lodgings. When Heloise became pregnant, Abelard offered to marry her to avert a scandal, but instead of being delighted, as we might expect, Heloise was horrified. In one of her later letters to Abelard, she quotes the example of women such as Eve and Delilah, who had been responsible for the downfall of their men as she had ruined Abelard: she put the catastrophe that overtook them entirely down to the fact that they had got married. Intelligent woman though she was, Heloise had completely internalized the myth of feminine evil that had crept into Christianity in the late books of the New Testament. She saw nothing honourable in the estate of holy matrimony. Abelard tells us that she protested vigorously that she would prefer to be his concubine rather than his wife. She had listed an impressive number of authorities, including Paul, Jerome and Augustine, to prove that marriage to a woman was an unworthy state for an important man. Abelard had a sacred vocation; philosophy was a full-time pursuit, and marriage far too sordid for this lofty calling:

> What harmony can there be between pupils and nurse-maids, desks and cradles, books or tablets and distaffs, pen or stylus or spindles? Who can concentrate on thoughts of Scripture or philosophy and be able to endure babies crying, nurses soothing them with lullabies, and all the noisy coming and going of women about the house? Will he put up with the constant muddle and squalor which small children bring into the home? The wealthy can do so, you will say, for their mansions and large houses can provide privacy and, being rich, they do not have to count the cost nor be tormented by daily cares.[15]

Heloise shows that even before celibacy became obligatory for Roman Catholic clergy, marriage was seen as an ignoble calling that could only drag a man down. At this point it does not seem as though Abelard had been ordained as a priest nor even that he intended to be. But in order to become a scholar he would have had to take minor orders, since learning and teaching were the sole prerogative of the clergy. It seems unlikely that women in Western Christendom would find that the vocation of marriage brought them the respect their Jewish and Muslim sisters often enjoyed.

Heloise did not prevail. Abelard was convinced that he was in honour bound to marry her and she succumbed sadly, 'amidst deep sighs and tears, murmuring: "We shall both be destroyed. All that is left us is suffering as great as our love has been."'[16] Later, looking back on the tragedy, she explained to Abelard that the Devil knew very well that 'men are most easily brought to ruin by their wives . . . so he attacked you by means of marriage when he could not destroy you through fornication.'[17] Abelard and Heloise did get married in a hole-in-the-corner ceremony and Heloise was left in a convent with her baby. The sequel is well known. Fulbert found out, had Abelard castrated, and for the rest of his life the great philosopher was prey to paranoid delusions and depression, even though he became a successful Churchman. Heloise herself became the Abbess of the convent of La Paraclète but was perpetually torn by longing, remorse and frustration. The story shows that women saw themselves as wholly incompatible with the learning and dignity of the clerical state. They were not helpmeets but a calamitous temptation.

Not all accepted the Church's estimate of their sex, however. The fourteenth-century writer Christine of Pisan, the first Western woman to make her living by her pen, shows her painful conversion to the woman's cause in *The Book of the City of Ladies*. She was an aristocratic woman who had been unusually well educated but discovered that in all her wide reading she could not find a single male scholar who had a good word to say for the female sex. When she looked at her own life and those of her friends, she could find nothing to justify this misogyny but for a long time she could not simply shrug it off. This view of womankind as the repository of vice was so engrained in her culture that she assumed that her intellect was too unformed and she too ignorant to see the truth of the matter. Yet this brought her to the brink of a despair which made her doubt the goodness of God:

> And I wondered how such a worthy artisan could have deigned to make such abominable work, which, from what they say, is the vessel as well as the abode of every evil and vice. And as I was thinking this, a great unhappiness and sadness welled up in my heart, for I detested myself and the entire feminine sex, as though we were monstrosities of nature.[18]

In our own day, Christian women have spoken of the pain they have experienced when they have encountered the contempt and hostility towards their sex which lies behind much of the opposition to women in priesthood. A religion that alienates half the human race in this way is in trouble. The purpose of any faith is to cultivate a sense of ultimate value in the flawed and tragic conditions of mundane life, yet it is often used – in all religions – to breed a sense of superiority and exclusion. Women are not the only people who have felt the contempt of the Christian world: the Jews of Christendom were also demonized and ostracized. Such exclusion can lead people to accept the valuation of their oppressors and to regard themselves with disgust. Intelligent women like Christine clearly felt that they were being driven away from the male world into an unholy sphere of their own.

The only solution that Christine could find was retreat. She had a vision of three ladies who comforted her and told her to build a city that would be a 'refuge and defence' for women,[19] a sort of female ghetto. For too long women had been vulnerable, 'exposed like a field without a surrounding hedge'. Christine's job was to build 'a particular edifice, built like a city wall . . . where no one will reside except all ladies of fame and women worthy of praise'. This was a fantasy, but in real life some women were voluntarily withdrawing from the world of men into walled convents, where they found a new power and dignity. As we have seen, virgins had constituted an *ordo* in the Church since the third century. It was a minor order and the virgin was only consecrated not 'ordained'. Nevertheless the Order of Virgins was a sign that was revolutionary at a time when it was obligatory for all women to marry. We have seen, too, that a virgin reflected the image of God for such spiritual men as Gregory of Nyssa. The virginal *ordo* showed that an unmarried woman was not a misfit but that, even though she was not attached to a man, God could touch her soul intimately. Originally virgins had lived in their own homes or, like Macrina, with their like-minded friends. But gradually the male hierarchy looked askance at this female autonomy and fenced in their virgins with rules and obligatory enclosures to 'protect' them. By the twelfth century, a measure that gave women space to be themselves and a certain independence was seen in canon law as a sign of their essential inferiority. As the twelfth-century canonist Gratian explained, the religious life of women must be controlled by men, since

> It is natural order among humans that women be subject to their husbands and children to their parents, because it

is only right in such matters that the greater serve the
lesser . . . woman was not made in God's image . . .

Therefore it seems most evident that man is the head of
woman. On that account without his permission she is not
allowed to make any vows to God of abstinence or of a
religious nature.[20]

Paul's 'headship' doctrine had been transposed, in the light of
Christian medieval misogyny, into an outright assertion that
women had not been created in the image of God.

Nevertheless some nuns were able to acquire a status and
power that many men would envy. One of the most extraordinary of these virginal women was Gratian's contemporary
Hildegard, Abbess of Bingen (1098–1179). As a small child,
Hildegard had had visions which terrified her, since they bore
no relation to any other experiences she knew. She kept quiet
about them until she was forty years old, fearfully hiding her
secret from the world. These 'visions' were not apparitions of
Jesus or the Virgin Mary but startling intuitions accompanied by
flashing lights. When Hildegard finally did tell people about
these ideas that broke upon her as if from another world, they
seemed so original and intelligent that it was assumed that they
must have been divinely inspired. How else could an unedu-
cated, sickly woman have conceived such extraordinarily brilliant notions? Pope Eugene II himself could only conclude that
God had revealed his secrets to Hildegard as to his prophets of
old. In secular terms, we can say that Hildegard was a natural
genius or prodigy who had the advantage of not being stifled by
a cumbrous scholastic education. As she explained in her
autobiography:

In that same [experience of] vision I understood the writings of the prophets, the Gospels, the works of other holy
men and those of certain philosophers, without any
human instruction and I expounded certain things based
on these, though I scarcely had any literary understanding, inasmuch as a woman who was not learned had been
my teacher. But I also brought forth songs with their
melody, in praise of God and the saints, without being

taught by anyone, and I sang them too, even though I had never learned either musical notation nor any kind of singing.[21]

Hildegard's music, some of which is still performed, is of considerable beauty. Her talents were outstanding. It has been said that in the Middle Ages her range was equalled only by the Muslim philosopher Avicenna. Her writings cover cosmography, medicine, ethics, poetry and aesthetics. Yet Hildegard constantly referred to herself as 'a poor little woman'. Her attainments, she always insisted, were not her own: only God could have raised her above the limitations of her sex in this way.

Women were scorned and pushed into a marginal position by the institutional Church but, as in primitive Christianity, personal charisma could liberate them despite their ecclesiastical superiors. Hildegard was almost certainly the most powerful woman of her day. She corresponded with three popes as well as with Conrad III of Germany, Henry II of England, his wife Eleanor of Aquitaine and the Holy Roman Emperor Frederick Barbarossa, feeling quite confident enough to rebuke them sharply if necessary. Women were usually forbidden to reverse the order of nature by teaching men but a papal chapter confirmed that Hildegard's 'visions' were authentic, and leading clerics, such as Odo of Cluny, wrote to ask her advice about thorny theological problems. Hildegard's status as inspired prophetess enabled her to exercise powers that were normally conferred only on priests at their ordination. Instead of keeping a submissive silence, she went on three preaching tours and exorcized demons, two functions that were now inseparable from a priestly ministry.

Hildegard's visions also enabled her to take pride in her sex. She taught her nuns to glory in their womanhood and even to flaunt it – an astonishing attitude at that time. They used to wear elaborate tiaras, as a symbol of their royal dignity as virgins. They did not wear the black veil of an *ancilla*, or servant girl, but white veils in token of their purity. Hildegard was trying to emulate the radiant, celestial beings she somehow sensed in her visions, which symbolized the divine Wisdom or

Holy Church. Femaleness was not a mark of shame but a badge to be worn with pride, though it is noteworthy that powerful women were also neglecting the old virtues of the *diakonia*.

Others evaded ecclesiastical control by becoming members of the so-called Third Orders instead of joining regular convents. This enabled them to live at home as freelance contemplatives. One of the most famous of these Tertiaries was Catherine of Siena (1347–80) who defied her family's marital ambitions for her and became a member of the Third Order of St Dominic. She became famous for her visions and austerities and this charisma for solitude and contemplation actually enabled her to enter the world of men. Again, like Hildegard, she became an irresistible force. In the 1370s she embarked on a campaign to prevail upon Pope Gregory XI to return to Rome from his 'captivity' in Avignon as a prelude to the reform of the Church. She came to dominate him to such an extent that at her behest he walked to the Vatican barefoot, as a sign of penitence. Holiness, which had always involved a radical separation from the profane, seemed to put Catherine into a sphere of her own, enabling her to transcend the constraints of gender. As Christ said to her in some of her visions: 'Resist no longer the Holy Spirit that is calling thee – for it will be hard for thee to kick against him. Do not let thyself be withheld by thine own lukewarm heart, or by a womanish tenderness for thyself, but be a man, and enter the battlefield manfully.'[22] The vivid religious experiences of saints like Catherine resulted in what has been called a 'radical obedience'. This did not consist of a submission to male, human authority but to what they perceived as a divine imperative, even if this meant that they had to defy such institutions as the family, the State or the Church. The most famous of these virginal saints was perhaps Joan of Arc, who was revered as the saviour of France. She heard 'voices' which enabled her to overcome extraordinary obstacles, breaking powerful taboos, in order to wear men's clothes and lead an army into battle. Saints like Catherine or Joan did not glory in their femaleness as Hildegard had done: they saw their emancipation in becoming honorary men.

During the Middle Ages there had been a quiet revolt against the masculine tenor of much Western Christianity. People seemed to want a less aggressive, androcentric spirituality that saw the divine from what we might call a female angle. This spiritual rebellion centred on the figure of the Blessed Virgin Mary, who had not figured much in Christian piety until the medieval period. During the twelfth century, however, her cult blossomed in Europe: cathedrals were built throughout Christendom in her honour and she quickly replaced soldier saints, such as St Michael the martial Archangel, in popular piety. In some of these popular legends, which were not endorsed by the Church, Mary was made to voice an unspoken dissatisfaction with a harsh, demanding spirituality that found its major outlet in the holy wars of the Crusades. In popular ditties and songs, Mary becomes a rebel against the masculine demands of Jesus and God the Father; she becomes the champion of the poor and dispossessed, able to rescue people who had been condemned to Hell by an intransigent Father God. But even powerful members of the establishment helped to build the cult of the Virgin Mary. Thus two Churchmen who were deeply embroiled in the savage crusading project – Adhemar, Bishop of Le Puy, who died on the First Crusade, and Bernard, Abbot of Clairvaux, who masterminded the disastrous Second Crusade – are believed to have composed the 'Salve Regina', the hymn that expressed this yearning for a more balanced spirituality:

Hail Queen, Mother of mercy; hail our life, our sweetness and our hope. It is to you that we cry, exiled children of Eve; it is to you that we sigh, groaning and weeping in this vale of tears. Therefore do you, our advocate, turn your merciful eyes toward us and after our exile show us your son Jesus. O clement, O loving, O sweet Virgin Mary.

The cult of Mary gave an outlet to those nurturing, softer virtues that are usually associated with femininity but were being pushed out of the Church with the women who were being banished to the sidelines. The huge popularity of this Marian devotion can be seen as an unconscious revolt of the psyche, an attempt to summon up an image of sweetness, compassion and kindness which people seemed to find not in Christ but in Mary: in the 'Salve Regina' the repeated and emphatic *'ad te'* (to you) makes this clear. In our own day, some have seen the importunate appeal for a female clergy fulfilling the same demand and bringing some of these gentler virtues into a religion that has become too narrowly patriarchal.

In the Middle Ages, some attempted to find a female aspect of God, impelled by the same desire to bring a better sexual balance to Western Christianity and make it represent humanity in a fuller, richer way. The fourteenth-century mystic Julian of Norwich (1342–after 1416) did not exercise such dramatic power as Hildegard, Catherine or Joan but she did inhabit a space that was uniquely her own – even physically. Instead of joining an enclosed religious order, Julian became an anchoress, one of the many recluses who shut themselves away at this time to pray in solitude. We can still see the foundations of her anchorage in Norwich next to the church which is now called St Julian's. An anchoress was interred in her room in an impressive, if disturbing, ceremony during the Mass for the Dead. She would publicly don her religious habit and walk into the cell as into her grave, while the bishop sprinkled ashes in her wake. Thenceforth she would live alone, dead to the world, receiving the Sacraments through a window in her wall. She had become a new creature, had acquired a mental freedom in her confined space. She had made a virtue out of her exclusion from male affairs. An anchoress was believed to bestow great benefits on a town; every district liked to have one; she was a focus of holiness and people would go to her for counsel and advice, as to a priest.

Even though God was above gender, he was usually described in male imagery. In her *Revelations of Divine Love*, Julian wrote of God the Mother: 'In our creation, almighty God is the Father of our nature, and God, who is all-Wisdom, is the Mother of our nature together with the Love and Goodness of the Holy Ghost.'[23] In the mystery of the Trinity, Julian saw three divine attributes: Fatherhood, Motherhood and Leadership. Jesus may have been a man while he was on earth but we Christians can experience him as a mother:

> We all know that our mothers bore us painfully, sometimes even dying in their labour, and look at what our true

Mother Jesus, the all-love, has done! He has borne us to joy and to eternal life, blessed be he! He has carried us within himself lovingly; he has laboured until the time came for him to suffer the sharpest pains and the most grievous agony that has ever been endured and, finally, he died.[24]

Like a mother, Jesus feeds us with the Eucharist and sustains us with all the Sacraments. He educates us like a mother, helping us to become familiar with our failings and working through grace with the baser parts of ourselves. He hastens to pick us up when we fall and comforts us with the tenderness of a mother. Sometimes, like a mother again, he allows us to get hurt to teach us a lesson, but as an earthly mother will never allow her child to die, so Jesus will permit none of his children to perish. Julian reminds us still that to describe God solely in terms of power and masculine strength is limiting. This representation of the divine needs to be qualified by other imagery which stresses the tenderness of the beneficence that we feel around us when we experience what we call God. People who have campaigned for the ordination of women in our own day have often pointed to Julian to prove that the transcendent and ineffable reality of the divine can be just as easily re-presented by feminine as well as masculine imagery and that women priests could remind Christians of that important fact.

In the early Church, the heretical sects seem to have given women more power than the orthodox. Similarly, some of the medieval heresies were often distinguished by the active ministry of women. Thus the Cathars, who preached a form of Gnosticism, and the Waldenses, who practised a radical poverty in imitation of the early Church, originally allowed women to preach. In the thirteenth century, the little sect of the Guglielmites was particularly interesting for our purposes, since it believed that the Holy Spirit had been incarnated in a woman. Guglielma had been a novice in the convent of Chiaravalle near Milan and had died in 1279. After her death, like Jesus, she was said to have appeared to her disciples. Shortly she would cause a new and more spiritual Church to rise out of the ashes of the old. When the papacy had been abolished, her followers maintained, the Vicar of Christ and the cardinals would all be

women. Since salvation had come into the world by means of a
woman, this time around, the priests of the new Church would
all be women. The Gospels would be superseded and four new
scriptures would take their place. This Church would be far
more successful than the Roman Catholic Church: Guglielma's
disciples would baptize the Jews, the Saracens and all the other
enemies of Christendom. Already the leader of the sect, May-
freda of Piravano, who was the future pope, used to say Mass
on Guglielma's grave in preparation for her glorious return as
the Paraclete Incarnate. All the heresies of the Middle Ages can
be seen as a rejection of the worldliness, wealth and cruelty of
the papal Church. But no sect expressed its dissatisfaction with
an exclusively male priesthood on such a grand scale as the
Guglielmites. It was a revolt, similar to the rise of the feminine
ideal in the cult of the Virgin Mary and the Mother God of Julian
of Norwich, against the expression of the divine in narrowly
male terms. But their protest was small and easily contained.
Only forty-six Guglielmites were discovered by the Inquisition;
three of these were put to death in 1300 and Guglielma's
remains were exhumed and burned.

At about this time, however, some orthodox historians
claimed that in the ninth century there had actually been a
female pope. The story of Pope Joan has never ceased to ·
fascinate. The first account of her life was written by the
Dominican historian and Vatican official Martin Polonus,
whose *Chronicum Pontificum et Imperatum* became a medieval
best-seller in about 1265. In it he gives a brief account of the
scandalous episode of John Anglicus, a woman who posed as a
man and managed to get herself elected to the papacy. The tale
caught on and was repeated, with various embellishments, by
many other historians until it became accepted as fact. She was
later known as 'Pope Joan' but none of the medieval chroniclers
gives her female name. All agree, however, that she was pope
after Leo IV, who reigned from 847 to 855 and before Benedict
III, who is normally said to have reigned from 855 to 858. She
was said to have been of German origin and to have studied in
Athens before coming to Rome disguised as a man and winning
a great reputation for scholarship. After she had been elevated
to the papacy, she reigned for two or three years (accounts

vary) but then became pregnant by the companion with whom she had travelled from Germany. Her reign ended when she scandalously gave birth to her child in the public street during a splendid pontifical procession. The chroniclers conclude that because of this episode, the popes have since avoided the street where the female pope gave birth when processing between the Lateran Palace and St Peter's basilica. Some say that a plaque marked the infamous spot, which read: 'Petre, Pater Patrum, Papisse Prodito Partum' ('O Peter, Father of Fathers, betray the childbearing of the woman pope').

The story of Pope Joan has been proved by modern scholarship to be a fabrication. There is no time in which she could have reigned and the brief accounts of her pontificate in the earliest chronicles have been shown to be later additions. But the myth gained wide credence because it appealed to the medieval imagination. The fifteenth- and sixteenth-century depictions of Pope Joan, wearing her papal crown and embracing her baby, are clearly meant as blasphemous inversions of the image of Madonna and child. The story was particularly popular among the enemies of the papacy and was repeated enthusiastically by Protestant Reformers in the sixteenth and seventeenth centuries. Joan had broken a taboo. She was a parody of the powerful virgins of the medieval period, who must have inspired such mixed feelings in the male breast. Like Joan of Arc she dressed in male clothes, a crime which had filled the saint's enemies with special horror. But unlike Joan of Arc, the female pope had masqueraded as a priest; she had held the holiest office in Christendom and, in the eyes of some, had tainted it beyond repair. Pope Joan had been no virgin but a strumpet, who had soiled the papal throne with the impure blood of childbirth. It was said that to prevent this catastrophe from occurring again, a newly elected pope had to sit on a special chair in St Peter's so that his masculinity could be verified. Thus in his Lives of the Popes (1479), Bartolomeo Platina, the prefect of the Vatican library under Pope Sixtus IV (1471–84), tells the story of Pope Joan and concludes: 'Some have written that because of this . . . when the popes are first enthroned on the seat of Peter, which to this end is pierced, their genitals are felt by the most junior deacon present.'[25] Platina argues that this interpretation is the result of a misunderstanding, but later authors had no such reservations and gleefully repeated the scurrilous details.

The fact that the papacy could be impugned because a woman had once assumed this office shows the profound aversion and distaste for the feminine that was by this time current in Europe. The idea of the High Priest of Christendom giving birth publicly to a child filled the enemies of the popes with a gloating horror. The priesthood and the female were so incompatible that the Pope Joan story was felt to have a kind of truth, despite its huge improbabilities, precisely because it violated a sacred taboo and spoke the unspeakable. It also expressed the widespread dissatisfaction with the established Roman Church. During the sixteenth century, this discontent erupted in the massive series of religious changes that we usually call the Reformation, which addressed many important complaints but also made Christianity a more aggressively masculine religion than ever.

The Reformation and the
Triumph of Patriarchy

ALL THE Reformers of the sixteenth century wanted to
return to the piety, practice and doctrines of the primitive Church. Nowhere was this more evident than in
their various attempts to reform the ministry. Those Reformed
Churches which would later be called 'Protestant' abolished the
institution of a sacrificial priesthood, pointing out quite correctly that the only person given the title of 'priest' in the New
Testament was Christ himself. Bishops should simply be called
'supervisors', like the *episkopoi* of the early Churches, 'priests'
should be called pastors or presbyters as of old, and the liturgy
should reflect the priesthood of all the faithful. Caught on the
defensive, the bishops of the Roman Catholic Church met at the
Council of Trent, which began its deliberations in 1545, to
define their own position. To counter the Protestant critique
they reaffirmed the sacrificial role of their ordained priests. Yet
Roman Catholics had begun to reform their clergy long before
Luther nailed his declaration to the church door in Wittenburg.
Zeal for Reformation was in the air. Catholic Reformers, such as
the High Chancellor of Castille, Cardinal Ximenes, founded the
University of Alcala to improve the education of priests; Jean
Standonck reorganized the College of Montaigu (*alma mater* of
both John Calvin and Ignatius of Loyola) to provide clerics with
an education in the classics and the humanities; Gian Matteo

Giberti, Bishop of Verona from 1524 to 1543, fought consistently and effectively against clerical corruption and ignorance in his diocese.

There was certainly a great deal of corruption to correct among the clergy of Europe, but today scholars warn us against seeing this in a simplistic way as one of the chief 'causes' of the Reformation. Western Christendom had become more sophisticated. Even the laity were now beginning to be educated to a high standard and had become more concerned about religion than ever before. Consequently, they needed to rethink their faith to enable it to meet their changed circumstances. Some of their ideas about religion and salvation as well as the whole issue of Church government entailed major change in the practice of the Church because it no longer worked. Precisely because of the new interest in religion, people were no longer willing to accept immorality and ignorance in their clergy, nor, if they were laymen, were they willing to continue in such a marginal role. Unfortunately, however, this reshaping of the religious experience of Europe, which marked a major change in Western consciousness, did not extend to women. Indeed, there is a case for saying that during the sixteenth and seventeenth centuries, Christianity in both the Protestant and Catholic denominations became even more masculine in tone.

For Protestant Reformers such as Martin Luther (1483–1546) and John Calvin (1509–64), problems of liturgy and ministry were high on the agenda. Indeed, for Calvin they were a priority since he was never particularly interested in theology. Luther is often credited with the formulation of reformed doctrine but in fact he was only giving voice to religious opinions that had been well aired by Roman Catholic theologians during the fifteenth century. When he left his religious order in 1524, however, and married Catherine von Bora, a Cistercian nun, Luther had taken a step that had symbolic import. He was convinced that there should not be two kinds of Christian. The laity should not feel separate and inferior to a celibate, priestly caste, since the gospel summons applied to everybody. He pointed out that in this sense there were no priests in the New Testament, because every single Christian had a priestly vocation. The practice of ordaining priests to a separate and superior rank was a distortion of the gospel. It was, he wrote, an 'invention' to maintain that bishops, priests and monks formed a spiritual estate (*standes*), while farmers, artisans and aristocrats were regarded as seculars. Because we are all priests of equal standing, he wrote in a statement to the German nobility, a 'priest' was only an office holder, and if he ceased to hold office he should go back to being a peasant or a townsman like anybody else. There was no special priestly character; there was nothing in the Bible to suggest that ordination was a sacrament. The whole idea of a sacrificial priesthood should be abandoned, since it had resulted in a most unChristian tyranny.

This was indeed a return to the spirit of the New Testament, though in other respects Luther, an irascible man and a dedicated anti-Semite, seemed far from its message of loving kindness. He was careful to stress the importance of community, however. A minister received his call from the community; any office he might hold belonged to and existed for the sake of the community. It was the community which received the priestly call, as the New Testament made clear. Nobody, Luther wrote in the same declaration to the German nobility, should push himself forward and take the ministry upon himself, without the consent and election of the people. No one could dare to take upon himself something that was common to all unless he had the consent of the Christian congregation. Luther was no populist, however. True, all Christians were priests, but that did not mean that everybody was free to preach or to administer the Sacraments. That was the prerogative of the ministers who were duly appointed by and for the community. When the peasants of Germany declared war on the nobility in 1524 Luther became terrified of the power of the mob. He looked to a virtuous prince, the secular ruler, to preserve law and order together with the officials he himself had appointed to oversee the Reformed Churches. In effect, he found that he had re-created the episcopate all over again. The difference was that the office lost the sacred aura it had acquired over the centuries; these new Lutheran 'bishops' were simply 'superintendents', like the *episkopoi* in the early Church.

In 1535 Luther even went so far as to create his own rite of ordination. Having got rid of the papacy in his Reformed Christianity, he had found that he needed to establish some kind of mundane authority. All power on earth derived from God, but Luther saw Church and State working harmoniously with one another: the Reformed Churches would ally themselves with the autocratic monarchies that were beginning to assert themselves all over Europe. But Luther's superintendents were simply administrative officials. They did not form a separate *ordo* from the other ordained ministers. When a Lutheran pastor was ordained by the laying on of hands, he did not receive powers to enable him to offer sacrifice and consecrate bread and wine. The pastor was primarily a teacher. He did not wear priestly vestments but the black gown of the academic. His chief task was to make the Word of God present in his own preaching. In Luther's reformed Eucharist, Christ the Word Incarnate was made present through the inspired words of scripture, and it was the task of the pastor to utter that Word and make it clear and luminous. The centre of the service was the gospel account of the institution of the Eucharist, which was read not as a purely historical narrative but as the manifestation of Christ 'in his own words', communing with his people. There was nothing that indicated a human offering to God; there were no offertory prayers and the Catholic Canon had been abandoned. All that remained was the elevation of the bread and wine by the minister as a symbol of Christ's endless offering of himself. As the New Testament had made clear, Christ was the only true priest. All that his people could do – minister and congregation alike – was to respond to his Word in a faith evoked by the scriptural readings and expressed in such prayers as the Creed, the Sanctus and the Lord's Prayer.

Calvin was equally determined to return to the simpler ministry of the early Church but found that the New Testament was neither clear nor consistent about the various offices. Jesus had issued no definitive directives and even St Paul was little help to somebody setting up a new kind of Church in the sixteenth century. Paul mentioned apostles, prophets and evangelists who had been necessary in the early stages of Christianity but were neither needed nor possible so long after the death of Christ. The offices of apostle and evangelist had been temporary and provisional. The only ministries of the primitive Church that still had relevance in Calvin's view were the offices of pastor and teacher (Calvin tended to combine the two), elder and deacon. Yet Calvin never quite made up his mind even about these offices and proposed a variety of formulae in his writings. His hesitations and changes of heart show that it may not be as easy as people sometimes imagine to reproduce traditional Christian ministry in a later period. Nor is it as easy as one might think to discover what the early Church actually thought about such issues.

Like Luther, Calvin relied on a partnership with the 'godly prince', who was, it must be remembered, the coming man in Europe, promising independence of the papacy. There was to be no absolute divide between clergy and laity but a working partnership in Calvin's churches. As in the Lutheran Church, his pastors wore no special vestments and offered no sacrifices; their chief job was preaching. The pulpit, not the altar, was the centre of a Calvinist church. The faithful were nourished by the Word of God, communicated in scripture and sermon. The Eucharist was simply a symbol of this verbal communion with God. The act of receiving bread and wine was a symbol of the mutual indwelling of Christ and the believer.

The Protestant Reformers had not been able to come up with a perfect Christian solution, however. Luther claimed that he had been born again in a transfiguring conversion, which had revealed to him his theology of justification by faith, yet he remained in many ways a bitter, angry man who believed, for example, that all rebellious peasants should be killed. Calvinism tended to put too much emphasis on guilt and sin. The proliferation of Reformed sects, all preaching complex doctrines that were all deemed essential for salvation, produced widespread anxiety among the people of Europe. There was now too much doctrinal choice. The bloodbath in which Catholic persecuted Protestant and vice versa ultimately discredited religion in the eyes of many. Yet in seeking to close the gap between clergy and laity and in attempting to bring the liturgy back to the people, the Reformers performed a great service which the Roman Catholic Church was unable to perceive.

When the bishops were summoned to the Council of Trent in the Tyrol in 1545, they were defensive and determined to fight Protestantism tooth and nail. When they came to discuss the Eucharist in the second session of the Council (1551–2), they would make no concessions. To allow the Mass to be said in the vernacular, as the Reformers desired, or to assert the priesthood of all the faithful, would have seemed like selling out. Consequently the bishops reaffirmed the old doctrines: the priestly 'character', the Mass as sacrifice, the validity of the private Mass. The Roman Catholic priesthood had become almost entirely cultic: an ordained minister's chief function was to offer sacrifice, like the Jewish priests of old, in order to appease God and atone for sin. The priest stood between God and the laity: it was only through confession of sins to a priest in the sacrament of penance that forgiveness of grave sin was possible. The priest was set apart from the people in general and from women in particular by his vow of celibacy. The Council attempted to peel away the accretions of centuries and to reform the liturgy but, sadly, by this time the Eucharist was regarded in practical terms as an exclusively clerical activity. Nobody thought of encouraging the laity to participate, and the Mass remained a one-man job. Gazing at the priest's back as he went through an incomprehensible and largely silent ritual, the faithful continued with their private devotions, marginalized and distanced from the heart of their faith.

The English Reformation is usually dated from King Henry VIII's rupture with the papacy in 1531 yet Henry always regarded himself as a Catholic and had no sympathy with Luther's ideas. His quarrel with Pope Clement VII, who had refused to nullify his marriage to Catherine of Aragon, was purely political. Although he declared himself to be 'protector and supreme head of the church and clergy of England' he dissociated himself from the Reformation when he ordered the publication of the *Institution of a Christian Man*, which adhered scrupulously to all tenets of the Roman Catholic faith except the supremacy of the Pope. Reformation doctrine was fostered in England during the reign of his son Edward VI (1547–53). In 1551 Thomas Cranmer, Archbishop of Canterbury, had published the final version of his *Book of Common Prayer*, which presented Calvinist doctrines on such matters as the Eucharist in a largely Catholic liturgical form. This type of compromise between Protestant and Roman Catholic ideals would characterize the new Church of England which finally emerged under Queen Elizabeth I, who reigned from 1558 to 1603. It represented a *via media* between the two positions.

In 1571 the Thirty-nine Articles defined the faith of the Anglican Communion in terms that can fairly be described as Calvinist. The Articles, for example, formally condemned the Roman Catholic doctrine of transubstantiation and some of the Lutheran interpretations of the Eucharist. The writings of Calvin and his leading disciples were reprinted in London and Elizabeth's bishops frequently cited Calvin as a leading theological authority, even going so far as to accept the highly controversial Calvinist doctrine of predestination in 1595. Yet despite their theological loyalty to Calvin, the Anglican bishops refused to follow him in matters of liturgy and ecclesiology, preferring a Church that remained more Catholic in its style of worship and organization. Thus they encouraged their parish priests to wear traditional vestments rather than the simple academic robes preferred by the Calvinists. They also preferred to keep the government of the Church in the hands of bishops appointed by the Crown. Elizabeth's own religious preferences are not clear: she kept her opinions to herself. This compromise may have been necessary because of the religious conservatism of most of the lay people of England, who could not understand the doctrinal changes and preferred the familiar ways of worship.

Like the Reformed Churches, however, the new Church of England was happy to submit to the rule of a 'godly prince'. As John Whitgift, Archbishop of Canterbury from 1583 to 1604, explained, the monarch had supreme authority in the realm. She administered civil power through her Chancellor and religious power through the Archbishop of Canterbury. The Thirty-nine Articles had reaffirmed the old Catholic orders of bishop, priest and deacon, although there was some difference of opinion on this matter. Such leading Anglican divines as Whitgift himself and John Jewel did not believe that any one ministry was essential to a true Church. Even Richard Hooker,

author of the magisterial *Laws of Ecclesiastical Polity*, who
eventually had a lofty conception of the role of the bishop,
admitted that the office had not been prescribed by Christ
himself but had been an invention of the Apostles. It is possible
therefore that the Anglican Church could have moved towards
a more fully Protestant and less 'priestly' conception of
ministry. Hooker, for example, thought that the original title
of 'presbyter' or 'elder' was more in accordance with the spirit
of the Gospels than 'priest'. But in 1572 some radical Calvinists,
who were known as 'Puritans' because of the righteous purity
of their views, demanded of Parliament a more thorough
Reformation and a greater equality among the ministers of the
Church of England. This incipient revolt caused the moderates
to retreat to a more conservative position, to uphold the order of ·
episcopacy and to retain a Catholic conception of priesthood.

This did not mean that the Church of England severed
relations with the Reformed Churches, however. During the
sixteenth and seventeenth centuries, the Anglican divines came
to see their peculiar compromise as an historical necessity. The
abuses of the medieval Church had brought the office of bishop
into such disrepute, they argued, that the early Reformers had
been obliged to abolish it and had depended instead upon the
'godly prince'. But in England and Sweden, circumstances had
made it possible to retain the old episcopal method of Church
government and yet to instigate a thorough liturgical reform. If
the Roman Catholic Queen Mary – and, later, the Puritan ruler
Oliver Cromwell – had lived longer, this would have been
impossible, because the line of succession would have come to
an end. As it was, the Church of England could claim that its
bishops had received their orders from the successors of the
Apostles. Even though the Roman Church absolutely refused to
accept Anglican orders as valid, the Church of England would
continue to see itself as Catholic, which would be of major
importance in the debate in our own day about the ordination
of women. The Church of England would develop its own
distinctive character, however, as well as its own liturgy.
Thomas Cranmer's Order of Communion (1552) had created a
Reformed service based on the spoken Word rather than on a
propitiatory sacrifice.

The Catholic and Protestant Reformers addressed many important questions, but they did not make the Christian experience happier for many of the people of Europe. During the sixteenth and seventeenth centuries, a heightened sense of sin and guilt manifested itself not only in Catholic sectarians such as the Jansenists, who developed their own dark theology of predestination, but in many of the emphases of Luther and Calvin as well. There was a growing conception of the world as a place that was incompatible with a truly religious life. The great Carmelite Reformer Teresa of Avila had a terrifying vision of the place especially reserved for her in Hell. For about twenty years she suffered acute distress about her religious inadequacy and inflicted severe penance upon herself, on one occasion crawling into the convent refectory with a basket full of boulders strapped to her back. Like Julian of Norwich before her, she lay for days in a kind of cataleptic swoon and was thought to have died before she was finally converted to Christ. Women were not alone in feeling this type of extremity and remorse. Ignatius of Loyola, founder of the Society of Jesus, used to weep so copiously during Mass that his doctors warned him that he might lose his sight. The great Catholic scientist and philosopher Blaise Pascal experienced a terrifying desolation when he contemplated the vast expanse of the universe.

This strain and imbalance were accompanied by a further deterioration in the position of women in Europe. Like other major religions, Christianity had become an aggressively patriarchal institution over the centuries. The Reformed Churches had made it more masculine than ever, now that the cults of the Virgin Mary and of the women saints had been suppressed. Luther may have left the male world of the cloister to get married but he was no lover of the female sex. Thoroughly Augustinian in his theology, he also saw sexuality as inherently sinful though inescapable. Nothing could have convinced him that the sexual act was sinless and though marriage was the only realistic option, it was simply a hospital for sick people, he said: it covered the base act with a veneer of respectability so that 'God winks at it'.[1] Not surprisingly, Luther seems to have projected a great deal of this sexual disgust on to women.

A woman's function was to have as many children as possible to bring Christians into the world, but that was all she was good for. Her punishment for the sin of Eve was to stay in seclusion from the world of men and public affairs:

> The rule remains with her husband and the wife is com-
> pelled to obey him by God's command. He rules the home
> and the state, wages war, defends his possessions, tills the
> soil, builds, plants, etc. The woman, on the other hand, is
> like a nail driven into the wall. She sits at home . . . the
> wife should stay at home and look after the affairs of the
> household as one who has been deprived of the ability of
> administering those affairs that are outside and concern
> the state.[2]

Women could expect little reformation of their lot. It was Luther who coined the famous phrase 'A woman's place is in the home.'

Calvin had a more positive view of women. In his theology, God had not created the institution of marriage for the sole purpose of procreation but to provide companionship: without women, men were incomplete. But Calvin's Geneva was a man's world and gave a very subordinate role to women. Gradually, however, the Reformed Churches would build a new Christian ideal: that of holy matrimony. Celibacy was no longer the primary Christian vocation. To sacralize the state of the vast majority of women in this way was a healthy develop-ment. Only an élite had been able to afford the dowry to win them entry to a convent. Yet it did mean that Protestant women no longer had an outside chance of the autonomy that the virginal life at its best had offered. Henceforth they would be more dependent than ever upon their men. With its feasts and festivals, processions and liturgies, Catholicism had been a sociable religion. In the more extreme Protestant Churches, this public ceremonial was abolished. Christianity became a religion of the heart and women lost that public dimension as well as the confessor whom they could consult privately. This was particu-larly apparent in that Calvinist form of Christianity known as

Puritanism, which had a crucial influence in both England and the United States.

The Puritans developed a highly patriarchal view of the family, basing it on the model they perceived in the Jewish scriptures. The Protestant belief in the priesthood of all believers did not extend to women. In practice, the husband and father ruled the religious life of the family and became a priest in his own home. It was he who led the family prayers, a rite that had a major impact on his dependants. It was now he who interceded with God on their behalf, he alone who addressed the Almighty. Husband and wife no longer knelt side by side while a priest, who was independent of the family, prayed for them. The husband and father was both priest and bishop. His word was law; he could punish his family in God's name and exact total obedience as God's representative. The family was now the only world to which a woman belonged. During the seventeenth and eighteenth centuries, her isolation was increased by the rise of capitalism, which deprived women of many of their traditionally productive activities, made estate management an exclusively male concern and turned women into mere consumers.

Anglicans also relegated their women to a subordinate role as they developed the new cult of Christian marriage. They too saw the husband as God's representative in the family, hence he must be obeyed implicitly by his women. 'The extent of wives' subjection doth stretch very far,' wrote the seventeenth-century Anglican divine William Gouge, 'even to all things.' Women were no longer regarded as intrinsically evil; they were simply weak and fragile. This was a direct result of the Fall. As Gouge explained, a wife needed her husband's good government, 'that she who first led man into sin should now be subject to him, lest by the like womanish weakness she fall again'.[3] From 1562 onwards, parsons were ordered to read a set homily on marriage every Sunday. This described woman as 'the weaker vessel, of a frail heart, inconstant, and with a word soon stirred to wrath'.[4] She was not endowed with 'strength and constancy of mind': 'Therefore they be the sooner disquieted, and they be the more prone to all weak affections and dispositions of mind more than men be; and lighter they be and more vain in their fantasies and opinions.' The new 'together-ness' of holy matrimony in the Reformed Churches did not, therefore, lead to a more just conception of women.

The Roman Catholic Church would also build a more positive conception of marriage to meet the challenge of the Reforma-tion. Celibacy remained and remains the prime vocation for Catholic men and women, however, and during the Reforma-tion period a new kind of nun emerged. We have become so accustomed to the idea of religious orders of women involving themselves in education, social work and nursing that we do not always appreciate that this is a relatively new phenomenon. Before the Reformation, all nuns had to be cloistered and cut off from the world, as decreed by canon law. The enclosed con-vent, which nuns never left, and which was forbidden to seculars who could only address its inmates through a grille, symbolized the segregation that the Church had come to desire for its women. The imagery was that of a prison. Indeed, the Protestant vision of the home, into which a woman was driven as a nail into a wall (to use Luther's astonishing image), shows that the Reformed Churches harboured similar fantasies. Dur-ing the seventeenth century, however, the religious orders were created for women who wanted to engage in an active ministry beyond the convent walls. These nuns refused to remain in the prison of the cloister but undertook a *diakonia* in the world like men. They became teachers and cared for the poor. Thus Louise de Marillac, with the help of Vincent de Paul, founded the Daughters of Charity; Angela of Merici and Jane Frances de Chantal founded the two teaching orders of the Ursulines and the Visitation; in England Mary Ward founded the Institute of the Blessed Virgin Mary on the model of Ignatius of Loyola's Society of Jesus. She set up schools and colleges for Catholic girls in England, Flanders, Germany, Austria and Italy, clearly answering a perceived need since girls were eager to enter her schools and join the Institute.

These activities seem unexceptionable, but the women were aware that they were pioneers and were in some sense breaking a taboo. They aroused in clergy and laity alike a hostility that is not dissimilar to that provoked by the spectre of women priests today: they were invading a male sphere in the name of God and breaking out of the boundaries men had set on their influence. Louise de Marillac reminded her nuns that women could be as heroic as men in the active apostolate, and Angela of Merici referred to the example of Judith in the Old Testament, who had cut off the head of Holofernes – a castrating image for many men. Mary Ward came in for particular abuse from the Church since, like the Jesuits, she insisted that she was bound by obedience to the Pope alone and thus avoided all other male authority. The Church was horrified. A board of cardinals reviewed her case and declared that women were incapable of doing any good to anybody but themselves in the religious life. In 1631 Pope Urban VIII suppressed her order of 'Jesuitesses' since they had dared to ape male priests and had 'carried out works by no means suiting the weakness of their sex, womanly modesty, virginal purity . . . works which men most experienced in the knowledge of sacred scriptures undertake with difficulty and not without great caution'.[5] Mary herself was arrested as a heretic and imprisoned in a convent of Poor Clares in a room apart from the rest of the community. The punishment was to fit the crime: Mary had sought liberation from the cloister, so she must be forcibly imprisoned and isolated. The ceiling was low, the two tiny windows boarded up, it was airless and, since a nun had been dying in the room before Mary's arrival, it also stank. The harsh treatment meted out to Mary was a measure of the degree of threat experienced by the Church at the prospect of active women abroad in the world. It desperately sought to contain and confine this release of female creativity. After a few days, Mary became ill with a virulent fever which brought her to the brink of death.

It was little better for her nuns, who had been turned out on to the streets when the Institute had been suspended. By now there were some three hundred of them, many of whom became penniless. Not all could rejoin their families: it was dangerous even to be a Catholic in England at this time, let alone an ex-nun. Many had to beg for bread, and when one sister actually had the temerity to enter a church dressed in her habit she was beaten by the sacristan and driven out. Eventually the Pope relented and pardoned Mary Ward, who recovered from her sickness and was permitted to live privately in Rome with five of her companions. The women had been treated as criminals for doing charitable work, since their ministry was perceived as subversive. Independent women who dared to model themselves on male religious, who undertook a masculine ministry and refused to submit to male control, seemed to have aroused many of the emotions that have surfaced in our own day in the debate about the ordination of women to the priesthood.

The other active orders founded during the seventeenth century fared little better. Vincent de Paul advised the Daughters of Charity to call themselves 'religious sisters' instead of 'nuns', a ploy which active religious orders of women have used to this day to escape their legal obligation of strict enclosure. The Ursulines and the Visitation nuns were forced back into the cloister and became conventionally enclosed nuns again: in their case, too, the Church had succeeded in bringing them to heel. On both sides of the Reformation, the position of women was characterized by subordination and segregation. It has been said that in Protestant Churches their relation to men was 'together but unequal', and in the Roman Catholic Church 'separate but unequal'.

Some of the women in the more radical Reformed sects encountered similar hostility. The first members of the Society of Friends, popularly known as the Quakers, preached a doctrine of strict equality which included women. The seventeenth century had seen a new professionalism among the clergy in both the Roman Catholic and the Reformed Churches, and a fairly stringent academic qualification was now required. The Friends realized that this attempt to educate the clergy had in fact alienated them from many of their parishioners. Some of the women Quakers courageously braved the male preserves of Oxford and Cambridge. Thus in 1653 Mary Fisher and Elizabeth Williams preached to a crowd outside the gate of Sidney Collegè, Cambridge, and debated religious subjects with the young theologians there. They were publicly scourged at Market Cross by order of the mayor. The following year Elizabeth Fletcher and Elizabeth Leavens did the same at Oxford and were dragged through a muddy pool and suffered the frightening punishment of having water siphoned into their mouths at a pump. Again, the punishment was made to fit the crime: women had dared to violate the biblical command to remain silent, so their mouths were shut for them. Quaker women in the American colonies suffered even more savage reprisals. In Boston Elizabeth Hooton was tied to a cart and dragged through the streets to the whipping posts of Cambridge, Watertown and Dedham. There she was stripped to the waist, beaten and abandoned in the forest where, it was hoped, she would be devoured by bears and wolves. She disappointed her captors by surviving to preach again. But in 1660 Mary Dyer, who repeatedly exercised what she claimed was her God-given right to preach in public, was hanged in Boston.

Women who dared to preach or to exercise an active ministry in the world had clearly broken a taboo. As yet no women in either the Reformed or the Roman Catholic Churches were asking to be ordained priests or ministers. That would have been beyond the realm of possibility, when a woman who aped a male ministry inspired such dread and murderous violence. But women had been linked to priesthood in a terrible fantasy. The sixteenth and seventeenth centuries saw the great Witch Craze, which swept through Europe and killed thousands of men and women. It was an exclusively Western phenomenon – in the Orthodox world of eastern Europe and Greece there were no witch hunts. In the rest of Europe, the craze would flare up in one area, then cease with sinister abruptness, only to break out again in the same place years later. The panic was equally intense in Protestant and Roman Catholic communities, transcending the doctrinal divisions of the time. Some parts of Europe suffered more than others, however. Spain, Italy, Portugal and Holland had only limited and sporadic witch hunting. Hundreds of women were hanged for dabbling in the occult in England but this was different from the kind of panic that raged in Scotland, France, Germany and Switzerland and even briefly in Salem, Massachusetts. At the end of the fifteenth century, the old pagan belief in witchcraft was transformed into a Christian heresy when Pope Innocent VIII published the astonishing Bull *Summa Desiderantes* in 1485.

The Pope claimed that an epidemic of sexual anxiety and sterility had erupted in Germany. Men were impotent and their wives barren. It was claimed that they had been bewitched by women who had become the lovers of demons. Women and sexuality, which had long been tainted with an aura of evil in the Christian imagination, had now been finally and graphically demonized. Pope Innocent commissioned two learned Dominicans, Jacob Sprenger and Heinrich Kramer, to look into the matter. The result was Sprenger's *Malleus Maleficarum* (The Hammer of Witches), which was endorsed somewhat reluctantly by the University of Cologne in 1487 and went through nineteen editions, becoming a major handbook of the papal Inquisition. To a modern reader, the *Malleus* is a bewildering document, since it is difficult to see how anybody could take it seriously. Alternatively, the explicit nature of this fantasy, from a psychoanalytical point of view, shows how profoundly threatening women had become at this time. Our two Dominican scholars tell us that women have been stealing men's penises. A particularly enterprising witch had a whole collection of them in a bird's nest and when she kindly allowed a young man to reclaim his penis, she prevented him from taking the largest one: that belonged to the parish priest. Clearly, castration fears were very close to the surface.

Later, men would be accused of witchcraft alongside women but never in the same numbers. Many Inquisitors shared Sprenger's view that witchcraft was an exclusively female heresy. He claimed that witchcraft was caused by carnal lust, which was insatiable in women. They needed to satisfy their rampant sexuality with demon lovers. Sprenger thanks God devoutly that men are freed of this curse, 'since [Christ] was willing to be born and to suffer for us'.[6] The implication is that Christ had not died to save women. Women were more vulnerable than men since they were defective and misbegotten: the first woman was created from a bent rib, 'which is bent as it were in a contrary direction to a man'. Hence she is chronically deceitful. Even the word *femina* derives from *fe* and *minus*, 'since she is ever weaker to hold and to preserve the faith'.[7] The *Malleus* depicted women as monsters:

> You do not know that woman is the Chimera, but it is good that you should know it; for that monster was of

three forms; its face was that of a radiant and noble lion, it
had the filthy belly of a goat and it was armed with the
virulent tail of a viper. And he means that a woman is
beautiful to look upon, contaminating to the touch and
deadly to keep.[8]

In this fantasy, which delineates the seductive as well as the
repellent power of women, there is a final and deadly segregation. Women no longer seem human, are not really saved by
Christ, but have been abandoned to the realm of evil.

By this period, Christians had long evolved equally terrified
fantasies of Jews and Muslims. Jews were said to murder little
children and mix their blood with the Passover bread; Muslims
were accused of monstrous and unnatural sexuality and were
believed to be dedicated to the overthrow of Christendom. The
fantasy of the 'witch' should be seen as linked to these other
phobias about dehumanized enemies. All show a profound dis-
ease in the Western Christian psyche, which was hag-ridden,
haunted by monstrous and fearful enemies that it had created
out of its own image and likeness. The fantasies about Jews
betray anxiety about the Eucharist and an almost Oedipal
dread of the parent faith; the sexual accusations that Christian
scholars levelled against Muslims (with a good deal of ill-
concealed envy) were projections of their own fears of sexuality
on to their powerful enemy. It had been at a time when
Christians had been fighting their own brutal holy wars in the
Near East against Muslims that they had learned to call Islam
a religion of the sword, even though Muslim generals like
Saladin often behaved with far greater restraint and compassion than the Crusaders. The fantasies of the witch should be
seen as a similar projection of worries about their own identity
on to womankind, the ancient enemy of the male sex.

There has been much scholarly debate about the exact nature
of the Witch Craze in Europe but it seems evident that there
were no real witches. The mythology that developed was a
collective fantasy, shared by both Inquisitors and their
victims. Later witch hunters developed Sprenger's work. Where
Sprenger had simply accused witches of casting a spell on their

hapless victims and 'fascinating' them, sixteenth-century scholars added new touches that rendered women even more diabolical. Witches were now believed to fly through the air at night to take part in orgiastic meetings where Satan was worshipped instead of God. Like Jews and Muslims, they were engaged in a giant international conspiracy to destroy Christendom: their meetings were called 'sabbaths' and 'synagogues'. These charges of sexual orgies and cannibalism were not new: the Romans had levelled them against the early Christians, and Christians had accused heretics such as the Cathars of similar crimes. These stock fears that imaged some profound psychic terror of the outsider and aroused murderous hostility were now attached to the diabolical female sex.

In the fantasy of the Black Mass in honour of Satan we can see an unconscious but compulsive revolt against a religion which everybody accepted on an intellectual level but which was causing deep anxiety. The Black Mass can be seen as a parody of the Eucharist: instead of the Communion with God, there was communion with the Devil, achieved through the consumption of human flesh (instead of bread and wine) and an obscene kiss. Massive orgies took the place of the sacred and remote ritual of the Catholic Eucharist and rampant sexuality replaced priestly celibacy. The 'priests' of Satan were mostly women instead of exclusively men. Even though men were arrested as witches, tortured until they confessed to these atrocities and executed by the Inquisition, many more women were killed. Major witch hunters, such as Henricus Institoris, the humane and scholarly Girolamo Visconti, Sylvester Prierias, Lupa da Bergamo and the Jesuits Peter Thyraeus and Paul Laymann, all believed that witchcraft was primarily a woman's vice. It was, therefore, mainly women who were imagined priestesses of Satan, presiding over a ceremony that was a parody of the Eucharist ordained by Christ and celebrated by male ministers. The fantasy of the Black Mass was an unconscious and symbolic rejection of a religion which many found too demanding and frightening.

It may well be that some of these old fears and phobias remain, even in our apparently more rational age. Certainly terms that once referred to the witches and their heresy are commonly used today and are the stock-in-trade of language describing women. Words such as 'charm', 'glamour' and 'fascination' now seem innocent enough but during the Witch Craze they were accusations of diabolical vice. The craze raged for two centuries in Europe and thus had time to make a profound impression. It had not come out of the blue but had systematized a centuries-old Christian misogyny and taken it to an extreme conclusion. By the eighteenth century it was spent; it could not survive the cooler climate of the Enlightenment. Nobody today seriously believes in witches' sabbaths, but it is possible that traces of the demonic still cling to women in our culture, just as the old witch vocabulary has survived and been absorbed. In any event, the only priesthood that was deemed possible for women during the Reformation period was the satanic priesthood of the Black Mass.

— 7 —

Suffragettes, Church Feminists and the End of Silence

THE VICTORIAN period was a watershed. In England there
was an explosion of sexual disgust which inevitably
proved detrimental to the position of women. Historians
have noted that since the Reformation it has been particularly
difficult for the Western world to maintain a sexual equilibrium.
In a manner that is not apparent in other cultures, a period of
relative permissiveness is succeeded by a severe puritanism,
which nearly always coincides with a religious revival. Christianity, as we have seen, has found it difficult to accommodate
sexuality and it has rarely experienced such a violent revulsion
from these facts of human life as during the nineteenth century.
The rational temper of the Enlightenment was succeeded, in
both England and America, by a wave of religious enthusiasm,
which was expressed in various ways: Evangelicalism, Methodism and the Oxford Movement. Long linked with sin in the
Christian imagination, sexuality was seen as an incurable
scourge by the Victorians, an ungovernable evil. Men lived in
terror of the fearful effects of masturbation and nocturnal
emission, children were supervised with Draconian rigour to
guard them from a chronic impurity and women were banished
yet again into a separate sphere, away from all the nastiness
that their menfolk could not accept within themselves.

In the Middle Ages, virginity had given some women a

certain power and prestige. This was still possible to an extent in some of the radical sects which broke away from the main-stream Churches. The most dramatic example of this phenom-enon had occurred during the eighteenth century and persisted in America well into the Victorian age. The Englishwoman Ann Lee had found sex terrifying and sad. She had loved her husband but had borne four children with immense difficulty and danger: all had died in infancy. Turning her back on sex, she had found some release in a branch of Quakerism whose members were known as 'Shakers' because of their ecstatic dancing and singing. One night after she had been thrown into a Manchester jail for disturbing the peace with the noisy Shaker celebrations, Ann Lee had had a revelation. She had seen a vision of Adam and Eve before the Fall and realized that sex was the cause of the primal sin: Jesus told her to preach the holy gospel of celibacy throughout the world. With a small band of disciples, Ann Lee emigrated in 1770 to America and there, unlikely as it may seem, her Shakers enjoyed astonishing success. Whole families joined the Shaker colonies, selling their houses and living in total chastity. Men and women worked together by day but slept in separate dormitories. The sect flourished briskly until the 1840s; like Mormonism which intro-duced polygamy and the nineteenth-century Oneida group which advocated free love, Shakerism showed that many men and women in the American colonies were far from happy with the conventional sexual and familial *mores*. The fanatical enthu-siasm for 'family values' that American Christians evince today may be a more modern attempt to accommodate the same anxiety.

In the breakaway sects of Christianity, women had often been powerful and effective in the early stages. So too Mother Ann Lee, as her followers called her, and her successor Lucy Walker were the Shakers' unquestioned leaders. At about the same time, Methodist women were also able to pursue an active preaching ministry and were prominent in the Evangelical movement on both sides of the Atlantic. John Wesley (1703–91) had evolved a form of Anglicanism which combined a revivalist fervour with the ideals of the Enlightenment in a movement that became known as 'Methodism' because of its efficiency and method in spiritual exercises. Wesley's mother Susanna had been a remarkable woman and may have influenced him in favour of women preachers, though he also showed a strange fear of women in his personal life. Susanna had turned her Sunday evening family prayers into a public service often attended by as many as two hundred people. When her husband had understandably objected, Susanna had replied:

> It came into my mind that though I am not a man nor a minister of the gospel, and so cannot be employed in such a worthy employment as they were, yet if my heart were sincerely devoted to God, and if I were inspired with a true zeal for his glory and did really desire the salvation of souls, I might do something more than I do.[1]

When he had started his classes in Bristol in 1739, Wesley had appointed women as teachers. Sarah Crosby, who had been converted in a violent born-again experience in 1735, soon found that she had almost two hundred people in her class and Wesley was forced to give her and other women permission to preach. When his colleague John Fletcher died, Wesley had encouraged Fletcher's wife Mary to take over many of his parish duties; consequently she preached to huge crowds, some of which numbered three thousand people, and Wesley described her preaching style as 'smooth, easy and natural', a 'fire' that conveyed 'both heat and light to all who heard her'.[2] Mary Fletcher herself appealed to the women in the New Testament when accused of immodesty:

> No, I do not apprehend Mary could in the least be accused of immodesty when she carried the joyful news of her Lord's resurrection, and in that sense taught the teachers of mankind. Neither was the woman of Samaria to be accused of immodesty when she invited the whole city to come to Christ. . . . Neither do I suppose Deborah did wrong in publicly declaring the message of the Lord.[3]

Wesley never approved of the formal ordination of women but the success of the women Methodist preachers had forced him to give a formal recognition to their active ministry. Yet again, personal charisma had given women power and influence that would not be possible in the more bureaucratic and conventional Churches.

But this type of charismatic leadership rarely lasts. Shakerism petered out until it consisted of a handful of isolated women in the 1980s. During the nineteenth century, Quaker and Methodist women both had their ministries curtailed. In the mainstream Churches, too, women were strictly confined to the private domain. In the Victorian ethos, the home became a latter-day convent, hushed, holy and removed from the strife of public affairs. It protected the purity of the Wife and Mother who may not have been technically virginal but was unmoved by sexual passion. In his immensely popular poem, the English Catholic poet Coventry Patmore called her 'The Angel of the House'. Other writers encouraged their women to be childlike and innocent and some, like John Ruskin and Lewis Carroll, preferred little girls to fully developed women. It was Ruskin who most memorably extolled the Victorian cult of the home, seeing it and the woman who presided over it as the objective correlative of the Victorian ideal, asexual and uncontaminated by the world:

> This is the true Nature of Home – it is the place of Peace; the shelter, not only from all injury, but from all terror, doubt and division. In so far as the anxieties of the outer life penetrate into it, and the inconsistently-minded, unknown, unloved, or hostile society of the outer world is allowed by either husband or wife to cross the threshold, it ceases to be home; it is then only a part of that outer world which you have roofed over and lighted fire in. But in so far as it is a sacred place, a vestal temple, a temple of the earth watched over by Household Gods . . . so far it vindicates the name and fulfils the praise of Home.[4]

This vestal shrine was, Ruskin concluded, 'the woman's true place and power'. Women who had been demonized two centuries earlier were now placed on an equally fictitious

pinnacle of perfection in one of those extreme swings of attitude that characterize the Western perception of sex and
gender.

The ideal woman in anti-Catholic England at this date was
the Virgin Mary but this Marian devotion no longer had subversive potential as in the Middle Ages; rather, it was part of a
male fantasy of a prelapsarian perfection. The French writer
Hippolyte Taine described the typical British beauty of the·
Victorian age as a 'fair maiden – lowered eyes, blushing cheeks,
purer than a Raphael Madonna, a kind of Eve incapable of Fall'.
In the early Church, virgins such as Macrina had also been seen
as a type of unfallen humanity but this had made them the
spiritual equal of their men. In the Victorian period, the new
Eve and the new Madonna were characterized by submission.
Churchmen lavished praise on the home of the Holy Family of
Nazareth; they hymned the faith, constancy and modesty of
Mary. They looked back to the Creation stories in the Bible and
argued that the inferior position of women in society was not a
punishment, as Luther had claimed, but a woman's glory and
pride. Thus in 1844 the prominent ecclesiastic J. W. Burgon
argued against the education of women on the basis of Genesis
and St Paul. Eve had been created as 'Man's helper . . . a second
self but not a rival self'. Paul's endorsement of this 'primeval
decree' was valid 'for all time'.[5] In the same year, Christopher
Wordsworth, Bishop of Lincoln, expressed a similar view in a
sermon on 'Christian Womanhood'. This was surprising, since
he was generally supportive of women: his daughter Elizabeth
would become the first Principal of Lady Margaret Hall,
Oxford, and the Bishop encouraged her endeavours. Yet he was
also convinced that woman's 'existence was not only subsequent to that of man but was derived from it. She was after man,
out of man and for man.' Anything that threatened this fundamental subordination 'weakens her authority and mars her
dignity and beauty. Her true strength is in loyal submission.'[6]
Despite the egalitarian tendency of primitive Christianity, the
subordination of women was regarded as basic to the faith. It is
a view still held today by those who oppose the ordination of
women on the basis of the 'headship' doctrine. Then as now it
was endorsed by prominent women. Thus the prolific Victorian

novelist Charlotte M. Yonge was committed to maintaining 'the inferiority of women', because Eve's physical weakness was a punishment for her original sin.[7]

The exalted language in which Ruskin and others invested the home showed that religious and spiritual values were beginning to be identified with the private sphere. This process had begun in the Enlightenment separation of Church and State and continued in the nineteenth century, fostered by the rise of industry. This encouraged some to see religion as an essentially private and, by association, feminine activity. Women became the carriers of all the virtues and men often felt themselves to be brutish, sexual and worldly by comparison. Woman, Ruskin maintained, was 'incapable of error; enduringly, incorruptibly good, instinctively, infallibly wise'. The heroines of male novelists such as Charles Dickens were often described in heavenly terms as the guardians of all virtue. This created a new ambivalence between clergy and their women parishioners: since the female nature incarnated a particular aptitude for goodness or religion in the Victorian imagination, this was dependent upon her remaining in the private cloister of the home. Again, many women subscribed to this myth, which still manifests itself in some of the more radical feminist spirituality. Such 'difference feminism' as it is called tends to see the piety of women as essentially different and somehow superior to that of men.

The feminization of religion in England was reflected in Church activities. By about 1880 there tended to be more women than men at services, a trend that continued into the twentieth century. Indeed, the 1861 census showed that there were more women than men in Britain *tout court*. Many were finding the shuttered sanctity of home stifling and, despite the prevailing ethos, had taken up philanthropic work, often under the aegis of the Churches. By 1893 it was estimated that half a million women were occupied as volunteer workers in the parishes and slums.[8] Religion was certainly one motive for this surge of activity outside the home but there were others. There was a strong sense that it was all too easy for women to fritter away their lives on trivialities, and practical charity seemed the answer for those who longed for 'something real'. As the writer

Edward Monro explained in his book *Parochial Work* (1850), such women were aware 'that they are responsible beings approaching an eternity in which they will have to render an account of hours given for higher uses but spent perhaps on vain trifles'.[9] Others were inspired by patriotism, a desire to contribute to the British effort. Some were anxious to stem the tide of revolutionary violence, the fear of which gripped Churchmen and laity alike during the Victorian period. Literally thousands of women worked as parish visitors, Sunday school teachers and missionaries in nearly all the major denominations. As the Victorian feminist Frances Cobbe remarked, many women chose philanthropy rather than academic study to fill their lives.

In 1919 a Church of England Commission appointed by the Archbishop of Canterbury attributed much of the renewed effectiveness of the Church to the activities of women since 1850. Yet despite their valuable contribution, they were usually treated as dogsbodies and unpaid menial help. Many of them were wives and daughters of clergymen who were expected to take part in a very wide range of activities that demanded a number of skills, such as music, teaching and social work, yet they were constantly reminded that there was an impassable gulf between them and the vicar. As Louise Creighton (1850–1936), herself the wife of the Bishop of Peterborough, remarked, the parson's wife had a sphere and a function in the parish, 'but it is an entirely subordinate one, more subordinate than that of any other wife'.[10] Not only was she inferior as a mere female but she also lacked the training and qualifications that were now deemed essential for Christian ministry.

Unlike his Roman Catholic counterpart who received a special seminary formation, the Church of England clergyman had had no professional training before the Victorian period. His duties were not markedly different from those of any other English gentleman. Like any squire, the parson often acted as doctor, social worker and Justice of the Peace in the parish. A special theological or pastoral qualification was deemed unnecessary. But by the 1860s other 'professionals' – solicitors, policemen, teachers and physicians – were beginning to take over some of these functions and the parson was obliged to concentrate on his specifically clerical duties: he had become a professional. Not only did clergymen begin to dress distinctively to mark their separate status but they had also started to form professional clerical bodies and to require a theological training at university. The clergyman now had three main duties: he presided at the liturgy, preached and was responsible for such pastoral duties as parish visiting and Sunday school. Women parish workers could assist him in this third ministry – indeed, they often made it possible – but were debarred from the ministries of liturgy and preaching.

Lay men were allowed an increasing share in both the liturgical and teaching ministries of the professional clergy. They could if they wished participate actively in the Eucharist as altar servers and choristers, wearing the appropriate dress, and by the 1860s they were also permitted to read the lessons in church and even to preach occasionally. In their pastoral ministry, women had also been affected by the enthusiasm for professionalism. They were no longer willing to be devout stooges but insisted that their work be taken seriously. In a report to the Congress of the Church of England in 1894, Louise Creighton argued that women Church workers should also be professionals and accorded a proper respect. A woman 'should not be merely a parochial drudge but a fellow-worker with the clergy, within her own sphere and subject, of course, to the control of the head of the parish'.[11] Creighton was obviously no radical feminist but she was convinced that a woman should not be considered as a mere appendage and convenience. She herself combined motherhood of seven children with a career as a writer and, in the early years of the twentieth century, in Church politics. In 1899 she was a delegate to the International Congress of Women, which discussed the role women could play in prisons and reformatories and among the poor. She was three times President of the National Council of Women Workers and from 1920 to 1930 a member of the Assembly of the Church of England. A forceful and highly respectable woman, she was willing to work within the institutional structures of the Church and society. Yet she was always aware that her Church should respond more boldly to the challenge of the times. Why, she asked at the Church Congress of 1899, were the most advanced and intelligent women in the country no longer willing to work for the Church? Because the bishops and clergy were not sympathetic to the women's movement.

This was, of course, the age of the suffragettes. Women were beginning to rebel against the impossible constraints imposed upon them by male society. It may well be that the cult of the home had had the reverse effect of what had been intended. The radical educationalist Emily Davis (1830–1921), who founded Girton College, Cambridge, found the boredom and irredeemable triviality of her life as a young girl insupportable. She was convinced that many women were driven to extreme misery and ill-health by a life of total seclusion and idleness. By the end of the nineteenth century, more adventurous spirits were able to endure it no longer. Leading feminists demanded the institutional reforms that would enable them to take their place in society as men's equals. Emmeline Pankhurst and her daughter Christabel campaigned for the vote, while education- alists like Davis insisted that women be educated to exactly the same standards as their brothers. Other feminists applied the same principles to the Church and by the end of the century had started to campaign for a more just share in Church government: after all, they were already doing a great deal of the work. In May 1897, the bishops of the Upper House of the Canterbury Convocation adopted six resolutions to encourage the laity to form parish councils. The fourth of these proposals stipulated that the lay councillors be *male*. This was scarcely surprising. But it was significant that a motion to delete the word 'male' was defeated by only two votes. It was the first sign of a changing spirit in the Churches.

A few months later, in February 1898, 1100 Anglican women presented a petition to the House of Bishops, protesting against the ban on women councillors. The ensuing debate showed that this sudden eruption of feminism into Church affairs caused the kind of grave disquiet and dis-ease that we have noted earlier. Some of the bishops were sympathetic to the women. The Bishop of Salisbury pointed to an anomaly in the legislation. He had two women who served as churchwardens and, by virtue of this office, they were *ex officio* members of the parish council. Robert Gregory, Dean of St Paul's, noted that women were often the most devoted members of the Church. After all, he argued, women who stood for election to the parish council would not have to make speeches or anything of that sort. Archdeacon E. G. Sandford of Exeter believed that this demand for representation on the parish council heralded an even more preposterous demand. St Paul had made it clear that women had not been created by God to take part in public discussion. They should therefore keep silent in the Church assembly and their voices should not be heard on the parish council. Sandford concluded that 'The very fact that a large body of women were agitating in this very matter seemed to show that there was something behind and beyond the mere wish that had been expressed that day.'[12]

What was this dread 'something' that was too fearful to be named? This was made clear five years later by Dr E. S. Talbot, Bishop of Rochester. In an attempt to keep abreast of the growing enfranchisement of men in secular society, Convocation had decided in 1903 to create a body of lay men to share in the legislative processes of the Church of England. One day, it was hoped, this House of Laity would achieve constitutional status, a dream fulfilled in the Synod. As one might expect, there would be no women in this legislative group, but the bishops had decreed that women should not even be permitted to vote for the delegates. There was an outcry. Even the most conservative women, who had no desire to take an active role in either ecclesiastical or secular politics, felt insulted. In the ensuing discussion in Convocation, Bishop Talbot described this exclusion of women as a great injustice. It was also short-sighted and inexpedient. Unless the Church of England paid greater attention to that sexual equality which was fundamental to Christian teaching, some women might be driven to insist that it be applied indiscriminately, even going so far as to demand admission to the priesthood.[13]

In the next twenty years, the spectre of a woman breaking the silence supposedly imposed upon her by St Paul and speaking in a Church assembly would continue to inspire fear of the ultimate abomination: a woman priest. But in fact the Church of England had already been prepared to allow some women to preach and teach in a missionary capacity at home and abroad.

Pandora's box had by now been opened. Way back in 1857, Mrs L. N. Renyard began to recruit what she called Bible Women to evangelize the urban poor in the Seven Dials district in London. They sold bibles and held mothers' meetings for reading, sewing and instruction. In 1860 the Honourable Mrs Taylor had founded the Parochial Mission Workers. These women missionaries to the poor had spread from London to Durham, Newcastle, Exeter, Liverpool and Rochester. Other women were going overseas. The Church Missionary Society had sent the first woman missionary to Sierra Leone in 1820 and women had since been given increasing scope for Church work abroad. They were not yet able to preside at the Eucharist but they were allowed to teach and instruct as missionaries to the heathen and to the deprived. Why could they not perform this ministry to their own kind?

Other women in Victorian England had even received ordination of a kind at the hands of a bishop – though not an ordination to the priesthood. The Catholic Emancipation Act of 1829 had seen the return of nuns to England, some of whom were now permitted by their Church to pursue an active ministry in teaching or nursing. The Oxford Movement had resulted in the appearance of Anglican nuns in the Church of England. In 1845 Dr Edward Pusey had founded a sisterhood to work in his parish of Christ Church, Oxford, and three years later the community of St Mary the Virgin was founded near Wantage, also for parish work. Soon there were some twenty communities of Anglican sisters in various parts of England. But in 1861 a different kind of religious order was instituted when Elizabeth Ferard founded the Community of St Andrew which claimed to have revived the ancient Order of Deaconesses 'for the purpose of engaging in works of Christian usefulness'.[14] In 1862 Elizabeth Ferard was 'set apart' by Dr Archibald Tait, Bishop of London. She was the first deaconess to be ordained by a bishop in England since the Middle Ages. Others joined her. The following year there were already three fully fledged deaconesses, six candidates and eight assistants. By 1873 it was necessary to move to larger premises in Tavistock Crescent.

Dr Tait was enthusiastic about the revival of the Order of Deaconesses for work among the urban poor. It appealed to him more than the Bible Women, who were not subject to episcopal control, and he knew that it had been revived with great success by the Lutheran Churches in Europe. By 1861 there were 220 deaconesses and 120 probationers at Kaiserswerth in Germany, where Florence Nightingale had done her nursing training. They ran hospitals, rescue homes for 'Magdalenes', sanctuaries for released women prisoners and schools. Candidates were 'set apart' for this ministry by their pastor in a laying on of hands, as in the early Church. The Kaiserswerth order had also inspired another English institution at Mildmay in North London, which had been founded by the Reverend W. C. Pennefather and his wife Catherine. This also grew quickly so that by 1884 there were 200 deaconesses and 1500 associates. Other communities about which we have less information at present were founded at Chester and Ely. Kaiserswerth's association with the ancient Order of Deaconesses was part of its appeal for Anglican women in these early years. The Oxford Movement had elicited an enthusiasm for such revivals. It had also encouraged Anglicans to regard what John Henry Newman (1801–90) had called the apostolical succession as essential to the priesthood. In the first of his *Tracts for the Times*, addressed to the clergy and published in 1833, Newman had explained that this direct link with the very first Christian community was indispensable: 'The Lord Jesus Christ gave his Spirit to His Apostles; they in turn laid their hands on those who should succeed them; and these again on others; and so the sacred gift has been handed down to our present Bishops.' We have seen that this view of early Church ministry has symbolic rather than historical authenticity. But Newman concluded that therefore 'we must necessarily consider none to be *really* ordained who have not *thus* been ordained'.[15] For many Anglicans today, as for Roman Catholics, this view of the priesthood is crucial to the integrity of any Church and has affected their view of the ordination of women.

The revival of the Order of Deaconesses in England can be seen as part of the attempt of the Church of England to root itself in the Christian past and share in the continuity and universality which the Roman Catholic Church had always claimed for itself. Dr Tait and the other clerics and theologians who master-minded this revival did not intend the communities of deaconesses to resemble the sisterhoods. They envisaged something more flexible for women who felt called to good works. The Order had not been intended by them as a permanent vocation; there need be no training, no vows, and the women could leave the Order when they chose. They were to be professional religious on a par with the ordained male ministers. The bishops were particularly pleased that the deaconesses worked under them; unlike the Bible Women and the nuns in the sisterhoods, they could be controlled. Again and again, the Order of Deaconesses was praised for being 'under authority', thereby conforming to the Victorian ideal of submissive womanhood. In 1875, the Reverend Arthur Grove praised the deaconess for her submission to her pastor: 'He is the head, she the ministering hand.'[16] There was no conflict here with the doctrine of 'headship'. It will be recalled that in the fourth century, *The Apostolic Constitutions* had used similar imagery to describe the women deacons of its own day. Yet we are far from St Paul's metaphor of the body of Christ which stressed the equality of the various members rather than the subordination of some parts of the body to others.

The deaconesses themselves, however, were developing a different conception of their vocation. In 1887 Isabella Gilmore, sister of the Pre-Raphaelite painter and designer William Morris, was ordained as a deaconess at Clapham. Widowed in her early forties, Gilmore had desired some form of Christian ministry. She had trained as a nurse at Guy's Hospital with this in mind but had at first disliked the deaconess orders. The communities she visited seemed petty and their conventual lifestyle seemed to thwart any sense of personal initiative. Gilmore thought that deaconesses should be independent and self-reliant, and when she founded her own Order she insisted that it be organized less as a sisterhood than in a way that was closer to the ministry of the male clergy. Once their probationary period was over, her deaconesses would not regard her as a sort of Mother Superior but, like any priest, would work directly with the bishop and clergy of a particular diocese. She

also insisted that the vocation was for life, like that of a male
cleric. As she saw it:

> A Deaconess is then a woman, who . . . is solemnly set
> apart by a Bishop, in the midst of the Church by the laying
> on of hands. . . . Her life and all that she has is dedicated
> to God's service. She is the servant of the Church, and
> works only and absolutely under the parochial clergy, to
> whom she is licensed, and is one of the Church officials.[17]

It was Gilmore's ideal that would become the norm, although
the St Andrew's Community, founded by Elizabeth Ferard on
more conventual lines, is still in existence for those who want
some kind of communal life. Most deaconesses would live and
work independently in the parishes, subject only to the bishop
and his vicars.

Yet even though the Order of Deaconesses was no threat to
the male hierarchy, the Church seemed curiously reluctant to
give these obedient helpers any official recognition. Many
balked at the whole idea of an *ordo* of women. The deaconesses
themselves believed, and were sometimes encouraged in this
belief by the Church, that their laying on of hands was a
ceremony that admitted them to Holy Orders. But, as we shall
see, after the First World War there would be much debate
about the nature of this 'ordination'. It was not until more
radical women took a more militant line about the ministry of
women that the Church of England saw the value of this more
submissive Order. But by that time, it was too late to turn back
the clock.

A new type of Anglican woman appeared in the first decades
of the twentieth century. Maude Royden (1876–1956), for example, had been educated at Cheltenham Ladies College and
Lady Margaret Hall. Subsequently she became a parish worker,
an extension lecturer for Oxford University and a suffragette.
She published books about the political, religious and sexual
status of women. As a leading member of the Church League
for Women's Suffrage, which sought to secure for women a
share in Church government, she was not prepared to wait
meekly until the male hierarchy deigned to share its privileges.

At a rally in 1915 she declared that there was no theological reason to exclude women from the priesthood. During these war years, women had perforce been given more opportunities in the Church as well as in the secular sphere, while their men were away at the front, and afterwards they would not be prepared to retire to the sidelines. Daringly, papers such as the *Church Times* and *The Christian Commonwealth* suggested that it might be acceptable for women to lead the singing in church, provided of course that they did not wear clerical cassocks, or take the collection during the war emergency. So far, so good; there was little objection. But when it was suggested that a woman might conceivably speak in church, all hell was let loose. On 10 February 1916, the wife of a country parson wrote to the *Guardian* asking why women should not read in those churches 'where there is no man who could, or would, read the lessons'. For a whole month the letter column was crammed with angry effusions of protest.

A few months later, Dr Randall Davidson, Archbishop of Canterbury, called a National Mission of Repentance and Hope to lighten the darkness of the war. He was particularly keen to involve the laity and, since most of the men were away, this meant that women did the bulk of the work. Maude Royden proposed a motion, which was passed by the Church Council for the National Mission, that women be permitted to speak as official Messengers of the Mission in the churches. The Bishops of London and Chelmsford also agreed that women Messengers be permitted to speak at the special meetings for other women and girls, provided that they did not address the congregation from the pulpit, lectern or chancel steps. Again, there was an uproar. Mr Athelstone Riley, a prominent lay member of the Council, organized a protest in the press. It was, he wrote to the *Church Times*, 'sheer nonsense' to say that men and women were equal in the sight of God. Maude Royden was engaged in 'a conspiracy to capture the priesthood, step by step'. It was a 'feminist plot'.[18] The secular press took up the cry, splashing the words 'plot' and 'conspiracy' across their pages. The very idea of a woman speaking in the sacred precincts of the church had aroused a profound but irrational dread. The bishops were forced to withdraw their permission for the scheme. Bishop Winnington-Ingram of London, horrified by the anger he had unwittingly unleashed, protested that he did not support the ordination of women to the priesthood, as did the Bishop of Chelmsford, who promised, however, that after the Mission the House of Bishops would discuss the whole issue of women preaching and reading aloud at Church services.

Those who supported the ideal of equal opportunities for women did not give up. They immediately raised a crucial question: how could the Church claim to express the divine humanity of Christ when half the human race was entirely excluded from its government and teaching ministry? Other women went further, not content with verbal protest. It had proved to be necessary for women to fight a hard battle for equal rights and just treatment within the Church as well as outside it. If suffragettes had not campaigned so vigorously, women would never have been given the vote. If education-alists had not pre-empted all the arguments against the advanced education of women by founding colleges and schools, women would have remained excluded from the male preserve of academe. If Elizabeth Garrett Anderson had not trained and practised as a doctor in the teeth of determined opposition, women would have remained debarred from the medical profession. It might have been hoped that Churchmen would have been more amenable to the notion of equal rights for women, since that was enshrined in the Gospels, but this proved yet again not to be the case.

Women were considered too frail and vulnerable for such masculine pursuits as medicine or scholarship. This is a myth that survived the political and social emancipation of women in the nineteenth and early twentieth centuries. As late as the 1970s it was argued that women would be unable to read the news on television since they would be overcome by their emotions. It is, therefore, easy to imagine how entrenched the opposition was to allowing women to enter the professions a century ago. Some ten years before she founded Girton College, Cambridge, in 1873, Emily Davis had gathered material for a pamphlet she intended to write about the myths that were current about women. Men believed that if women had anything else to do they would be reluctant to marry, she found. Others were convinced that public life was harmful to women who had been created specifically for the domestic sphere, that it was dangerous to interfere with the laws of nature, that women were naturally indolent and that ambitious courses of study could only unhinge the fragile female brain.[19] Throughout her career, Davis had to contend with eminent male doctors who warned parents of nervous breakdowns if they allowed their daughters to attempt a mental exertion that was beyond their natural, female capacity. Nearly every day she received letters from perfect strangers expressing their 'repugnance' at the idea of 'the competition between the sexes'. 'Girls are different from boys,' wrote one correspondent, 'their brains are light, their foreheads too small, their reasoning powers too defective, their emotions too easily worked upon to make good students.' Women would become 'too strong-minded' if they neglected their needlework and music for more academic pursuits: how could they be 'good sisters, wives, mothers and nurses' and 'make evenings delightful'? How could a man possibly marry a woman who was better educated than himself?[20] Even the leading specialist Henry Maudsley (1835–1918), who introduced important reforms in the treatment of mental illness, subscribed to these myths. In an article on 'Sex in Mind and Education' published in May 1874, he argued that 'study is the cause of ill-health in women'.[21] It was because of the ambitious educational system to which some women were subjected in schools and colleges that the American girl was becoming sexually incapacitated for her duties as wife and mother. These opinions were not based on empirical evidence or concocted in a spirit of cold calculation. They were accepted implicitly and uncritically as obvious truths but they also expressed a deep fear of women and some buried doubts about the institution of marriage. The only way of dispelling such prejudice was by demonstrating their falsity, as pioneers like Emily Davis did.

While some feminists set about proving that women could become good academics and doctors, others were determined to show that they were capable of exercising a priestly ministry about which there were similar taboos. Maude Royden wanted to fulfil her vocation to the priesthood, despite the opposition to women priests in the Church of England. She became a distinguished preacher and in 1919 was invited to preach the three-hour Good Friday Service at St Botolph's, Bishopsgate. At the last moment the Bishop of London withdrew his permission, but the Rector of St Botolph's got round the prohibition by observing the letter if not the spirit of the law which forbade women to preach or read at statutory services in church. Royden preached in a room adjoining the church. It was packed: people even crowded round the windows outside. Despite passionate opposition, Royden's Good Friday Services became an annual event. Once she had broken the ice, other women followed. The suffragette and Church feminist Edith Picton-Turbeville preached in Lincoln, Dublin and Geneva, wearing a cassock and surplice. It was true that only a very few radicals were willing to go to these lengths but the opposition took their campaign very seriously. Thus in 1916, Arnold Pinchard published *Woman and the Priesthood*, voicing objections that have remained crucial to the debate. We have always spoken of God as masculine; Jesus was a man: how could a woman adequately re-present this male God at the altar? Men and women had different spheres of activity: 'There is given to the male a certain superiority . . . priority of initiative and decision . . . a kind of final responsibility.'[22] Other people protested that Jesus had chosen only male disciples; the very idea of a woman priest was indecent, a 'wicked return to the ideals of heathenism', which could drive men away from the ministry and from the Church itself.[23]

Compared with the demands of such radical Christians as Royden, the more handmaidenly Order of Deaconesses suddenly seemed immensely desirable to some of the clergy. Isabella Gilmore had always made it clear that she did not consider her Order a step towards the priesthood. Yet Churchmen were aware that the war years had wrought a major change in the position of women in England. They were anxious not to alienate the most advanced and educated women but wary of offending more conservative Christians, as well as of damaging ecumenical relations with the Roman Catholic Church. Enhancing the role of the deaconess seemed to some to be the best compromise. Consequently the position of women was debated at the Lambeth Conference of 1920. It declared that a deaconess was indeed admitted to Holy Orders, even though her *ordo* remained a minor one. Anything more was quite unacceptable: 'the idea of women being admitted to the priesthood [is] . . . wholly contrary to the immemorial and consistent custom of the Catholic Church'.[24] Henceforth deaconesses would be allowed to speak in Church buildings but *not* at the Eucharist, Matins or Vespers.

During the debate, some bishops were clearly afraid that permitting a woman to speak in services would put the Church on the slippery slope to a female priesthood. Dr Sparrow Simpson argued that the subordination of women was fundamental to the order of nature and to the Bible. Gascoyne Cecil, Bishop of Exeter, felt a profound unease at mixing the religious with the sexual instinct, which 'were too close to be allowed to be brought into close contact'. Hinting darkly at menstruation, Henry Wace, Dean of Canterbury, noted that 'there were differences not only in the physical but in the psychical constitution of women which rendered the office of regular public preaching unsuitable for them'.[25] It was much the same kind of argument as Dr Maudsley had used to declare women unfit for advanced education. Seeking reassurance on these disturbing issues, the Lambeth Conference asked the physician and feminist Dr Laetitia Fairfield to comment privately on the medical aspect of women's ministry. She robustly rejected the menstrual myth, concluding that it reflected a buried belief in the old taboos about ritual impurity. Yet she realized that it was of fundamental importance. The reluctance to admit women to the ministry 'cannot be founded on a lack of spiritual worth . . . nor on mental quality'. It must be the result of the primitive conviction that 'a woman's liability to periodic illness makes her permanently defiled by her sex in a way that a man is not'.[26] It was this 'defilement' that made it psychologically impossible for so many men and women to accept the idea of a woman entering the pulpit or the chancel.

Yet it seemed that the British felt more squeamish about including women in worship and active ministry than Anglicans in other parts of the world. In Canada, Dr Lloyd, Bishop of Saskatchewan, welcomed the findings of the Lambeth Conference. He immediately appointed a deaconess to perform all the duties of a deacon and soon deaconesses were given votes in the Synod. In South Africa they were immediately included among the clergy and in Australia they were allowed to conduct services. In the United States, while the Order of Deaconesses had never really caught on, a report of the Episcopal Church stated that the deaconess had a distinctive place in the Church. American Episcopalians were aware that women in other Churches, which did not have an ordained priesthood, were already being admitted to the preaching ministry. By 1927 there were 100 Congregationalist women ministers, the Methodist Episcopal Church had begun to ordain women as local preachers in 1924, and in 1930 the Presbyterian Church, while drawing the line at full ordination, did permit women to become elders. But in these Churches, ministry was a practical matter. Ministers were not seen as 'priests', as in the Anglican, Roman Catholic or Greek Orthodox Church. They were not mediators who interceded with God on behalf of the faithful and represented the person of Christ. The idea of a woman priest standing at the altar, handling the sacred vessels and elements, seemed to touch on a primitive but powerful fear.

At this point the Roman Catholic and Greek Orthodox Churches did not even consider the question of the ordination of women. In the Church of England, Anglo-Catholics who held a 'high' notion of priesthood were profoundly unhappy at the idea of a woman being admitted to Holy Orders. People objected vigorously to the new liturgical functions given to the deaconess by the Lambeth Conference. On 3 September 1929, the leading article of the *Church Times* was given the provocative heading: 'The Coming of Women Priests'. Fending off this hideous prospect, the writer argued: 'There is one claim that we can never allow, and that is the claim to admit women to Holy Orders. . . . Who can believe that even if they think that they have banged, barred and bolted the door against a female priesthood these bolts will hold?' This was the language of fear rather than of reason. But at the Lambeth Conference of 1930, the bishops went back on their earlier ruling and decided that a deaconess was *not* in Holy Orders. She could baptize and officiate at the churching of women but there was no question of admitting women to any other ministry. The Order of Deaconesses was 'the one and only' branch of ministry open to women and it was *not* equivalent to the Order of Deacons, which was a step towards full priesthood. The women's Order was simply a ministry of physical and spiritual succour, 'distinct from and complementary to the great Orders of the Church',[27] the episcopate, presbyterate and diaconate. But this retrograde step caused immense confusion. The deaconesses who had been ordained between 1920 and 1930 had naturally been convinced that they *were* receiving Holy Orders. Some had begun to hope for the priesthood. It seemed that uncertainty and ambivalence now surrounded their ordination, and numbers dwindled.

The Churches which had preserved the office of priesthood seemed convinced that they must continue to fight off the ordination of women. Even the small endorsement of deaconesses had proved too much for many of the British clergy. But was there a theological reason for this prohibition or was it simply culturally conditioned, like the taboos against women's education? For the next sixty years, Anglicans would continue to debate this question, but not before the first woman had been ordained to the priesthood.

— 8 —

1944–1992: Towards the Priesthood

A   s THE SECOND World War entered its final phase, a
       deacon and a bishop agreed to meet at Xing Xing in Free
       China in January 1944 to make a fateful decision. A
priest was needed for the Chinese Anglican Community in
Macao but because of the Japanese occupation of southern
China it was impossible for a member of the regular clergy to
get through. A deacon was already installed in Macao, however, and had been given special permission to celebrate the
Eucharist occasionally in these exceptional circumstances. This
troubled R. O. Hall, the Anglican Bishop of Hong Kong, who
believed that the liturgy should be celebrated correctly by a
fully ordained priest. For two days he and the deacon from
Macao prayed and talked together. Bishop Hall believed that he
could see the God-given charisma of priesthood in the deacon
and on 25 January, the feast of St Paul, 1944, in the small
southern Chinese town of Zhaoqing, he duly ordained her.

The deacon was Florence Tim Oi Li, one of the most zealous
members of the Chinese Church. Bishop Hall was aware that he
had taken a momentous step. He was no radical and had
thought long and hard before inviting Florence Li to meet him
at Xing Xing, so that they might decide together whether it was
indeed God's will that she be ordained a priest. In a letter
written two days after her ordination on St Paul's day, he wrote:

'I have had an amazing feeling of great conviction about this as if it was how God wanted it to happen.' He was entirely cut off from his brother bishops and unable to ask their advice. Nevertheless this wartime expedient seemed the best way of effecting the major innovation of ordaining the first Anglican woman to the priesthood. A formal registration before the event, Bishop Hall wrote in the same letter, 'could result in women who "claim the right to be priests" pressing into ordination even where there is no real need for them as priests'.[1]

The ordination of Florence Li was revolutionary but it was also deeply traditional. The three monotheistic religions had always been distinguished from such religions as Hinduism and Buddhism by the great significance they attached to history. From the time of Abraham, Jews, Christians and Muslims have believed that the divine imperative which they have called 'God' has revealed itself in current events in the mundane world. They have analysed history and have found a transcendent meaning in current events, in political catastrophe or victory, listening hard to the inner logic of what has happened. It is possible to see Bishop Hall contemplating the political situation of war-torn China to find a way forward in this manner. His decision had resulted in a deeply settled conviction: it was no mere superficial expedient. When the news of Florence Li's ordination broke on an astounded Anglican world after the war, there was, as one might expect, a deeply negative reaction. The ordination could not be undone, of course, since the 'character' of priesthood was indelible, but Geoffrey Fisher, Archbishop of Canterbury, demanded that Bishop Hall suspend Florence Li from office. Hall found that he could not in conscience comply. On 30 September 1945, he wrote to Fisher: 'I write with intense personal regret to say that I am unable to accept your advice. I must, therefore, as you ask, give my reasons in writing. I have only one reason. I acted in obedience to our Lord's commission. I do not believe that he wishes me to undo what I have done. That is my reason.'[2] The situation was saved by the Reverend Tim Oi Li herself. When she heard that Bishop Hall would probably have to resign, she voluntarily gave up her orders. She was a very tiny person, a mere worm, she said, and her influence was very small. The Bishop's position in the world was important. Her priesthood could never be erased but to enable him to continue in office, she would relinquish the name of priest while continuing her work for the Church.

But the Anglicans of Hong Kong were extremely upset by this repudiation. After the 1946 Synod of the Chinese Anglican Church, Bishop Hall sent out a circular letter to all the diocesan synods: 'Members of the Synod found the attitude of the Church in the West impossible to understand,' he wrote. 'The Reverend Lei Tim-Oi's ordination seemed to them natural and inevitable and her work as pastor has been quite outstanding. She has shown in life and ministry that God has given her the charisma of the parish priest.' He went on to argue that God was using China's age-old respect for women and traditional confidence in women's gifts for administration and pastoral care to 'open a new chapter in the history of the Church'. Western Churches had to learn to expect things like this to happen when Christianity took root in a civilization as old and as different as that of China. He had far too few priests as it was. Because of the provincial and limited views of the Churches back home, one of his pastors had been seriously limited in her work, 'and the whole Church in South China has been spiritually wounded and most grieved at heart. We consider such discrimination against women in the Church of Jesus Christ unreasonable, unChristian and unscriptural.'[3]

The controversy surrounding Florence Li's ordination set up a pattern that would be repeated in subsequent Anglican debates about women priests. The younger Churches, which were not hampered by centuries of Christian misogyny, would usually prove to be far more ready to accept the ordination of women than the Church of England itself. They often drew a parallel with the first-century dispute about the admission of gentile converts to the Jewish sect of the Nazarenes, which had threatened to split the primitive Church down the middle. The letters of St Paul and the Acts of the Apostles both make it clear that the mother Church in Jerusalem, headed by the Twelve Apostles, was deeply reluctant to break with centuries of Jewish tradition and admit gentiles, who had not been circumcised and did not observe the Law of Moses in its entirety. It was Paul's converts in the younger daughter Churches of the Jewish Diaspora, where Jews often had a more positive view of the *goyim*, who realized that it was time to break with tradition and make this revolutionary change. It was their view which ultimately prevailed. The Jewish Nazarenes died out and Christianity became a predominantly gentile religion.

One might have expected the Chinese Anglicans to have been horrified by the idea of women in a position of authority. We are all too aware in the West of the cruel practice of footbinding which had literally hobbled women and impeded their progress. But it is also true, as Bishop Hall had pointed out in 1946, that as in Jewish and Muslim society, women have been very influential in the Chinese family. In China there had been less emphasis on childbearing and more stress on the mother's pastoral role in teaching and counselling her children. The mother-in-law had always been a force to be reckoned with and women's authority was still important in the family. Chinese clergy naturally expected women priests to fulfil this role in the family of the Church. They had been particularly responsive to the restored Order of Deaconesses. After the 1920 Lambeth Conference had declared deaconesses to be in Holy Orders, the Anglican Church of China had moved quickly. In 1922 Dr J. Hind, Bishop of Fulkein, had six missionaries ordained as deaconesses. A few years later, the Synod of the Chinese Anglican Church went far beyond the 1920 Lambeth Conference and made new legislation. Canon XV now declared unequivocally that 'the ordination of a deaconess confers on a woman Holy Orders and this status is permanent'.[4] Like the male clergy, a deaconess in the Chinese province was henceforth an *ex officio* member of Synod, of the parish council and the vestry. In England, the Lambeth Council had only given deaconesses leave to preach occasionally, outside regular services. In China a deaconess could read and preach regularly in church and was also allowed to baptize women and girls.

It is important at this stage to note that the various provinces of the Anglican Church are not bound to the Church of England in the same way as Roman Catholics to the Vatican. The provinces of the United States, Australia, New Zealand, India,

China and Japan formed an alliance that was not dissimilar to the British Commonwealth. The Archbishop of Canterbury is not Supreme Pontiff but first among equals. The decisions of the Lambeth Conferences and the Anglican Consultative Committees are respected by the member Churches but are not obligatory; each province retains its independence, since no part of the Anglican Communion can impose a decision about faith and Church order on the others.

The Anglicans in China were frankly bewildered by the Western response to Florence Li's ordination. Christian missionaries had taught them that foot-binding was wrong and that the emancipation of women was a gospel value. They said that male and female were both created in God's image and were one in Christ. They saw women missionaries holding responsible public positions as teachers, nurses or college principals. The ordination of women seemed the next logical step, and the cries of dismay from the Church of England appeared unChristian. Why should they submit to this double-think? It is also important to note that the Chinese language did not encourage people to think of God as masculine. In Chinese all pronouns are pronounced in the same way, so that there is no means of distinguishing between male, female, an object, an animal or God except in writing. The divine was 'other', in a separate category beyond gender. 'It' might have become incarnate in Jesus Christ but could – and should – be represented by both male and female priests in order to express the whole mystery of divinity as fully as possible. Thus Chinese Christians did not have the same problems about gender and the divine as their brothers and sisters in the West.

During the 1950s, when the Churches of China were cut off from the West, they continued to recognize the ordination of Florence Li. She became a teacher of theology in the Christian Theological Seminary of Canton and when it was closed down in 1957 it was she who celebrated the last Eucharist there, vested as an Anglican priest. In the meantime, the Anglican Church of Hong Kong had become even more isolated, since it was no longer in contact with the Chinese Church. This Hong Kong diocese remained a pioneer in the ordination of women, way ahead of the Churches in the West. In 1958, with the enthusiastic support of his diocese, Bishop Hall ordained Jane Hwang as a full deacon – not just as a deaconess. Four years later he also conferred the diaconate on the English missionary Joyce Bennett. Since the diaconate was a step in the progress to the priesthood, both women were waiting in the wings, ready to take the final step when they got a green light from Canterbury. We shall hear more about Hwang and Bennett later in this chapter.

Meanwhile, in the West, those Christian denominations which had abandoned the institution of priesthood continued to ordain women as ministers. When a minister was not supposed to re-present Christ or officiate at a sacrificial liturgy, as in the Anglican, Roman Catholic and Greek Orthodox Churches, there was not the same resistance. Nevertheless these women ministers inevitably suffered from the sexist attitudes that informed the Churches as much as the rest of society. Their victory only revealed new problems. Women ministers generally faced longer periods of unemployment than their male contemporaries, lower salaries and few opportunities for responsibility. Since women in these Protestant congregations tended to be appointed one by one on the basis of their personal merits rather than by the decree of a synod or council, they were often having to fight an isolated battle for acceptance, cut off from one another. In the 1960s, the Reverend Ruth Matthews, a Baptist minister, was the only woman in her training college in Oxford:

> I did feel terribly discriminated against. Everything was oriented to the fact that they were all men; in small ways, like the rule saying you could not be alone with a *woman* in college, with the door shut. Pastoral problems were always dealt with from that angle and when I said, 'And how am *I* expected to deal with *men*' all I ever got was a big laugh from everybody. If you are the only woman at anything they will always make jokes. And when we were away at Conferences and things, they always had prayers for wives and families. And then I had the discrimination

of not finding a job, when everybody else was going to find one easily. You were told you were a problem.[5]

Matthews was the first Baptist minister in England to be allowed to continue her ministry after she got married: it was generally assumed that women ministers would be celibate – yet another instance of the distaste for female sexuality in Christianity. When she shared an appointment with her husband, who was also a minister, she would always be introduced as 'our minister's wife' though he was never introduced as 'our minister's husband'.

In the Anglican and Roman Catholic Churches there was little movement on the ordination question until the early 1960s. In 1959 Pope John XXIII summoned a general Council of the Roman Catholic Church to Rome to begin a programme of *aggiornamento*, renewal. Even though only one woman was invited as an observer, the St Joan's Alliance, a Catholic women's organization, submitted this request to the Second Vatican Council:

> The St Joan's Alliance re-affirms its loyalty and filial devotion and expresses its conviction that should the Church in her wisdom and her good time decide to extend to women the dignity of the priesthood, women would be willing and eager to respond.[6]

There was little official response to this modestly worded statement but some of the more radical nuns and theologians began to marshal arguments for the cause and, as we shall see, some fourteen years later forced the Vatican to confront the issue. In the early 1960s, it seemed that Roman Catholic women would probably be ordained before their Anglican sisters in England and the United States, but even here there were signs of incipient change. Thus in 1956 the Episcopal Theological School in Cambridge, Massachusetts, decided to admit women to the degree courses that trained male candidates to the priesthood. In this way a body of theologically qualified women was ready and waiting to act twenty years later.

In England the question of women priests was reintroduced as a topic of Anglican debate by a rather different route. In 1962, a small committee headed by the Dean of Westminster produced a report entitled *Gender and Ministry*. Inevitably it mentioned ordination to the priesthood but its prime object was to ensure that women parish workers were paid a decent salary. By asking what women should be and do in the Anglican Church, the report noted an ambiguity of attitude which needed to be cleared up. There was still confusion about the Order of Deaconesses, for example: were they or were they not in Holy Orders? Obviously women were physically and intellectually capable of performing some of the duties of a priest, such as celebrating the Eucharist and blessing the congregation, but the fact remained that they were not called to a sacramental ministry in the Church of England. What were the real reasons for this exclusion? The report concluded:

> We think that the various reasons for this withholding of the ordained and representative priesthood from women, reasons theological, traditional, instinctive, anthropological, social, emotional, should be much more thoroughly examined.[7]

Even the knowledge that this question had been reopened would 'lessen the sense of frustration from which many of the most able women in the Church are suffering today'.[8]

The committee which had prepared the report included Mother Clare, the Superior of the Deaconess Order of St Andrew, and Christian Howard, who would play a leading role in the ensuing debate about the ordination of women, even though she herself did not feel called to the priesthood. The daughter of a suffragist – though not, she is careful to add, a suffragette – Howard had studied for the Lambeth diploma in theology during the 1930s as a young woman of twenty-three and had become a teacher and a lay worker in the Church. As Secretary of the Board of Women's Work in the Church, she had long been concerned about the muddle and inconsistency that prevented Anglican women from being used to the best advantage. Did the Church want women to work for it or not?

In the York province, for example, women had been allowed to read and preach at church services since 1950, but this was not permitted in the southern province of Canterbury until 1964. Deaconesses were not allowed to read or preach anywhere, even in the York province, because of some outdated legislation. It was still not at all clear whether they were in Holy Orders or not. These questions needed serious consideration, since the muddle threatened both the efficiency and the integrity of the Church.

The *Gender and Ministry* report was discussed in the Church Assembly on 7 November 1962. The Dean of Westminster opened the debate by explaining that the committee was well aware that by opening up the controversial question of the ordination of women, it was asking Anglicans to address an issue that 'went down very deep below their rational selves to their instinctive selves'. What might seem to be mere prejudice could be attributed to those 'fears' and 'instinctive reactions' which were shared not only by priests and lay men but also by women themselves. He was careful to stress that the report had not proposed that women *should* be admitted to the priesthood but that the group 'would not dare to say that never, *never*, in the future history of Christendom as a whole could women enter upon Holy Orders!'[9] The Anglican Church of New Delhi had also asked that the matter be discussed; the whole Church must remain open to the guidance of the Holy Spirit. The Assembly should note that the bulk of the report was concerned with the priesthood of the whole Church, however. The groups simply asked that women be allowed to perform the same functions as lay men, who were allowed to read and preach in church. Traditionally there were four orders in the Church of England: bishops, priests, deacons and laity; at present, because of these anomalies, there were in fact five: bishops, priests, deacons, lay men and women.

Dr O. W. H. Clark, who would become a veteran of the opposition, feared that women would not be content with the right to speak in church and lead the congregation in prayer: the next thing would be an outright demand for the priesthood. The Reverend H. Cooper of London dismissed the phrase 'priesthood of the laity' as nonsense. Women had many ways of serving God: 'in maternity, housework or whatever it might be'. The report had suggested that there was no theological reason to exclude women from the priesthood, but it was wrong. The doctrine of Creation, which declared women to be subject to men, made this perfectly clear and he 'hoped on any future committee there would be somebody who understood these things'.[10] The tone as well as the dubious theology of this effusion convinced many members of the Church Assembly that a new committee should look carefully and objectively into all the reasons – theological, traditional, instinctive, anthropological, social and emotional – against the ordination of women as priests.

This report, *Women in Holy Orders*, was published in 1966 and discussed in the Church Assembly on two occasions in the following year. The debate was given new urgency by a similar report which had been presented in July 1966 to the Methodist Conference. The Methodists had come to the conclusion that there were no valid theological objections against women priests and had affirmed that 'women may properly be ordained to the ministry of the Word and Sacraments'. They did not want to act unilaterally, however, and asked for discussions with the Church of England. *Women in Holy Orders* was less decisive than the Methodist report. It decided that it was impossible to find conclusive evidence for or against ordaining women to the priesthood. It appended a report by one Dr Demant, which argued that since God was conceived as male and the Logos or Word of God was a male principle, it might not be appropriate for women to represent the divine as priests. Even though the whole Christian tradition is unanimous that God is beyond gender and that both male and female were created in God's image, this question has continued to surface throughout the debate and touches something fundamental in the Christian psyche. Dr Demant had gone so far as to say: 'To have a twin priesthood of males and females could be more disruptive of the Christian Church than any doctrinal heresy or deviation. That is because we are here dealing not only with the conscious, intellectual and ethical side of Christianity but with the deep-hidden roots from which religions and their distinctions spring.'[11] The issue of God's masculinity and the abhorrence experienced by many people for the idea of women priests touched the personal sexual identity of each member of the Church of England, clerical or lay, male or female. This was an area that could not – and possibly still cannot – be assuaged by logical arguments from scripture, since it lay far below the rational and cerebral. Questions of sexuality and gender had been problematic for centuries within Christianity and had produced some bizarre and aberrant behaviour, as we have seen.

The profound unease that many felt at the mere thought of a woman priest presiding at the altar was abundantly clear in the debate on the report in the Church Assembly, which took place in February and July 1967. A lay woman like Mrs M. A. Rawlinson could admit that there was no logical reason for the exclusion of women from priesthood, but 'I am against it, so deep is my prejudice or instinct, which I think common to my generation.'[12] Prebendary J. H. B. Andrews told the Assembly that women often preached in his church in North Devon and were received with admiration and approval. 'However, I am advised that a woman priest speaking as a woman from the pulpit would appear very different from a woman as a priest at the altar,' he explained, going to the heart of the question. 'I do not think that people would be able to say why. They would only say that it would not seem right or that they did not like the idea.'[13] Miss P. M. C. Evans from Winchester admitted that hackles would rise at the thought of a woman taking the Eucharist. But this was a prejudice and in other matters, on questions of race and colour, for example, we tried not to let our prejudice overcome our Christian behaviour. The Church should try to help people overcome this instinctive revulsion by getting them used to the idea gradually. Why not let a deaconess administer the chalice, like the male deacons?

This instinctive repugnance must always be borne in mind when the question of the ordination of women is discussed. For centuries, as we have seen, women and their sexuality had been regarded askance in Western Christendom; women had been demonized and linked with evil in the Christian imagination.

The inability to deal with these facts of life in a balanced way had been a symptom of a profound dis-ease in the Christian psyche that seemed part of the Western mentality. As the debate about women priests progressed, people would often speak of their whole faith, their entire world view being radically undermined by the idea. This fear and horror had long excluded women from the sacred, and the suggestion that they now be allowed to enter the Holy of Holies was – and remains – profoundly disturbing. But the issue was crucial for thousands of women in the Church. As Mrs M. B. Ridley explained, because women were debarred from the priesthood, the Church of England had somehow been unable to develop any full-scale ministry for women. This had a depressing effect on the position of Christian women in almost any situation. Who could believe in a God who discriminated between the sexes in such a way?

Some tried to stave off the evil hour by pleading that the time was not ripe for such a catastrophic change; it would split the Church asunder and damage ecumenical relations with the Roman Catholic and Greek Orthodox Churches. But others rose to insist that this was a matter of urgency. In an impassioned speech, Miss V. J. Pitt of Southwark told the Assembly that the remarks she had heard about women in the course of this debate had made her angry. 'The wholesale rejection of a call to the ministry for a particular sex is a very serious matter,' she insisted. 'It is a grave responsibility for the Church to say to its members, "No, you are under an illusion" . . . knowing that this will inflict misery upon the persons who feel themselves to be so called.'[14] The Church could not take this responsibility unless it could prove conclusively that women must for ever be debarred from the priesthood. Many delegates had pleaded that ordaining women went against two thousand years of Christian history, had argued that only the lunatic fringe had considered women suitable for the priesthood. But this appeal to the past was based on a common Anglican fallacy. Anglicans took history seriously; they maintained that their particular form of Christianity was the result of historical events in the sixteenth and seventeenth centuries. 'Because our faith is rooted in history', Miss Pitt concluded, Anglicans often believed 'that history is theological'.[15] Thus two of the delegates had argued, quoting Genesis and St Paul, that a woman could not be the head of a man. She herself was head of a division and had five men working under her. Was she therefore in a state of sin? How would they have fared if they had dared to argue thus with Queen Elizabeth I? We constantly reinterpret our relationship with God, and a slavish reliance on historical tradition is harmful and destructive if it imprisons us in outmoded patterns of thought.

Two academic theologians made an important contribution. The Reverend Professor G. W. H. Lampe of Cambridge University also believed that the Church had hesitated over this matter for too long. There were no good theological reasons against the ordination of women. Even St Paul had been hard pressed to find adequate reasons for insisting that women wear veils when prophesying: 'When he has ploughed his way through some obscure theological argument, in the end he is reduced to saying "We have no such custom."'[16] Professor Lampe rather suspected that some of the so-called theological arguments against ordaining women that had been raised during the debate were a similar attempt to ward off innovation. Some of these arguments were based on an anachronistic view of history, as, for example, that there were no women among the Twelve. If the Assembly could not find conclusive arguments against the ordination of women, it should come clean and say so! In its July session, Professor Lampe proposed the motion that 'this Assembly, believing that there are no conclusive theological reasons why women should not be ordained to the priesthood but recognizing that it would not be wise to take unilateral action at this time',[17] would welcome further discussion with the Methodists and any other Church ready to enter into a dialogue. Professor Derek Nineham, also of Cambridge University, noted that this motion was very cautious. The Assembly should ask: 'Is there something about woman as such which makes it for ever contrary to the will of God that a woman be ordained to the priesthood?'[18] In his view, this was 'a terrible belief'. St Paul had said that in Christ there was neither Jew nor gentile, male nor female. 'If I meet a Jewish Christian and say there is no difference between us except that I can be a bishop or a priest but you cannot', is it then 'a sensible thing to say it to a woman?'[19]

People did not take history seriously enough, Nineham argued. God could not have become incarnate in a woman in the context of the first century, nor could he have depended upon female apostles. But times changed, often radically. At the present time, they were witnessing a liberation of women that was new and irreversible. There was no going back. Paul's observation in Galatians 3:28 meant that he 'could already see all that was involved in what Christ had done and been'. But

> It took the Church a long time to realize the practical implications of this even in regard to Jew and Gentile, and still longer to realize with regard to slave and free, and I believe that it has taken even longer to see the implications with regard to male or female as we are being asked to do now.[20]

The analogy with the abolition of slavery in the nineteenth century would often be drawn by supporters of women priests in ensuing years. Nineham concluded with another argument that was to become central in the debate. He did not believe that it was correct that the nature of God demanded a male priesthood, as was sometimes suggested. True, some aspects of the divine nature, such as Fatherhood, could only be represented by male priests, but there were other aspects of the divine life and affection 'which are better, or it may be only, represented by the female sex'.[21]

Throughout the debates, opponents of women priests referred to scriptural arguments that had been used again and again to keep women in an inferior position in the Churches. They pointed to the 'headship' doctrine: that Eve had been created after Adam and that after the Fall her punishment had been subjection to her husband. They referred to St Paul's prescriptions in 1 Corinthians about 'headship' and veils and referred to the verses that bade women keep silent in church meetings. They had argued, as Professor Nineham had pointed out, that as God was predominantly masculine and Jesus a man who had chosen only male apostles, only a traditional male priesthood was acceptable. But during the 1967 debates, there were signs that some were finding these arguments inadequate and irrelevant. As Mr R. S. Catmur of Bath and Wells pointed out: 'We who are in business have managed to keep women out so far, but they are coming in and we are going to have to put up with them.' It was pointless digging up texts to argue about: 'This is not theology; it is archaeology.'[22] The early Church had not proceeded by dredging up quotations to justify their innovations but had depended on the Holy Spirit. In this matter, the Church needed new insight, a new vision.

The motion was not carried but events were moving the Church forward almost against its will. Professor Nineham seemed to have been right in saying that the liberation of women – even in the Churches – was irreversible. In 1968 women were permitted to be elders in the Church of Scotland, a bastion of patriarchy, and the Lambeth Conference of Bishops put the ordination of women on to the agenda of the Anglican Churches. In the debate on 'Women and the Priesthood', Bishop Gerald Ellison of Chester reminded the Conference of the depressing effect a negative statement would have on the women in the Church. They were being lost to the pastoral ministry largely because the Church seemed to find it impossible to give them a responsible place in its life. Bishop Leonard Wilson of Birmingham, who had once worked with Bishop Hall of Hong Kong, recalled that everybody had a great deal of womanhood as well as manhood in his or her nature: the Church needed a whole ministry and was at present deprived of the great contribution that could be made by half its members. Bishop John Gilbert Baker, who had succeeded R. O. Hall in Hong Kong, showed that they had come a long way in the Church since the ordination of Florence Li: the resolution on the order paper circulated before the debate had found 'no conclusive theological reasons for withholding ordination to the priesthood from women as such'.

As one might expect, many of the bishops were not ready for this. Instead, the Lambeth Conference of 1968 passed an amended resolution saying that 'the theological arguments as at present presented for and against the ordination of women to the priesthood are inconclusive'. Church tradition was an important source of authority and guidance for Anglicans, as for Roman Catholics. They did not rely on scripture alone like the Protestant denominations. Consequently many argued that an all-male priesthood, an unbroken tradition of nearly 2000 years, was basic and binding. But the Conference also issued a report stating that Anglicans did not accept tradition blindly: any good teaching authority 'refuses to insulate itself from the testing of history and the free action of reason'. Supporters of women priests argued that an exclusively male priesthood was a peculiar tradition since it was based on a mistaken belief that the Bible taught the inferiority of women.The Lambeth Conference concluded that since ancient and medieval assumptions about the social role and inferior status of women were no longer acceptable, the appeal to tradition is 'virtually reduced to the observation that there happens to be no precedent for ordaining women to be priests'. As a final thought, the bishops added this telling maxim: 'The New Testament does not encourage Christians to think that nothing can be done for the first time.'[23]

There were four other related resolutions of a practical nature. First, each province of the Church should study the question of the ordination of women carefully and report their findings to the Anglican Consultative Committee (ACC). Second, the ACC would initiate discussions with Churches which did ordain women to ministry and with those which did not. Third, before a province made a final decision to ordain women to the priesthood, it should seek the advice of the ACC. Fourth, in the meantime, qualified women should be allowed to preach, baptize, read the lessons at Holy Communion and help to distribute the bread and wine.

The Church of Hong Kong, which had long been eager to have women priests, saw this as the sign they had been waiting for, but Bishop Baker was careful to fulfil all four of the above requirements. The various parishes of his diocese studied the question carefully and reported back to the Diocesan Synod in January 1970. Only two of the twenty-one parishes had not responded and all but one of the parishes which did respond either had a majority in favour or were unanimously in favour of women priests. The one dissentient voice, ironically, was

Macao, Florence Li's old parish: there the Church had suffered much from the terror of the Cultural Revolution and had received great support from the Roman Catholics; it was anxious not to disturb these good relations by ordaining women. Next, Hong Kong asked the ACC for permission to ordain the first women priests at its first meeting after Lambeth at Limuru, Kenya. This was passed by twenty-four votes to twenty-two, the balance being tipped by the African bishops whom many had expected to be against the idea. In fact the Africans had taken the matter very calmly, saying that the prospect of women priests seemed more of a problem to the Western Churches than to themselves. Professor Mbiti of Makevere University cited the various African cultures which gave women leadership roles.

As a result of this almost unanimous vote of confidence, Bishop Baker began to prepare for the ordination of his two women deacons, Jane Hwang and Joyce Bennett. Both were highly qualified for the priesthood, far more so than many men. Jane Hwang was fifty years old, had university degrees in theology, had built up St Thomas's parish from scratch in a densely populated resettlement area and since 1967 had been vicar of Holy Trinity, Kowloon, one of the largest parishes in Hong Kong. Joyce Bennett had been a missionary in China since 1949, had a London university degree in theology and had built up a new style of education for Chinese girls in the College of Kulun Tong. Nevertheless the decision to ordain these two women was controversial and caused dismay in most other Anglican Churches. This was the thin end of the wedge with a vengeance, since henceforth, whatever anybody said, there would be two legally ordained women priests in the Anglican communion.

Bishop Baker was not a radical by temperament. He was known as a quiet, cautious and indecisive man. His daughter used to say that he found it almost impossible to decide what train to catch or what kind of wallflowers to plant. But on this major decision, he had absolutely no doubts: he felt that he was simply the agent of the inevitable. Later he used to say simply, 'I could do no other.' On 28 November 1971, he ordained Jane

Hwang and Joyce Bennett in the Anglican Cathedral of Hong Kong.

In the United States, the Episcopal Church was also moving inexorably towards ordaining women candidates to the priesthood, though it would proceed by a more revolutionary route. For a decade there had been theologically qualified women who by 1970 were equipped to fight the apathy and reluctance of the male hierarchy. In 1970 hopes were high: that year women were allowed to become full members of the General Convention of the Episcopal Church and deaconesses were declared to be on a par with deacons. Since the diaconate was traditionally a step *en route* to the priesthood, many women assumed that it would soon be possible for them to become priests. But in 1973 these hopes were dashed when the General Convention of Louisville voted against the ordination of women. This was particularly hard to accept since it had been achieved by a technicality. A majority of members had been in favour but the motion was defeated by a voting procedure.

The American opponents of women priests were vocal and passionate. The Reverend George Rutler of Pennsylvania could not countenance a sacramental role for women. He seemed to see salvation in highly sexual terms. A priest could act as God's instrument since his maleness was 'a symbol of the seminal initiative of God'. God 'had singled him out in his maleness to be Christ for the people, the summation of the naked man before his mother at Golgotha and the white-robed man before the harlot [sic] in the Garden'. Sexuality was inseparable from the Eucharist, Rutler concluded. A priest with an 'identity crisis' would be one who did not understand that his central job was 'to be a man at the altar'.[24] There had always been a bias against women priests in monotheism, since they recalled the pagan priestesses of antiquity, but in seeing the priest as a stand-in for Christ in such literal terms, Rutler had more in common with the old cults than with St Paul. American opponents of women's ministry seemed to see initiative as an exclusively male attribute. Women, presumably, were essentially passive and receptive – a gross over-simplification in the 1970s. Of course God was not male, wrote Bishop Kilmer-Myers of

California in October 1971. The male imagery simply symbolized God's initiative of salvation. The priest 'partakes of Christ's
priesthood, which is generative, initiating, giving. The generative function is plainly a masculine kind of imagery, making
priesthood a masculine conception.'[25] The Reverend A. J.
Dubois went so far as to say that because 'the male has the
initiative in creation', the sacrament of Holy Orders could only
be effective for a male human being. Anybody could validly say
'Bless us', but to say 'Bless this' was 'to initiate a creation. In this
the male priest reflects the creative activity of God the Father.'[26]
There is an almost pagan sense in these arguments of the divine
fructifying the world through the sexual channels of temple
priests, were it not for the fact that there are no priestesses in
this scheme, no balancing female activity.

The decision of the Louisville Convention enraged some of
the men as well as the women. Forty bishops called it an abuse
of moral justice, and there was much ferment. Some believed
that since the ordination of women was not expressly forbidden
by canon law, it would be permissible to proceed independently. The General Convention was supposed to represent
the whole Church, but at Louisville women had been under-
represented: only 14 per cent of the lay delegates had been
women. Leading Churchmen such as Dr Charles Willie, Vice-
President of the House of Deputies, and Edward Harris, Dean
of the Philadelphia Divinity School, called for immediate ordinations. Finally, on 29 July 1974, the feast day of Martha of Bethany,
eleven women were ordained as priests by three bishops who
had retired from office. Instead of waiting for further study and
endless vacillation, American women and their friends had
simply decided to act and make women priests a reality.

Deacon Ellen Warburg had chosen not to be priested that
day. Like all the candidates, she knew that this revolutionary
act would probably make any normal priestly ministry in the
Episcopal Church impossible. There would be reprisals and
black lists. But on the day of the ordinations, Warburg denied
that she had chosen the 'better part', like Mary of Bethany.
These illegal ordinations were a prophetic act, which had given
women like herself a new voice. Nobody would be interested
otherwise in what she had to say, she told a Press Conference:

Were it not for my sisters and their radical, shocking
obedience to God's claim upon their lives – an obedience
which gives dramatic witness to the urgency of our common vocation to priesthood and summons the whole
Church to attention – there would be few to hear me or
take seriously my own deep sense of having been called to
priestly ordination.[27]

One of the ordinands, Emily Hewitt, saw the ceremony as the
end of her priestly ministry. She believed that at Philadelphia
God had asked her to give up her personal vocation for the sake
of the cause. Afterwards she entered law school and has never
performed a priestly, sacramental act.

At Philadelphia women had shown that they could also take
the initiative and that their submission to what they saw as
God's will must come before obedience to mere men. In August
1974, the House of Bishops met at Chicago and declared the
ordinations invalid. But many theologians, Roman Catholic as
well as Anglican, believed that the bishops were incorrect. The
Philadelphia ordinations were certainly irregular but it was by
no means clear that they had been invalid. The Jesuit Franz
Joseph Van Beeck, for example, compared them to the baptisms
performed in the third century by the Donatist heretics, which
the Church had pronounced valid. The bishops may not have
complied with the letter of canon law but they had the power to
ordain and the right intention. In September 1974, Bishop
George Barrett showed his independence of the Chicago decision by ordaining four women in Washington, DC. The
momentum seemed unstoppable. The new women priests celebrated the Eucharist all over the country. Finally, at the 65th
General Convention of the Episcopal Church at Minneapolis in
1976, a majority of delegates in both houses declared that
women had the right to be ordained. Some Episcopalians
pleaded that they could not in conscience accept women
priests. Bishop John Allin, for example, declared that women
could no more be priests than husbands or fathers. Consequently, the bishops revived the old 'conscience clause', giving
individual bishops the right to refuse ordination to a woman.

In America Roman Catholic women were no less active. Some were even more radical than the Episcopalians. Theologians like Rosemary Radford Ruether and Elizabeth Schussler Fiorenza declared sexism to be a sin. It was pointless admitting token women to the clerical caste. In the Protestant Churches which had ordained women ministers, the women were forced to shore up the old patriarchal, sexist attitudes. Priesthood itself had become corrupt: it had been disfigured by power. The priority was to restore the old Christian ideal of *diakonia*. This was no passive idealism, however. In 1976 Catholic women organized an impressive Conference on Women and Orders at Detroit, on a scale which would have been impossible for women in other denominations. Roman Catholics had the advantage of nuns who had been radicalized by the Second Vatican Council and were already mobilized and ready for international group action. The Detroit Conference forced the Vatican to respond. In January 1977, the Pope issued *Inter Insigniores*, its *Declaration on the Question of the Admission of Women to the Ministerial Priesthood*. Women could not be ordained, since they did not have a 'natural resemblance' to the maleness of Christ. Jesus's own choice of male disciples had revealed the divine will once and for all.

Like any of the theories that made biology and the 'Y' chromosome the chief qualifications for priesthood, the declaration was on shaky ground. The stress on the physical resemblance of male priests to Christ focused on gender in a way that seems almost obscene and obsessive. As theologians like Rosemary Radford Ruether have tirelessly pointed out, if taken logically, it would mean that women could not be baptized 'into Christ' either. It was a fundamental denial of the universality of the salvation wrought by the Incarnation which had declared that *nothing* human was marginal or profane. To push women on to the sidelines of the divine plan was not merely the result of a slightly prurient concentration on Christ's masculinity but was totally opposed to the spirit of the Gospels.

There were no such dramatic initiatives in the Church of England. As the British feminist writer Sara Maitland has observed, in England the sense of personal vocation to the priesthood is balanced by a strong sense of the necessity for that call to be ratified by the community. This collegial or communal view of the Church and priesthood was stronger in Britain than in the United States, where a more individualistic sense of calling prevailed, perhaps because of the ideal of the pursuit of happiness enshrined in the Constitution. In 1973, after the Louisville Convention had refused to ordain women, Donald Belcher, a lay deputy, had risen to his feet:

> I rise on a point of personal privilege. There is a priest in the diocese of Pennsylvania who has counselled many of us lovingly and wisely . . . two nights ago I sat alone and wondered what I could possibly say to that loving and wise priest . . . I decided I would say 'thank you for your gifts so far. . . . Do not despair, Suzanne Hiatt, for in God's eyes you are a priest indeed.'[28]

A woman like Suzanne Hiatt, one of the Philadelphia Eleven, believed that she was a priest because of her intense inner conviction: this could only be ratified by the Church. In England there was a greater sense that a future priest must also be called by the Church and community – a view that has a long tradition in Christianity.

As in the United States, there were many bishops, priests and lay people who were passionately opposed to the ordination of women. Much of the opposition was fuelled by that instinctive repugnance we have already noted, and was frankly admitted by those who spoke against women priests in the Church debates during the 1970s. But they also had theological reasons. The two key arguments remained those of 'headship' and 'representation'. Evangelically inclined Anglicans, whose faith was based on a careful and and often literal reading of the Bible, tended to cite the 'headship' doctrine. Anglo-Catholics, who had a 'higher' conception of priesthood, stressed the argument that a woman priest could not represent the male Christ at the altar. Those who supported the ordination of women could point to such texts as Galatians 3:28 and urged that far from departing from Anglican tradition, the ordination of women would continue a deeply Christian bias towards egalitarianism.

They liked to look back at the decision to admit gentiles to the primitive Church. When St Peter had visited the Roman centurion Cornelius, who had asked for baptism, he had been profoundly perplexed. Admitting uncircumcised *goyim* into the Jewish sect went against his whole religious tradition, but he had come to the conclusion that 'God does not have favourites but that anybody of any nationality who fears God and does what is right is acceptable to him'.[29] As he spoke, the Holy Spirit had descended upon Cornelius and his household, ratifying this decision. Anglicans were faced with a similar decision, one which seemed to go against centuries of Christian tradition but which was God's will and would give new life and vitality to the Church.

The ordinations in Hong Kong in 1971 inevitably caused much heart-searching in the English Church. Christian Howard produced a balanced report and recalled that in general the Synod was pleased with her paper, which was debated on 8 November 1972, to decide whether the Church of England was still in communion with Hong Kong. Professor Lampe agreed with Howard that this was not a question of the rights of women: it was primarily a question about the Church, the Sacraments and the essence of the Christian vocation. For centuries, Christians had stressed the deep relationship that existed between the ministry of the Word and the ministry of the Sacraments. Traditionally, women had been unable to celebrate either in an active capacity but now women were permitted to read and preach during services. Yet they were still blocked from a sacramental ministry. Was it necessary for the sex difference to interpose a wedge between the Word and the Sacraments in this way? Baptism admitted both men and women into the priestly body of Christ on equal terms but a man could celebrate the Eucharist and give a blessing, and a woman could not. Was this sensible, just or consistent? An increasing number of women believed that they had received an inner call to the priesthood but they had not been called by the Church to exercise it. It was most important to work out a satisfactory way of relating the private and public aspects of vocation.

Yet there was fierce opposition. As Prebendary H. Riley argued, some questions, such as Sunday observance or monogamy, were not prescribed by the New Testament or Church Councils but were nevertheless 'deep down in the Christian lifestyle'.[30] The male priesthood was one of these. Why were there women prophets, queens and sages in the Old Testament, asked Prebendary H. Cooper of London, but no priestesses? Men and women had different vocations and different qualities. Men were cautious and more stable emotionally, while

> It is clear that a woman's character and her endowments centre much more normally and obviously upon home and family and she has those quick emotions which enable her to care for and to cherish children and make the home happy, although this is not to say that she could never go beyond it.[31]

He could not serve the Church in Hong Kong and would have to resign his orders if the Church of England decided to ordain women. Mrs U. Spencer Ellis of Carlisle agreed. It was blasphemous to suggest that Jesus Christ would have appointed women as apostles if he had been born in another time. Motherhood was a woman's true vocation and 'that she should wish to become a priest is an insult to her nature'. The priest before the altar was entirely sexless but 'to think of a woman in that position is quite wrong. I could not accept it.'[32] Miss L. M. Pobjoy of Wakefield also subscribed to the strange belief that a man could be detached from his gender in a way that women could not. It was this ability

> to stand before the altar as a representative of a sexless God, stripped of his sexuality, or, if you like, of his specific masculinity, which speaks to the most basic instincts of so many worshippers, and which causes them to feel appalled – I do not think this is too strong a word – at the prospect of a woman celebrating the Eucharist.[33]

Both Spencer Ellis and Pobjoy professed to believe that women were in many ways superior to men, but their contributions reveal a profound unease with their sexuality, which made them fall back on such old prejudices as 'all women from time to time are at the mercy of their hormones' and 'all women are basically in competition with men'.[34] The Churches had long tended to oversexualize women and had made Christians acutely conscious of their 'concupiscential parts', as Augustine had put it. The debate showed that in the post-Freudian period, the old myths were still alive and well.

The women's movement was in its infancy in Britain in 1972. Soon, as we shall see, this type of argument would be dropped from the opposition's agenda, but it is likely that the old feelings of dread and disgust have remained, subliminally. Mrs M. R. Ridley urged Synod to remember that these old feelings could change. She vividly recalled the prejudice against women doctors which had been common in her youth; but now people had come round to the idea. Referring to the 'headship' doctrine, she had been disturbed to note that some of the literature circulated before the debate had said categorically that the Bible forbade women to have authority over men. But the emancipation of women had been proceeding apace for decades. If this teaching was really so clear and fundamental, why had the Churches remained silent? They had reached a point where two of the countries with some of the greatest problems of the world now had women prime ministers:

> Surely this doctrine is so fundamental that it should have been proclaimed earlier, even if we failed to influence the world in this regard, and not saved up to be used now as an argument against the earth-shattering possibility that a woman may be Vicar of Much-Binding-in-the-Marsh in 1980 or Bishop of St Oggs in the year 2000?[35]

Of course there were problems of a practical nature, but women would be able to work them out and evolve their own style of priesthood as they had already done in the other professions.

Mr T. L. Dye of York had found some anomalies in the opposition arguments. Jesus had said that nobody should be called 'Father' or 'Lord': those titles were reserved for God alone. We were told that there were excellent sociological reasons for this departure from gospel principle, but when considering the ordination of women, delegates were told to take no heed of sociological arguments. He was also distressed by the *tone* of some of the contributions. Women, it was said, should not be priests because their God-given role was to follow, assist and submit. The attitude seemed to be: 'We are the Church and you have got to do as we say!' But was that a truly Christian stance? Jesus had come to serve. Was this triumphalism the reason why the churches were emptying? In the New Testament, people had not hunted for quotations to prove that gentiles should be admitted to the Church. The clinching evidence had been that the *goyim* had in fact received the Holy Spirit. So too today. God had already made up his mind. The Church had already seen the Spirit at work in women missionaries, for example. Ministers did not receive their authority from their masculinity but from the Holy Spirit.

At the end of the day, Synod voted non-committally to take notice of Christian Howard's report. But three years later, in 1975, the year after the Philadelphia ordinations, it was clear that the issue of women priests would not go away. The Church of England had to formulate its own position. Accordingly, on 3 July, Synod debated the motion 'that there are no fundamental objections to the ordination of women to the priesthood'. It was proposed by the Bishop of Oxford, who drew the attention of Synod to Christian Howard's maxim: it was not there to discuss women's rights but to further the gospel. All major changes in the past – the admission of gentiles, the Reformation and the abolition of slavery – had been based on a changing perception of the nature of God. The same applied today. 'To be truly representative of humanity,' the Bishop argued, 'I believe that the priesthood must be open to both sexes.'[36] We could no longer think of Creation in the same way as our forebears: few members of Synod believed that Adam and Eve had walked out of the Garden of Eden in 4004 BCE. 'The absolute distinction between the sexes, and the refusal to ordain them, had a parochial ring. It lacks the humility of a scientist's openness to the undisclosed mysteries of the universe.'[37] In the current debate, some, like Dr Demant in 1966, had argued that the Logos was a masculine principle; others had referred to Dame

Julian's God the Mother. But gender could only be applied analogically to the divine. New Testament writers like St Paul had seen the Incarnation in eschatological rather than historical terms: Jesus was not a divinized male but represented a new kind of humanity. Instead of claiming that priests should be men, we should learn to look ahead to the apotheosis of the New Creation in Christ when there would no longer be male or female. In this perspective, it was valid to have women as priests. How could the Church in charity deny women's request for ordination? People often said that it would damage the ecumenical relationship of the Church of England with other Churches, but if Synod believed that it was theologically correct to ordain women to the priesthood, it had a duty to say so to the Roman Catholics and the Greek Orthodox.

The Bishop of Chichester, who opposed the motion, believed that the comparison with the Reformation and the abolition of slavery was misleading. Synod had never been asked to make such a major break with tradition: 'What we are concerned with is a fundamental change in the Christian ministry as received from Christ and his Apostles and as handed down to our own day.'[38] There was passionate agreement from the floor. Mr G. E. Driffield argued that there *was* fundamental theological objection to the ordination of women: there had been no women among the Twelve; there were Paul's letters to the Corinthians and to Timothy. Those who supported the motion had brushed the Bible aside to pander pathetically to the fashionable doctrines of Women's Lib. The Bishop of Truro insisted that 'The Incarnation was in a male and I believe that it was left to our Lord to represent God.'[39] The Gospels showed that women had different vocations: they depicted the 'headship' of the male Christ in the service of the Cross and the motherhood of Mary.

In a thoughtful speech, the Archbishop of Canterbury could find no clear pattern of ministry in the New Testament. The early Church had been flexible, open to the new truth. Were they in danger of circumscribing the Spirit? The Archbishop asked Synod to consider the position of a deaconess counselling a dying person who eventually asked for the Eucharist. What precisely was it at that point that made it impossible for the deaconess to minister to her sister, who might not have the strength to start all over again with somebody else? This was the nub. He imagined an intelligent woman graduate who felt called to the priesthood, asking for her vocation to be tested. Was he to answer: 'No, you may not!' The thought caused him grave and deep anxiety.

The motion was carried at the end of the debate: Synod assented that there were no fundamental theological objections to the ordination of women to the priesthood but it rejected a further motion that proposed to set legislation in motion to allow this to happen. Consequently, the Synod debated the question yet again in 1978, two years after the Episcopal Church had admitted women to the priesthood. This time the motion, which again proposed removing legal barriers to women priests, was proposed by the Bishop of Birmingham, who reminded Synod that it had already ruled out the possibility of their being grave theological objections. It was a matter of truth, therefore, and truth must be paramount. As it was, the legislative process would take a good five years to come into effect. God was neither male nor female. The Greek Fathers of the Church had insisted that the Word had become *anthropos* (Man), not *aner* (male). It was, therefore, humanity not maleness that enabled a priest to re-present God to the people and the people to God. If it was to be truly representative, male and female priests were needed. There were already women priests in the Anglican Church: no decision of Synod could change that. The Roman Catholics would simply have to take Anglicans as they were. More time was needed? People always said that. The Church of England could not tolerate such difference of opinion between those who accepted women priests and those who did not? Why not? The primitive Church had been able to accommodate James, Jesus's brother, who had kept all 613 commandments of the Torah, as well as Paul, who had wanted to jettison it. Surely the Church of England could be similarly flexible?

In opposition, the Bishop of Truro argued that the issue was too big for Anglicans to decide alone. He quoted Archbishop Fisher: 'We have no doctrine of our own – we only profess the catholic doctrine of the Catholic Church.' Those who wanted women priests seemed ready to eviscerate scripture, seeing

Jesus and Paul as culturally conditioned and the Fatherhood of God a human creation. But as the 1662 Ordinal made clear, the priest represented the 'headship' of Christ; he was not a human leader, like the Queen. Jesus had been born a man in order to reflect the order instituted by God, in which 'headship' and authority were associated with maleness. If women became priests, this natural God-given symbolism would be confused and would evoke an entirely new response to God.

Professor D. R. Jones, of Durham and Newcastle Universities, seemed to think that this might not be a bad thing. The Judaeo-Christian tradition had been male-dominated. The cult of the Virgin Mary could be seen as a deep psychological protest against the patriarchal ethos. Jung had found it significant that children saw the Virgin Mary rather than Jesus in visions at Lourdes and Fatima. The collective unconscious was always at work. When Pope Pius XII had declared the Virgin Mary Queen of Heaven in 1950, Jung had considered this to be the most important religious event since the Reformation. Maybe, for the Anglican Church, the ordination of women was the best way to correct this male bias.

Why were so many of the opponents of the motion so fearful of female sexuality? asked Jean Mayland. 'They had only to hear the dread word "priestess" than [sic] they are faced with visions of sexual orgies and fertility cults.'[40] Female sexuality should be seen as a gift that could be of use to the Church. Canon A. C. Hall, the son of Bishop R. O. Hall of Hong Kong, recalled the ordination of Florence Li. The current situation reminded him of the Council of Jerusalem, when the mother Church of Palestine had listened to the joyous tidings of the Diaspora Churches which had admitted gentiles to their ranks. Perhaps the Church of England should follow the example of the Jerusalem Church and be open to the vision of younger Churches like Hong Kong?

This time the opposition did not focus so much on the usual arguments. Instead, speakers concentrated on the threat to Christian unity with other Churches and the fear of schism within their own ranks. But the motion was defeated, only to be reintroduced yet again in Synod on 15 November 1984. In the meantime, the Movement to Ordain Women had been founded, as a reaction to the 1978 defeat, and had kept the issue alive. When he proposed that Synod should consider legislation to enable women to be ordained, the Bishop of Southwark cited the example of William Wilberforce, who had brought his motion to abolish slavery before Parliament every year from 1791 to 1799, and again in 1804 and 1805, although he was often asked to give up, since it was said that neither the planters nor the slaves themselves felt that the time was ripe. People were becoming more accustomed to the ministry of women. This was evident in the shift away from many of the old arguments and texts. The Bishop believed that the only way to safeguard the doctrine of God, who was so often inadequately depicted in masculine terms, was to ordain women. In opposition, Mr O. W. H. Clark admitted that no conclusive arguments, for or against, could be found in scripture. This, in itself, showed how far the idea of women priests was in fact gaining acceptance, even in the most dedicated members of the opposition. In this debate, the stress was again on the threat to Church unity rather than to the 'headship' doctrine and so forth. Had the Church of England the authority to make a major change of this kind? The Archbishop of York expressed this memorably: 'Underlying the dilemma is the dread of so stressing our own autonomy that we seem to be setting ourselves up as some funny little independent entity.'[41] Was it possible to take unilateral action on this matter, while still remaining part of the Catholic Church? He reminded Synod that the Anglican Church had already departed from other traditions, not simply because it already had some women priests but because the innovation of the Synod and the democratic involvement of bishops, clergy and laity in the determination of doctrine and practice had already gravely complicated relations with the Roman Catholic and Greek Orthodox Churches, which went in for more autocratic rule.

The Bishop of Birmingham, who had led the 1978 debate, believed that the theological discussion of this issue had become sterile. Sociological surveys had shown that those who opposed women priests tended to hold more conservative views of family life and sexuality, but biological science showed that sex had evolved long before mammals appeared on the planet and that its purpose was to increase genetic diversity. It clearly had nothing to do with the ordination of women to the priesthood. Opponents of women priests seemed to be agreeing with Freud that religion drew its emotional strength from the memory of a father-figure, while their supporters were closer to Jung and his perception of the need for balance between animus and anima. It was essential to resolve the conflict; people on both sides were behaving in a wounding and insensitive manner.

This time the motion was passed and the legislation to enable women to be ordained began to be drafted. The first women deacons were ordained in England in 1987. The drafting was completed in February 1992 and put before Synod on 11 November. This historic debate was characterized by generosity and concern. Again there was fear of schism and discrimination within the Church of England against those who could not accept women priests. People also feared losing ecumenical links with the Roman Catholics and the Greek Orthodox. The old arguments about 'headship' and representation were mentioned, but little was said that was new. As Dr Christina Baxter of Southwark pointed out after a learned but inconclusive excursus on the exact meaning of the Greek *kephale* (head), neither side was as sure as they once had been about the meaning of 'headship' in the New Testament. Instead, most of the opponents concentrated on the specific legislation they had been asked to approve.

In his opening speech, the Archdeacon of Leicester ably summed up the main objections to the proposed legal changes. The legislation, he said, proposed irreversible change on the basis of an inconclusive theological argument which had no backing in either scripture or tradition. In asserting that it did not make it lawful for a woman to be consecrated to the office of a bishop, it made a false distinction between episcopate and presbyterate that was prejudicial to women. The legislation lacked consensus in the Church at every level and was biased in the direction of inexorably phasing out the opposition from seats of influence. But perhaps the most moving speech made against women priests that day was by the Reverend Peter Geldard of Canterbury. He emphasized above all that the

Church of England 'was but a part – and a very small part – of a wider Church'. The ministry was not theirs alone but part of something bigger, something that they shared with others. Therefore, 'we cannot with integrity mint our own coinage and claim that it is the same currency that we are sharing,' he argued. 'Yes, we can claim female ministers, we can do something *sui generis* to ourselves, but we cannot thereafter ever claim again that we share something with the wider body of Christ.'[42] The fear expressed by the Archbishop of York in 1984 that the Church would become a 'funny little independent entity' was clearly felt that afternoon. Finally, in an eloquent peroration, Geldard spoke of a deeper fear. There was an oak tree in his village which had stood there for many years. It was interwoven so deeply with the life of the village that it was hard to say whether the oak belonged to the village or the village to the oak. But recently, a voice which was 'very acceptable and sweet' had suggested that it should be cut down to give more light and space. Before yielding to this persuasive modern argument, however, Geldard asked his audience to remember two things about the oak tree:

> The first is that, unlike other things that the world possesses, because this is given by God we cannot improve upon it and if we try to change it we can easily destroy the thing itself. Second, and more important, they say that that which you see, grand as it is, is but a part and a very small part, for under the ground there are roots and sinews which are bigger and greater than any of us realize, and they go to areas that none of us fully understands.[43]

The exclusively male priesthood, with all that it implied about the nature of God and of Christ, the relationship between the sexes and, indeed, of personal sexual identity, seemed so pervasive that its removal could undermine the whole fabric of ecclesiastical and individual faith.

But the opposition did not have all the best speeches. The Reverend June Osborne made a moving plea: 'I long for you to allow me to minister the grace of God through priesthood. In the mercy of Christ and for the sake of our Church, I ask you:

please test my vocation.' The trouble with the traditional arguments about 'headship' was that the meaning of gender was
elevated out of all proportion. 'Where lies the relevance of my
gender when I exercise judgement, teaching, discipline, order
and spiritual endeavour?' she asked. 'If we elevate the significance of the gender of the priest we have seen how we very
quickly elevate the significance of the gender of Christ, and
thus we begin to denigrate women's role in the exercise of
faith.'[44] There were several references to the blue line on the
floor near the back of Durham Cathedral, which in the Middle
Ages had marked the limit beyond which no woman could go.
As Dr Ruth Etchells explained, in the thirteenth and fourteenth
centuries, women were confined to the margins of the Church
and barely allowed over the threshold. Those who made that
line were our Christian forebears; they were part of the 'tradition' that everybody was so concerned about. But since that
time, Christians had grown in understanding and women had
moved forward into the pews, into the lectern, into the pulpit
and recently, as deacons, into the Choir. There was still metaphorically a blue line around the altar itself. The Reverend
Susan Hope argued that the legislation did not mean the
importation of secular feminism but 'the making explicit of
what is implicit in the Pauline doctrine of the Church'. It would
show all Christians that there was only one priesthood:

> When the community of male and female, clothed in the
> seamless robe of Christ's priesthood, act as the icon of
> Christ, taking bread, blessing, breaking, it is the individual
> priest who images the action of Christ in his Body, a Body
> made up of both male and female.[45]

These speeches by women deacons showed how far women
had come. It would have been unthinkable a hundred years
earlier for women to have contributed to such a gathering. The
silence imposed upon them for centuries was indeed over. But
towards the end of the debate, two speakers put the question of
the oppression of women into a wider perspective. The Bishop
of Southwark reminded Synod of his Irish ancestry (he was
born in Belfast). He said that he could not 'with any degree of

integrity challenge the injustices within the Church which prevent women from testing their vocation to the priest hood'.[46] He noted with wry humour that the Anglican Church of Ireland, which was so often accused of being forty years behind the times, had crept ahead of the Church of England in this respect. It seemed to him that if the Church of Ireland had got on with the job, as had the Church of South Africa, 'in two lands where people's lives are being shattered by violence day after day, it may very well be that in those kinds of circumstance, they get even a thing like this in perspective'.[47] Finally, asked the Bishop of Durham, should they not be broken by the shame they were bringing on Christ and his gospel? 'Is it not shameful to be quarrelling as we are about women in the Church when the whole world is torn by poverty, strife and lostness, and to be doing it in the full glare of the media?'[48]

Indeed. But for centuries Christians had found it difficult to keep questions of gender and sexuality in perspective. After the debate, however, the Church of England finally 'got on with the job' and passed the legislation for the ordination of women by the necessary two-thirds majority. It brought to an end a debate which had begun in earnest thirty years earlier. It had aroused huge passions and fears. Women would now be priests in the Church of England. But would this crossing of the last frontier mark an end of oppression and prejudice or the start of a new era of conflict?

Epilogue:

Forward in Faith?

T HE DECISION OF the Church of England to ordain women to the priesthood has not brought peace. Rather, it seems merely to have intensified old divisions. Within a few hours of the vote, the Vatican had sent a negative message to the Anglican Church, saying – as expected – that the decision was a 'serious obstacle' to unity. The Greek Orthodox Church had already declared that admitting women to the priesthood would be an 'unpardonable transgression' that would render further attempts at dialogue with the Anglicans pointless. Further, the Church of England itself seemed about to be split asunder and, at the time of writing, it is not at all clear that these divisions can be healed. Has there been irreparable damage? The Anglican Church has long been famed for its tolerance: it has even been ridiculed for its readiness to compromise and to admit conflicting shades of opinion. But the ordination of women has been too much for many of the faithful to swallow. Clerics and lay people who have been able to accommodate rival theological opinions which, arguably, are far more important to the faith may find that the hideous spectre of a woman priest will drive them away from their beloved Church into the arms of Rome or a breakaway sect of their own.

The legislation approved by Synod in November 1992 had made provision for those who could not in conscience accept the ordination of women to the priesthood. They would be able to withdraw from the reform and the Church would compensate those priests who felt that they must resign their orders. In January 1993, the bishops of the Church of England voted unanimously to make provision for this minority by a system of three episcopal 'overseers' who would minister to its needs within the Church as a whole. That the bishops were so solidly united seemed a hopeful sign, but a month later this promise of unity and reconciliation proved ephemeral. On 17 February 1993, a hundred rebel Anglicans walked out of the General Synod of the Church of England and held a rival debate in a hall nearby. The group of traditionalist organizations which had orchestrated this exodus had formed a new movement which they called Forward in Faith. The Reverend John Broadhurst, its chairman, accused the Church of England of preferring 'the insights of our own contemporary culture to the constraints of the universal faith' and expressed his 'real distrust' of the bishops who had voted for the ordination of women.[1] Forward in Faith proposed to set up what has been termed a 'Church within a Church'. In this scheme, those Anglo-Catholics and Evangelicals who opposed women priests would form a third province of the Church of England, alongside the existing provinces of York and Canterbury. Clearly it would not have geographical boundaries but it would be governed by its own archbishop. John Broadhurst said that administrative structures were being put in place in every diocese and deanery in the land to function parallel to existing Church structures. If the Church of England allowed this, he said, Forward in Faith would be prepared to cooperate as far as their consciences would permit.

But the mood was aggressive and it was obvious that some ugly and sordid disputes about finance and property lay ahead. The Church of England was prepared to pay over £11 million in compensation, pension and housing provision to every hundred men who resigned their orders. The 'Church within a Church', however, proposed to withhold its current payments to diocesan funds to secure its own resources, a measure which would obviously hurt during a time of recession. Margaret Brown of Women Against the Ordination of Women said: 'We are going to go all out for our own buildings and a share of the assets. Why should we give our assets and buildings to a corrupt body? Our forebears did not build churches for them to be handed on to corruption.'[2] It depends, of course, how far these traditionalists are prepared to go back in their search for an authentic, uncorrupted Christianity. One could argue that the 'Fathers' might not have intended the Church to have assets or buildings at all. We are clearly far from the spirit of the early Church, which had no official buildings and celebrated the Eucharist in the homes of its various members. We are even further from the Son of Man who had nowhere to lay his head.

Other traditionalists do not subscribe to the solution of a Church within a Church. Instead, some Anglo-Catholics hope to take their parishes over to the Roman Catholic Church if they can make satisfactory arrangements with the Vatican. Cardinal Basil Hume, the Roman Catholic primate of England, has been enthusiastic. This, he has said, could herald the conversion of England for which Roman Catholics had been praying so long. Not surprisingly, this has raised many hackles in Britain, which has a long tradition of extreme distrust of popery and plots. Dr Graham Leonard, the former Anglican Bishop of London, heads this Roman option and seems to be hoping for some sort of package whereby he and his flock would become a permanent 'Uniate Church' in England, retaining Anglican traditions while owing some kind of allegiance to Rome. As Cardinal Hume explained, this would call for an acceptance of the authority of the Holy Father as Supreme Pontiff. But what exactly would this involve? Anglicans have traditionally jibbed at these papal claims but the fear of becoming a 'funny little independent entity' has driven them to a desperate expedient. In 1898, Pope Leo XIII declared that Anglican Orders were 'absolutely null and utterly void' and this continues to be official Roman Catholic policy. Is Bishop Leonard really willing to deny, publicly and unequivocally, all the confirmations, ordinations and Eucharists he has celebrated in the course of his long, distinguished career and accept reordination? Those who are prepared to be ordained again in the Roman Catholic Church will face financial problems, too. At present those Anglican priests who have trickled over to Rome over the years and have been reordained are usually given the few salaried posts available to Roman Catholic priests in England – as hospital or prison chaplains. This has enabled them to support their families but such a solution would not be possible on a larger scale.

That a significant number of priests and lay people are prepared even to contemplate this drastic step is a mark of their disquiet and distress. Ever since the Oxford Movement, the Anglo-Catholic wing of the Church of England has believed that it is a member of the family of Catholic Churches and that the Church of England can compare itself to the Churches of Rome and Constantinople. The Synod's decision on 11 November 1992 was Protestant, however: it showed that the Church of England was a national Church prepared to go it alone rather than to submit to the decisions of the Universal Church as a whole. It voted according to a democratic procedure which is deeply English but alien to either Roman Catholicism or Greek Orthodoxy. The Church is now prepared for the decision to be ratified by the national Parliament.

Bishop Leonard's supporters feel that their Christian identity has been shattered and that Rome is their only option. Yet Roman Catholics point out that they are in for a shock. Despite the Pope's negative statement after the Synod had voted, the St Joan's Alliance announced that it had set up a movement for the ordination of women within the Roman Catholic Church. Many point out that it would only need a more liberal pope for this dream to become a reality. The Vatican can act autocratically: for a pope who believed that it was right for his Church to admit women to the priesthood there would be no need to submit to Synod or discuss the matter with his brother bishops. *Inter Insigniores*, the 1977 Declaration that vetoed women priests, is not an infallible statement but a private papal opinion. As such, it is reversible at any time. The Roman Catholic Church has its own problems with ministry. The issue of obligatory celibacy alone has caused hundreds of priests to resign their orders. During the last twenty-five years, there has been a massive exodus from the Roman Catholic priesthood which has meant that the Church has lost about a quarter of its active work-force. Consequently thousands of Catholics cannot hear Mass or receive the Sacraments. This might make the ordination of women to fill these gaps an attractive option. As the Reverend Raglan Hay-Will, Roman Catholic Chaplain of the University of Sussex, told *The Times*, Bishop Leonard and his cohorts might have an unpleasant surprise: 'They think Catholicism will provide a safe haven free of all the dangerous liberal views they have had to live with in the Church of England. They are in for a shock when they find that the Catholic Church is full of priests, like myself, who believe, among other things, that women should most certainly be ordained.'[3]

Does this widespread dismay and disunion mean that Synod made a mistake? Or does it reveal a deeper malaise in the Christian psyche? In their flight to such desperate and divisive remedies, many Anglicans seem to be displaying the imbalance that has so long characterized the Christian response to questions of sexuality and gender. The fact that the very idea of a woman at the altar has unleashed such dread shows that in the Anglican no less than in the Roman Catholic Church, many Christians have been unable to integrate the female into their experience of the sacred. Religion is not about preserving Churches and dogma. Its primary function is not to uphold an institution. All religions have attempted to stop men and women from falling into despair; at best, they have enabled millions of people to cultivate a faith in the ultimate meaning and value of human life, despite the suffering that flesh is heir to. An inability to regard some major facts of life with equanimity must mean, as so many critics of Christianity have argued, that religion has in fact alienated people from the human condition. In all the major world religions, the iron test of religious experience has been the exercise of compassion. After experiencing enlightenment in solitude, said the Buddha, a religious person must return to the market-place in order to practise compassion for all living beings. As St Paul said in his famous hymn to charity, without love a Christian is no better than sounding brass or a tinkling cymbal. As some of the bishops pointed out in Synod, charity had been conspicuously lacking on both sides of the floor. Others noted that the spectacle of a Church squabbling publicly and intransigently about an issue that – as had been agreed – was not fundamental to the faith was disturbing and unedifying. It certainly seems a waste of energy and a preoccupation that is so misplaced as to be almost sinful. The world urgently needs the Churches to give a moral lead on such questions as the rise of neo-fascism in Germany, the genocide in Bosnia and the ecological threat to the planet. But instead of bringing the compassion of Christ to a world torn apart by hatred, greed and despair, Christians are paralysed by the internal question of women priests.

The three monotheistic religions have all warned against the dangers of idolatry. By this they have not simply meant the worship of false gods but the deification of purely human values, institutions and objectives. In much of the opposition to women priests there is a concern about the institutional Church which seems idolatrous since it raises a purely human creation to an exalted level, so that it almost seems to be an end in itself. Certainly, ideas about the Church seem to come before justice to women and appear to be preventing a serious consideration of widespread human misery in many parts of the world. But are either ecclesiology or a particular understanding of Christian ministry so important that they can divide Christians from one another in this way? Does a theory of the universal Church really eclipse St Paul's vision of a new humanity in which the divisions of race, gender and class have been abolished? Is it not an idolatry to raise these man-made doctrines and institutions to such a high level that they inspire a most unChristian division and prevent the Church from carrying out its mission to the world?

The Anglicans, Roman Catholics and Greek Orthodox who oppose the ordination of women to the priesthood argue that it will mark an unacceptable break with tradition. They accuse the Church of England of preferring the insights of contemporary culture to the constraints of two thousand years of Christian history. But the introduction of the priesthood into Christianity was itself a major break with the past. Like many other Jews of that time, Jesus and the first Christians did not ordain any of their number to the priesthood. The only priests they acknowledged were involved with the Temple cult, where the early Jerusalem Christians worshipped daily. The New Testament writers only speak of the priesthood of Christ himself. He had rendered a priestly representative unnecessary. Each Christian could now approach God freely, since Jesus, the new High Priest, had entered the Sanctuary on behalf of the whole of humanity. It was no longer essential to appoint specially trained individuals to brave the mortal perils of holiness on behalf of the community. Even gentiles, who had been on the outskirts of holiness, forbidden to step beyond the outermost court of the Temple, could now be united to God himself in the person of Christ who had abolished the old Temple priesthood.

In the primitive Church, the Eucharist does not appear to have been conducted only by specially ordained persons. Only gradually, when it became clear that Jesus's Second Coming was indefinitely postponed, did the early Church appoint its own officials. Not until the third century did they start to think of these as 'priests'. Since the priesthood itself seems to have been a human rather than a divine creation, is the introduction of women an innovation which flouts God's will? Will it be as radical a departure as the setting up of the institution of priesthood in the first place? Further, the office of priesthood and Christian ministry was constantly adapting to what the Reverend John Broadhurst of Forward in Faith has called the insights of contemporary culture. The very words 'ordination' and 'vicar' derive from Imperial Rome. Later, the Church saw the office of priesthood in terms of feudalism or, at the time of the Reformation, in the context of an absolute monarchy. In the Victorian period, the priest became a professional, like doctors, teachers and lawyers. All this was very different from the early Christian ideal of *diakonia* but it may have been a necessary part of the Churches' struggles to incarnate the Christian imperative into the flawed conditions of mundane life.

Like Jews and Muslims, Christians have taken their history very seriously. In each generation, they have reconsidered and restated their beliefs and practices. Only thus could they address the current condition. Christians have sometimes introduced daring and revolutionary doctrines to meet a current need. One example of this kind of doctrinal innovation was the definition of the divinity of Christ at the Council of Nicea in 325. In its own way, this decision was just as divisive as the 1992 decision to ordain women promises to become. It looked as though the Church was going to be split right down the middle. The controversy raged, becoming ever more acrimonious for two hundred years: sects proliferated – Arian, Nestorian, Monophysite, Monothelite – which interpreted the question of Christ's divinity differently and permanently ruptured Christian unity. It was not until Maximus the Confessor reached a satisfactory theological solution in the sixth century that the question was settled in the Orthodox Church. Today Anglicans, Protestants, Roman Catholics and Greek and Russian Orthodox can all recite the Nicene Creed without a qualm, have integrated its teaching and see it as fundamental to the faith. The old sense of shock and outrage occasioned by the controversial decision of the Council of Nicea that Jesus had been the uncreated and unbegotten Son of God has vanished. If Christians have been able to accommodate the Nicene doctrine of the Incarnation and regard it as fundamental, surely they can come to terms with a practical measure like the ordination of women for which they could find no substantial theological objection?

Some have argued that the ordination of women *is* a theological issue, however, since it has a direct bearing on the conception of God. In Britain an increasing number of people find the traditional view of God as a male personality unacceptable. Freudians, for example, maintain that this theology derives its power from the memory of a strong father-figure and has kept human beings in a state of permanent immaturity. The idea of God as a person who has created the world and organizes human affairs in the way that human beings make things or run institutions has resulted in some grave theological doubts about the possibility or the validity of such a being. Has this inadequate conception of the divine been perpetuated in part by an exclusively male priesthood, which claims to re-present 'Him'? Nobody has seen God, but we have all seen the priests who are ordained to stand in for Him. In the pagan world, both men and women re-presented the divine in ritualized drama and gave their congregation a living image of a reality which was inclusive of both sexes. When the idea of God emphasizes its utter transcendence of such human limitations as gender, the representative priesthood becomes problematic. This was one of the reasons why Jews and Muslims rejected the whole notion of priesthood, since it was impossible to re-present the ineffable and incomprehensible God.

Many Christians have found a priesthood helpful, however, since it has enabled them to cultivate a sense of God as a present, living reality in their midst. To be sure, any notion of priesthood will have its inadequacies: to think of the priest as an imperial official or as a professional will inevitably be limiting since he is supposed to represent a reality that goes beyond political organization or professional skill. In much the same way, an exclusively male priesthood is likely to evoke the image of a wholly male God which cannot adequately express the complexity of the divine. Indeed, a wholly masculine God has made many people fearful. As we have seen, those priests and theologians who have argued in favour of a male priesthood have stressed the initiative and power of God. This is all right as far as it goes but, like any human image of God, it needs qualification. All too often God has been presented as an oppressive and angry father or ruler. Jesus Christ revealed a very different God. He died because he had no power and said that Christians should avoid powerful titles, regarding themselves instead as slaves. A priesthood that stresses its *sacra potestas* is a disfigurement of the ideal.

Like all human institutions, the Churches have sometimes failed to live up to their ideals. There have been some unhappy and shameful blots on Christian history. One of the traditions of which Western Christianity is most rightly ashamed is the anti-Semitism which became an incurable disease in Europe. For nearly a thousand years, Jews were regarded as human monsters, God-slayers, infanticides and the powerful enemies of Christendom. As we watch the resurgence of a murderous racism in Europe today, we are acutely aware of the dangers of such distorted thinking. Anti-Semitism represented a profound fear of a shadow-self that was a projection of grave anxiety. We have seen that women have also been dehumanized in the Christian imagination: at one point during the Witch Craze of the sixteenth and seventeenth centuries, the connection of misogyny and anti-Semitism became explicit in so far as people spoke of witches' 'synagogues' and 'sabbaths'. When the opponents of women's ordination speak lovingly of tradition, they should recall some of the worst aspects of the Christian tradition which cry out for correction.

Today psychologists point out that it is dangerous – on an individual as well as on a social level – to deny the feminine. Within every individual and every society there are masculine and feminine aspects which need to be integrated and balanced creatively. Excluding women from clubs, professions and the Curia is an outward sign of inward imbalance, the obverse of a sacrament. We have seen that Christian history has often been characterized by the denial of the female and that this has resulted in psychologically damaging behaviour. Ever since the Jewish priestly tradition separated male and female, women have often been seen as a polluting influence. The anxiety evinced by members of Forward in Faith about the 'taint' of women priests looks directly back to the old taboos about menstruation enshrined in Jewish law. Christ was supposed to have liberated his disciples from this kind of thinking; this is why early Christians like St Paul declared that he had super-seded the Torah. But the survival of such primitive fears shows how superficial is our hold upon that rationalism of which we are so proud. If a religion cannot assuage such anxiety, it is not living up to the liberation that the gospel claimed to have brought. Throughout Christian history, women have been excluded and consigned to a separate sphere in a way that seems alien to the spirit of the primitive Church. From time to time the repressed feminine has attempted to break through, as it did, for example, in the cult of the Virgin Mary. The demand for women priests may be another such attempt to achieve balance and wholeness and, if so, it should be heeded carefully. The issue of ordination is not just a matter of women's rights but the furore it has inspired points to a wound that has long damaged the integrity of Christendom.

The notion of separation was central to the priestly ideal of ancient Israel, but by the time of Christ many Jews no longer felt that this kind of priesthood was appropriate. Certainly ideals of separation and exclusivity were alien to early Christianity. Over the centuries, however, the priest did become separate from the people; his back was literally turned to them, as we have seen, and the Latin words that he whispered as he celebrated Mass were inaudible and incomprehensible. The Reformation sought, among other things, to rectify this. To insist that the priesthood remains exclusively male is to perpetuate another type of separation. In their very different ways, the Churches have attempted to revive the old communal ideals of early Christianity during the twentieth century. At the Second Vatican Council, the Roman Catholic Church stressed the collegiality of the episcopate and the vocation of the whole People of God. The Anglican Church went further in reviving and extending the function of the Synod, in which bishops, priests and laity discuss Church doctrine and government in a democratic manner. There has also been a revival of the communal theology of priesthood, so that we can understand the patristic doctrine of the priesthood of the whole *laos*. It is not just the ordained priest but the whole community who offers the Eucharist. Every baptized Christian is an *alter Christus*, a representation of Christ the Priest. Consequently Christian priests do not approach God like Aaron, on behalf of the laity and in their stead. A priest is simply the sacramental focus of the congregation and, theologically, a woman can fulfil this role as well as a man.

Some feminists, as we have seen, have questioned whether priesthood is a valid goal for women. They argue that women, who have long been second-class citizens in the Kingdom of God, should not view ordination as entry into a privileged caste but should seek to reform and transform it from within. From the early days, the Gospels stressed the *diakonia* of women's ministry and suggested that women understood this ideal of service better than Jesus's male disciples. Certainly, once they have been admitted to the priesthood, women face a difficult journey. As ordained ministers, Lutheran, Baptist and Anglican women have all encountered the old sexism and discrimination in their brother clergy. To justify their entry into this oppressive club, perhaps women should work to revive the ideal of *diakonia* and to lay aside the old imagery and symbolism of priestly power. In the early Church there were no priests, but prophets were extremely important and influential. Women were prophets alongside men. In an established Church it is difficult

for priests to fulfil a prophetic role. After centuries of marginal-
ization and prejudice, women are not yet insiders and could
perhaps remind their brethren of the old prophetic function. It
would be a fine thing if male and female priests confronted
secular and ecclesiastical authorities in the spirit in which Isaiah
and Jeremiah once voiced unpopular views to their kings in the
name of God.

Finally, we have seen that in the very early days, priesthood
was about the re-creation of the world. A revival of a prophetic
priesthood could fulfil this mission socially and politically, but
today all priests must have a duty to cultivate a respect for the
environment. Even the disciplines of separation inculcated by
the Jewish priesthood were a reminder of stewardship: the
people of Israel were not to imagine that the earth was theirs to
do with as they chose. A masculine priesthood and a male God
have stressed the qualities of action, initiative and domination.
We have seen that Thomas Aquinas believed that women could
not represent the attribute of 'eminence' that was essential to
the priesthood. These traditionally 'masculine' virtues have
played a part in the political and environmental domination
that has led to the dislocations of colonialism and the savaging
of the planet. The presence of a woman at the altar could help to
qualify this aggressive, dominant theology and recall the more
nurturing and creative type of spirituality which since antiquity
has been associated with the 'feminine'.

Men as well as women have been damaged by the fears and
hostility of misogyny. It is no joke to be the heirs of Augustine,
Tertullian and Luther. The institution of priesthood has injured
men too, as can be seen in the great Roman Catholic exodus of
priests who refuse to accept the rule of celibacy and in the
dominant, oppressive behaviour of the Church in developing
countries. The admission of women to the priesthood could
help to reform an office that, like any human institution, needs
periodic examination and scrutiny. There is a great temptation
to cling to the *status quo* and endow it with an absolute, divine
sanction, which brings reassurance with the consolations of
familiarity. But the monotheistic tradition has always insisted
on the importance of moving forward. In all three of the
monotheistic religions, Abraham has been revered as the man

of faith *par excellence*. In Genesis, God is depicted as bursting into Abraham's life out of the blue and commanding him to leave his family and their pagan religion behind: 'Leave your country, your family and your father's house for the land I will show you.'[4] God was experienced as an imperative to action and change. He revealed no theological conception of himself to Abraham and formulated no creeds, but simply commanded a practical change of direction. Faith in this God should carry worshippers beyond themselves, taking them far from the consolations of normality into another country. It issues no guarantees but insists on a readiness to leave old attitudes and ways of worship behind.

It cannot be said that this is the spirit manifested by organizations such as Forward in Faith, which actually seem more concerned with looking backward. Throughout the religious world, there is at present a frantic desire to turn the clock back and to return – sometimes atavistically – to the past. The phenomenon that we call 'fundamentalism' has erupted in almost all the major world religions and seems to be a response to the peculiar strains of the late twentieth century. It claims to return to 'fundamentals' but often negates such essentials as the virtue of compassion. There is frequently a fierce resistance to change and modernity and, in many cases, the position of women becomes an image of fidelity. Something similar occurred in early Christian history, when theologians like Tertullian and Irenaeus saw submissive, veiled women as symbols of orthodoxy – as opposed to the more active women in the heretical sects. In a rather similar way, perhaps, the veiled women of Islamic fundamentalism are seen as emblems of true Muslim values, even though the Koran does not prescribe veils and seclusion for the whole female sex. Again, in a Roman Catholic country such as Ireland, women are officially prevented from using contraception and having recourse to abortion, almost as a sign of Irish Catholic solidarity against the secularism and laxity of the mainland.

Those who oppose the ordination of women to the priesthood do not conform to the popular image of the fundamentalist, but there are similarities. Like many other militant conservatives, they insist upon the importance of the historical institution of their Church, rather as others have made the political entities of 'Islam' or 'the Holy Land' supreme values. The opponents of women priests, like the fundamentalists, frequently interpret the scriptures in a literalistic way and feel obliged to take a stand against secular society. As we have seen, they are often impelled by a profound fear which is not dissimilar to the emotions which fuel religious radicalism in other parts of the world.

These fears must be addressed fully and with sensitivity. There can be no way forward until there is an honest, compassionate dialogue. The unhappy history of relations between the sexes in Christianity needs to be rehearsed. Present attitudes of misogyny and unresolved conflicts must be brought out into the open, and the pain experienced by women within the Churches must also be addressed. It will be a long, hard road, but there is no alternative if the profound disorders and injustices of the past are to be healed. Only thus can Christians progress to a healthier future and a more complete ministry.

Notes

Chapter 1: Priest and Priestess in the Ancient World

1. Pindar, Nemean VI, 1–4, in *The Odes of Pindar* (trans. C. M. Bowra) (Harmondsworth, 1969), p. 206.
2. Quoted in Asia Shepsut, *Journey of the Priestess, The Priestess Traditions of the Ancient World* (London, 1993), p. 92.
3. Anat-Baal texts 49.11.5. Quoted in E. O. James, *The Ancient Gods* (London, 1955), p. 88.
4. 1 Kings 12:28; 1 Kings 15:11, 2 Kings 21:3. All biblical quotations have been taken from the Jerusalem Bible.
5. Deuteronomy 33:9–10.
6. 2 Kings 23:7.
7. 2 Kings 23:14.
8. Deuteronomy 6:6–7.
9. Jeremiah 2:20–5; 7:18; 9:13; Ezekiel 8:14–16.
10. Ezekiel 8:10–12; 44:6–12.
11. Ezekiel 44:11-13.
12. 1 Kings 2:27–36.
13. Ezekiel 44:23.
14. Mary Douglas, *Purity and Danger* (London, 1966), p. 14.
15. Ibid., p. 4.
16. Genesis 9:3–4.
17. Isaiah 6:5.
18. Exodus 19:12–15.
19. Leviticus 20:6.
20. Leviticus 20:26.
21. Leviticus 19:11, 13, 14, 17–18, 34.
22. Exodus 31:12; cf. 39:32, 43; 40:2, 17; 31:3, 13.

23. Leviticus 8:34.
24. Leviticus 9:22, 24.
25. Leviticus 16:1.
26. Leviticus 26:3–5.
27. Leviticus 26:12.
28. Numbers 16:3.
29. Numbers 17:27; 18:1.
30. Genesis 1:27.
31. Leviticus 15:20–2.
32. Genesis 17:10.
33. Ezekiel 7:19–20; Ezra 9:11.
34. Exodus 19:15.
35. Judith Plaskow, *Standing Again at Sinai* (San Francisco, 1990).
36. Exodus 19:6–7.

Chapter 2: Jesus, Women and the Twelve

1. Luke 9:1–2.
2. Luke 10:16; Matthew 10:40.
3. 1 Corinthians 15:8.
4. 1 Corinthians 15:9–10.
5. Acts of the Apostles 1:26.
6. Luke 22:30.
7. Revelation 21:12–14.
8. Mark 16:17-18.
9. 1 Corinthians 7; Mark 10:17–22.
10. Luke 24:53.
11. Shabbat 31a.
12. Matthew 23:4–7, 25–6.
13. Midrash on Genesis 2:17.
14. Mishnah Tanhuma Wayyishlah 36.
15. B. Megillah 23a.
16. Aroth de Rabba Nathan 6.
17. Mark 10:42–5.
18. For example, 2 Corinthians 4:5.
19. John 13:14.
20. Matthew 23:9–11.
21. Luke 8:2–3.
22. Matthew 15:21–8.
23. Mark 5:34; 7:24–30; 12:41.
24. Chauvinist Matthew makes the mother of the sons of Zebedee, rather than James and John themselves, ask for privileged seats on the Last Day.
25. Luke 10:38–42.
26. John 11:21–7.
27. John 6:68–9; Matthew 16:16.
28. Mark 14:19.
29. Mark 14:24.

30. Matthew 26:28.
31. Exodus 24:8. See Exodus 24:1–8 for this pre-priestly Elohist account of the ratification of the covenant account of Sinai. It has also been pointed out that there is a reference to Isaiah 53:12, which depicts Israel as the Suffering Servant of God, who is symbolically depicted as a lamb led to the slaughter for the salvation of the 'many' – an early indication that some Jews believed that Israel had a mission to the whole of humanity.
32. Mark 15:40; Matthew 25:55–6; Luke 23:25; John 19:25.
33. 1 Corinthians 15:5–8.
34. Luke 24:11.

Chapter 3: Paul and the Ministry of the Primitive Church

1. Acts of the Apostles 2:2–4.
2. Acts 1:114.
3. Joel 3:1–2.
4. Acts 5:34–42.
5. Acts 6:1–6.
6. Galatians 1:15–16, cf Jeremiah 1:5.
7. Galatians 2:1–14.
8. 1 Corinthians 15:4.
9. 1 Corinthians 7:29–31; 1 Thessalonians 4:15–18.
10. Philippians 2:7.
11. Romans 15:15.
12. 1 Corinthians 7 passim.
13. 2 Corinthians 6:1; Romans 15:30.
14. 1 Corinthians 11:23.
15. 1 Corinthians 12:4–7.
16. Acts 13:1; 11:27.
17. 1 Corinthians 14:19.
18. 1 Corinthians 14:26–32.
19. Acts 16:12–15, 30.
20. Romans 16:1–2.
21. Romans 16:7.
22. Acts 18:18, 26.
23. Quoted in Ben Witherington III, *Women and the Genesis of Christianity* (Cambridge and New York, 1990), p. 11.
24. Galatians 3:28.
25. 1 Corinthians 11:3–16.
26. 1 Corinthians 11:13.
27. 1 Corinthians 7 passim.
28. 1 Corinthians 6:15–17; 8:7–13.
29. 1 Corinthians 11:3.
30. 1 Corinthians 11:7–9.
31. Genesis 1:27.
32. *Paradise Lost*, Book IV, lines 296–301.
33. 1 Corinthians 11:10.

34. Genesis 6:1–4.
35. 1 Corinthians 11:13–15.
36. 1 Corinthians 11:11–12.
37. 1 Corinthians 11:16.
38. 1 Corinthians 14:34–5.
39. Genesis 3:16.
40. Philippians 1:1.
41. 1 Peter 5:5.
42. 1 Peter 2:9.
43. Ephesians 2:12.
44. Ephesians 2:13–14.
45. Ephesians 2:15.
46. Ephesians 2:18.
47. Ephesians 2:19.
48. Ephesians 2:19–22.
49. Hebrews 9:11–12.
50. Hebrews 7:27.
51. Hebrews 9:24.
52. Hebrews 10:19–21.
53. *Didache*, 15.
54. *Didache*, 10:7; 13:3; 15.
55. Clement of Rome, *First Epistle to the Corinthians*, 40.
56. Titus 2:1.
57. 2 Timothy 1:6; cf. Tosefta Sanhedrin 1:1.
58. 1 Timothy 2:11–14.
59. 1 Timothy 2:15.
60. Colossians 3:16–22.

Chapter 4: The Patristic Age: Silent Women and Eloquent Fathers

1. *The Apostolic Tradition*, 3:3.
2. Ibid., 9:2.
3. Ibid., 9:3.
4. *Letters* 66:8.
5. Quoted in Herbert Musurillo (ed. and trans.), *The Acts of the Christian Martyrs* (Oxford, 1972), p. 65; cf. 1 Corinthians 1:26.
6. Ibid., p. 75.
7. 'The Acts of Perpetua and Felicitas', 10, quoted and translated in Peter Dronke, *Women Writers of the Middle Ages, A Critical Study of Texts from Perpetua to Marguerite Porete* (Cambridge, 1984), p. 4.
8. *On Prescription Against Heretics*, 41:5.
9. *On Baptism*, 17:4.
10. *The Veiling of Virgins*, 9.
11. *On Female Dress*, 1:1.
12. *Exposition on the Gospel of Luke*, 10:161.
13. Enchiridion, 27.
14. Letter 242:10.
15. *On the Trinity*, 3.

16. Fragment on 1 Corinthians, 74.
17. Sixth Homily on Isaiah, 3.
18. Stromata, 3.
19. *Didascalia Apostolorum* 3, 12:10.
20. Ibid., 2, 26:8.
21. *The Apostolic Constitutions*, 8, 28:3.
22. Ibid., 2, 26:6.
23. Ibid., 8, 20:1–2.
24. Quoted in Elizabeth Schussler Fiorenza, 'Word, Spirit and Power: Women in Early Christian Communities', in Rosemary Ruether and Eleanor McLaughlin (eds), *Women of Spirit, Female Leadership in the Jewish and Christian Traditions* (New York, 1979), p. 54.
25. *Pistis Sophia*, ibid., Chapter 96, p. 53.
26. Ibid., Chapter 36.
27. *The Apostolic Constitutions*, 3, 6:1–2.
28. Ibid., 3, 9:1–4.

Chapter 5: The Middle Ages and the End of Diakonia

1. *The City of God*, 20:16.
2. *On [his] Flight*.
3. *On the Priesthood*, 3:4.
4. *Letters*, 6:3.
5. *Sentences*, 4:53.
6. *Summa Theologiae*, IV, Part I, quaest. xcii, art. 1, 2.
7. John 1:1–4.
8. Megillah 23a.
9. Berakhot 20b.
10. Middot 2:5; Sukkah 5:1–4, 51b.
11. Kiddushim 1:7.
12. Valkut Shimoni; 1 Samuel 1:13.
13. Sefer Abadracham, *The Third Gate, Blessings Over the Commandments*.
14. Koran 33:35, in the translation by Muhammad Asad, *The Message of the Qur'an* (Gibraltar, 1990).
15. 'The Story of His Misfortunes, Abelard to a Friend', in Betty Radice (trans.), *The Letters of Abélard and Héloise* (Harmondsworth, 1974), pp. 71–2.
16. Ibid., p. 74.
17. Letter 3, ibid., p. 131.
18. Christine de Pisan, *The Book of the City of Ladies* (ed. and trans. Marina Warner) (London, 1983), 1, 1:2, p. 5.
19. Ibid., 1, 3:3, pp. 10–11.
20. Gratian's Decree, C12, 13, CXXXIII, q. 5; C20, CXXXIII, q. 5, quoted in James R. Cain, 'Cloister and the Apostolate of Religious Women', *Review for Religious*, 27 (1968), p. 262.
21. *Vita*, in Peter Dronke, *Women Writers of the Middle Ages, A Critical Study of Texts from Perpetua to Marguerite Porete* (Cambridge, 1984), p. 145.
22. Quoted in Vida D. Scudder, *Saint Catherine of Siena as Seen in Her Letters* (New York, 1911), p. 298.

23. *Revelations of Divine Love*, Chapter 56, in Karen Armstrong (ed. and trans.), *English Mystics of the Fourteenth Century* (London, 1991), p. 203.
24. Chapter 59 in ibid., p. 266.
25. Quoted in Rosemary and Darroll Pardoe, *The Female Pope, The Mystery of Pope Joan: The First Complete Documentation of the Facts behind the Legend* (Wellingborough, 1988), p. 32.

Chapter 6: The Reformation and the Triumph of Patriarchy

1. Commentary on Genesis, 3:9.
2. Ibid., 3:16.
3. Quoted in Lawrence Stone, *The Family, Sex and Marriage in England, 1500–1800* (London, 1977), pp. 197–8.
4. Ibid., p. 198.
5. Quoted in Mary Daly, *The Church and the Second Sex* (London, 1979), p. 64.
6. *Malleus Maleficarum* (trans. and ed. Montague Summers) (London, 1928), p. 48.
7. Ibid., p. 44.
8. Ibid., p. 46.

Chapter 7: Suffragettes, Church Feminists and the End of Silence

1. Quoted in F. Townley Lord, *Great Women in Church History* (London, 1940), p. 161.
2. Quoted in Thomas M. Morrow, *Early Methodist Women* (London, 1967), p. 98.
3. Quoted in Phoebe Palmer, *The Promise of the Father* (Boston, 1859), p. 11.
4. John Ruskin, 'Of Queens' Gardens'.
5. J. W. Burgon, *To Educate Young Women Like Young Men and With Young Men: A Thing Inexpedient and Immodest* (London, 1844), pp. 15–16.
6. Christopher Wordsworth, *Christian Womanhood and Christian Sovereignty* (London, 1844), pp. 16, 21.
7. Charlotte M. Yonge, *Womankind* (London, 1876), p. 1.
8. Baroness Burdett-Coutts, *Woman's Mission* (London, 1893), pp. 68–75.
9. Edward Monro, *Parochial Work* (London, 1850), p. 168.
10. Louise C. Creighton, *Life and Letters of Mandell Creighton*, 2 vols. (London, 1904), vol. 1, p. 8.
11. 'The Work of Women in the Parish', *Laity in Council*, Church Congress Report (CCR), 1894, p. 36.
12. *The Chronicles of Convocation* (CC), 1898, pp. 123–7.
13. CC (1904), pp. 13–14.
14. Janet Grierson, *The Deaconess* (London, 1981), p. 21.
15. Quoted in M. A. H. Melinsky, *The Shape of the Ministry* (Norwich, 1992), p. 104.
16. Quoted in Brian Heeney, *The Women's Movement in the Church of England, 1850–1930* (Oxford, 1988), p. 71.
17. Quoted in Grierson, *The Deaconess*, p. 31.
18. *Church Times*, 28 July 1916.

19. Daphne Bennett, *Emily Davis and the Liberation of Women, 1830–1921* (London, 1990), p. 37.
20. Ibid., pp. 49, 55–6.
21. Quoted in ibid., p. 156.
22. Arnold Pinchard, *Woman and the Priesthood* (London, 1916), pp. 7–8.
23. *Guardian*, 8, 15 April and 6 May 1910.
24. *The Six Lambeth Conferences 1867–1920* (London, 1920), p. 41.
25. Church Congress Report, 1919, II, p. 101; 1920, III, p. 36.
26. Laetitia Fairfield, 'Women and Lay Ministries', *Lambeth Conference*, 1920, CXXXVI, pp. 61–70.
27. *The Lambeth Conference*, 1930, p. 60.

Chapter 8: 1944–1992: Towards the Priesthood

1. Quoted in the Reverend Joyce M. Bennett, *Hasten Slowly, The First Legal Ordination of Women Priests* (Chichester, 1991), p. 4.
2. Ibid.
3. Ibid., pp. 4–5.
4. Quoted in Brian Heeney, *The Women's Movement in the Church of England, 1850–1930* (Oxford, 1988), p. 50.
5. Personal interview with Sara Maitland, *A Map of the New Country, Women and Christianity* (London, 1983), p. 89.
6. Quoted in ibid., p. 83.
7. *Gender and Ministry*, a Report prepared for the Church Assembly by the Central Advisory Council for the Ministry, Autumn 1962, p. 20.
8. Ibid.
9. Church Assembly, November 1992. The Verbatim Report. Debate on *Gender and Ministry*, 7 November 1962, p. 694.
10. Ibid., pp. 705–6.
11. *Women in Holy Orders*, a Report Prepared for the Church Assembly by the Archbishops' Commission (CA 1617), p. 101.
12. Church Assembly, February 1967. The Verbatim Report. Debate on *Women in Holy Orders*, 15 February 1967, p. 197.
13. Ibid., The Resumed Debate, 3 July 1967, p. 302.
14. Ibid., p. 310.
15. Ibid., p. 311.
16. Ibid., 15 February 1967, p. 216.
17. Ibid., 3 July 1967, p. 279.
18. Ibid., p. 280.
19. Ibid., p. 281.
20. Ibid., p. 280.
21. Ibid.
22. Ibid., p. 297.
23. *The Lambeth Conference, 1968, Resolutions and Reports* (London, 1968), p. 106.
24. George William Rutler, *Priests and Priestesses* (Ambler, Pa., 1973), pp. 85–6.
25. C. Kilmer-Myers, 'Should Women Be Ordained?', *The Episcopalian*, vol. 137, no. 2 (February 1972), p. 8.

26. Albert J. Dubois, 'Why I Am Against the Ordination of Women', *The Episcopalian*, vol. 137, no. 7 (July 1972), p. 22.
27. Press Release, July 1974.
28. Quoted in Maitland, *A Map of the New Country*, p. 106.
29. Acts of the Apostles 10:35.
30. The General Synod, November 1972. The Verbatim Report. Debate on *The Ordination of Women to the Priesthood*, a Report by the Advisory Council for the Church's Ministry (GS 104), p. 697.
31. Ibid., p. 706.
32. Ibid., p. 710.
33. Ibid., p. 716.
34. Ibid.
35. Ibid., p. 703.
36. The General Synod, July 1975, The Verbatim Report, Debate on *The Ordination of Women*, a Report by the Standing Committee (GS 252), p. 544.
37. Ibid., p. 546.
38. Ibid., p. 549.
39. Ibid., p. 571.
40. The General Synod, November 1978. The Verbatim Report. Debate on the motion: 'That this Synod asks the Standing Committee to prepare and bring forward legislation to remove the barriers to the ordination of women to the priesthood and their consecration to the episcopate', p. 1038.
41. Ibid., p. 1107.
42. *The Ordination of Women to the Priesthood*, the Synod Debate, 11 November 1992. The Verbatim Report (London, 1993), p. 28.
43. Ibid., p. 30.
44. Ibid., p. 27.
45. Ibid., p. 61.
46. Ibid., p. 63.
47. Ibid.
48. Ibid., p. 65.

Epilogue: Forward in Faith?

1. *The Times*, 18 February 1993.
2. Ibid.
3. *The Times*, 17 February 1993.
4. Genesis 12:1.

Index

Bible Women, 173, 174, 175
bishops, 92–7, 110–11, 117, 119–20, 122, 143
Black Mass, 160, 161
Blandina, 99–100
blood taboos, 36–7, 38
Broadhurst, Rev. John, 220, 225
Brown, Margaret, 220–1
Buddhism, 104, 121, 186
Burgon, J. W., 167
Byzantine Empire, 97, 119, 120

Cainites, 101
Calvin, John, 85, 106, 143, 144, 146–7, 149, 151, 152
Calvinism, 147, 149, 152–3
Canaan, 14, 18, 22
Carey, Dr George, 2
Carroll, Lewis, 166
Cathars, 139, 160
Catherine of Siena, 136, 138
Catmur, R. S., 199
Cecil, Gascoyne, 181
celibacy, 46, 108, 124–5, 131, 152, 154, 164, 191, 222, 230
Chantal, Jane Frances de, 154
charismatics, 81–2, 90, 91, 166
Charlemagne, Emperor, 120
childbirth, 36, 37, 38, 141
Chinese Anglican Church, 185–9, 200–2
Christ *see* Jesus Christ
Christine of Pisan, 132, 133
Chrysostom, St John, 112, 117–18
Church Missionary Society, 173
Church of England: allows ordination of women, 218, 219–22; as Catholic Church, 150; clergymen, 169–70; deaconesses, 173–6, 180–3, 192–3; debates ordination of women, 194–200, 205–6, 207–18; *Gender and Ministry*, 192–4; House of Laity, 172; independence of provinces, 188–9; missionaries, 172–3; nuns, 173; opposition to women priests, 1–3, 126, 182–3; parish councils, 171–2; Thirty-nine Articles, 149–50; threatened resignations, 219–22
Church of Ireland, 218
Church of Scotland, 199
Church of South Africa, 218
circumcision, 37
Clare, Mother, 192
Clark, Dr O. W. H., 193, 214

Clement, *episkopos* of Rome, 82–3, 84
Clement VII, Pope, 148
Clement of Alexandria, 90, 91, 96, 109
Cobbe, Frances, 169
confessors, 89, 97
Congregationalist Church, 182
Constantine, Emperor, 97
Cooper, Rev. H., 193–4, 208
Cornelius, 207
Corpus Christi, 124
Cranmer, Thomas, 148–9, 150
Creation, 10–11, 12, 31, 32, 33, 36, 75, 85, 102, 167, 194, 210
Creighton, Louise, 169, 170–1
Cromwell, Oliver, 150
Crosby, Sarah, 165
Cyprian, Bishop of Carthage, 96–7, 119

David, King of Israel, 48, 120
Davidson, Dr Randall, 177
Davis, Emily, 171, 178–9
deaconesses, 70, 110–12, 173–6, 180–3, 185–90, 192–3, 211–12
deacons, 52–3, 95, 97, 109–10
Dead Sea Scrolls, 48
Deborah, 36
Demant, Dr, 194–5, 210
diakonia, 52–4, 66, 68, 78, 82, 83, 95, 97, 229
Dickens, Charles, 168
Didache, 81–2
Didascalia Apostolorum, 109–10
dietary laws, Judaism, 28, 31, 32
'difference feminism', 168
disciples *see* Apostles
Douglas, Mary, 28, 37
Driffield, G. E., 211
Dubois, Rev. A. J., 203
Durham Cathedral, 217
Dye, T. L., 209–10
Dyer, Mary, 157

Edward VI, King of England, 148
Egypt, 18–21
Elijah, 23
Elizabeth (mother of John the Baptist), 54, 55
Elizabeth I, Queen of England, 149
Ellison, Gerald, 199
'Elohist', 39, 59, 78
Encratists, 73
Enheduanna, Princess, 14–15
Enlightenment, 161, 163, 164, 168
Enuma Elish, 12, 21

Tiamat, 21
Timothy, 83–5, 103, 211
Titus, 83–4
Torah, 49, 50, 51, 52, 57, 63, 67, 77, 126,
    212, 228
Trent, Council of, 143, 148
Trinity, doctrine of, 104, 138

United States of America, 202–5
Ur, 14–15, 16
Urban VIII, Pope, 155
Ursuline nuns, 154, 156
Uruk, 13, 16

Van Beeck, Franz Joseph, 204
veil, 72, 74–6, 128
Vermes, Geza, 55–6
virginity, 106, 108, 133–4, 141, 163–4
Visconti, Girolamo, 160
Visitation nuns, 154, 156

Wace, Henry, 181
Waldenses, 139
Walker, Lucy, 164
Warburg, Ellen, 203–4

Ward, Mary, 154, 155–6
Winnington-Ingram, Bishop of
    London, 178
Wesley, John, 164–6
Wesley, Susanna, 165
Whitgift, John, 149
widows, 108–9
Wilberforce, William, 214
Williams, Elizabeth, 156
Willie, Dr Charles, 203
Wilson, Leonard, 199
Witch Craze, 157–61, 227
Women Against the Ordination of
    Women, 220–1
Women in Holy Orders, 194
Women's Movement, 209, 211
Wordsworth, Christopher, 167

Ximenes, Cardinal, 143

Yahweh, 21–36, 49, 59
'Yahwist', 36
Yonge, Charlotte M., 168

Zadok, 27, 33
Zeus, 21–2